SMALLER
SLANG DICTIONARY

OTHER WORKS BY SAME AUTHOR

A Dictionary of Slang and Unconventional English: 16th–20th centuries. Cr. 4to, double-columned, xvi + 1230 pages; 5th edition, 2nd printing (Routledge & Kegan Paul.—U.S.A.: the Macmillan Company)

Slang Today and Yesterday: A History and a Study, British and American. 3rd edition, 2nd printing (Routledge & Kegan Paul.—U.S.A.: the Macmillan Company)

A Dictionary of the Underworld, British and American: 16th–20th centuries. Cr. 4to; 2nd edition, with Addenda (Routledge & Kegan Paul.—U.S.A.: the Macmillan Company)

A Dictionary of Clichés, with introductory essay. 4th edition, 4th printing (Routledge & Kegan Paul.—U.S.A.: the Macmillan Company)

Origins: An Etymological Dictionary of Modern English. Cr. 4to; 3rd edition (revised) (Routledge & Kegan Paul.—U.S.A.: the Macmillan Company)

Francis Grose's *Classical Dictionary of the Vulgar Tongue*: edited by Eric Partridge with a biographical notice. Royal 8vo; 2nd edition (revised), 2nd printing (Routledge & Kegan Paul.—U.S.A.: Barnes & Noble)

Comic Alphabets: a light-hearted history and study, illustrated by Michael Foreman (Routledge & Kegan Paul.—U.S.A.: the British Book Centre)

The Gentle Art of Lexicography: a memoir (André Deutsch.—U.S.A.: the Macmillan Company)

English: A Course for Human Beings. 4th edition; in one volume and in three separate books (Elementary, Middle, Advanced) (Macdonald & Co. (Publishers)—London and New York)

Usage and Abusage: A Guide to Good English. 5th edition, revised, enlarged, re-set (Hamish Hamilton.—U.S.A.: the British Book Centre)

The Concise Usage and Abusage. 3rd impression (Hamish Hamilton. —U.S.A.: Philosophical Library)

You Have a Point There: A Guide to Punctuation and its Allies. 4th edition, 3rd printing (Hamish Hamilton.—U.S.A.: the British Book Centre)

SMALLER
SLANG
DICTIONARY

by

ERIC PARTRIDGE

Routledge and Kegan Paul
LONDON AND BOSTON

First published 1961
by Routledge & Kegan Paul Ltd.
Broadway House, Carter Lane, EC4V 5EL
and 9 Park Street, Boston, Mass. 02108, U.S.A.

Printed in Great Britain
by The Redwood Press Limited
Trowbridge, Wiltshire

© *Eric Partridge 1961, 1964*

2nd edition
with a few corrections and additions
1964

Reprinted 1968 and 1972

ISBN 0 7100 1938 6

For
SIMEON POTTER
a humanist among the philologers;
a great philologist
with a generous sense of the humanities

*

FOREWORD

THERE exists no good short dictionary of modern British slang: slang importantly current either throughout or for a longish period of the 20th century.

To achieve this, I have abridged *A Dictionary of Slang and Unconventional English* (16th–20th centuries) to about one-twelfth the size of the original—a task very much more difficult than it sounds—by doing these three things:

(1) by excluding all material obsolete by the year 1900;

(2) by omitting nearly all the cant, as scholars call the language of the underworld;

(3) by omitting absolutely all matter that could offend against propriety or even delicacy.

This *Smaller Dictionary*, intended for general consumption, can therefore go into any home, any school, any library. Such a dictionary was badly needed.

ERIC PARTRIDGE

ABBREVIATIONS AND SIGNS

abbr.: abbreviated; abbreviation
adj.: adjective
adv.: adverb
app.: apparently
c.: cant (language of underworld)
C.: Century, as in 'C. 18'
ca.: about (the year)
cf.: compare
coll.: colloquial(ism)—midway
    between slang and Standard
    English
c.p.: catch-phrase
d.: died
dial.: dialect(al)
Eng.: English
esp.: especially
ex: out of, from: derived from
fig.: figurative(ly)
Fr.: French
gen.: general(ly)
Ger.: German
Gr.: Greek
i.e.: that is
imm.: immediate(ly)
It.: Italian
j.: jargon or technical(ity)
L.: Latin
lit.: literal(ly)
n.: noun
n.b.: note carefully
ob.: obsolescent (dying); cf. †
    below
occ.: occasional(ly)
O.E.D.: *The Oxford English Dictionary*
opp.: opposite; as opposed to
orig.: original(ly)
pl.: (in the) plural

Port.: Portuguese
ppl.: participial; participle
prob.: probable; probably
pron.: pronounced; pronunciation
q.v.: which see
resp.: respective(ly)
s.: slang
sc.: understand or supply
S.E.: Standard English
sol.: solecism; solecistic
Sp.: Spanish
U.S. or ⎫ The United States of America;
U.S.A.: ⎭ American
v.: verb
v.i. and ⎫
v.t.   ⎭ verb intransitive—transitive
vbl n.: verbal noun

—: (before a date) known to exist at
    least as early as
+: (after a date) recorded then and
    still existing
†: obsolete (dead); cf. 'ob.' above
>: becomes or become; became; has
    become
=: equal(s); is or are equal to

A Note on Etymology:
    The etymologies, when given at all,
are necessarily brief. They lean heavily
upon these four works:
    The Oxford English Dictionary;
    Ernest Weekley's *Concise*
        Etymological Dictionary (W);
    Webster's New International
        Dictionary;
    my *Origins: A Short Etymological*
        Dictionary of Modern English.

A

Abergavenny A penny: rhyming s.

Abo An aboriginal: Australian: late C. 19–20.

abso-bloody-lutely The most frequent of the *bloody* interpolations.

absolutely! Certainly! Coll. intensification of 'yes'. Slightly archaic.

accident An untimely, or accidental, call of nature: coll.

accidentally on purpose With purpose veiled: c.p.

ace, adj. Excellent; 'star': coll. *The Daily Express,* April 20, 1937, speaking of an orchestra: 'London's ace players improvising hot numbers.'

acid, come the To exaggerate; exaggerate one's authority; make oneself unpleasant; endeavour to shift one's duty on to another: originally military.

ack ack Anti-aircraft guns or their shells.

acker See *akka*.

acquire To steal; to obtain illicitly or deviously: Army euphemistic coll.

ad An advertisement: coll.

Adam, not to know someone from Not to know at all: coll.

Adam & Eve To believe: rhyming s.

Adam & Eve on a raft Eggs on toast.

Adam & Eve wrecked Scrambled eggs.

adj. Adjutant; esp. *the Adj.,* one's adjutant: Army officers'.

Admiralty ham Any tinned meat: naval: late C. 19–20. Bowen.

afters The second course; coll: thus 'Any afters?' = 'Any pudding?'

aft through the hawse-hole (Of an officer) that has gained his commission by promotion from the lower-deck: naval.

afto Afternoon: Australian.

1

agents, have one's   To be well-informed: Army and Air Force: since *ca.* 1939. With an allusion to 'secret agents'.

aid of?, what's this (occ. **that**) **in**   Esp. of something unexpected or surprising: what does this mean?—why?—a reference to *what* precisely? Originating in those Flag Days which began during the war of 1914–18.

agony, pile up (or **on**) **the**   To exaggerate: coll.

agony column   The personal column in a newspaper's advertisements (first in *The Times*).

ain't ain't grammar   A c.p. used jocularly in correcting someone saying *ain't*: since ca. 1920.

airs & graces   Faces: rhyming s.

akka, or **acker**   An Egyptian piastre: servicemen's. Ex the slang of Egyptian beggars: *piastre* corrupted.

alarm & despondency   War-time depression: 1940 +. Ex speech by the Rt Hon. Winston Churchill.

Alex   Alexandria (in Egypt).

all done by (or **with**) **mirrors**   Often preceded by *it's*. A c.p. uttered when something clever has been done. It presumably originated among stage magicians.

all dressed up & nowhere to go!   A c.p., from a song by Raymond Hitchcock, an American comedian.

all hot & bothered   Very agitated, excited, or nervous: coll.: 1937, in *The Times* leader. Ex the physical and emotional manifestations of haste.

all in, adj.   (Of persons, occ. of animals) exhausted.

all my eye (& Betty Martin)   Nonsense! Despite many ingenious theories, the origin remains a mystery. Slightly archaic.

all over the shop   Ubiquitous; confused, untidy. Also as adverb.

all right for you   Ironical c.p., addressed to those better off than oneself: Services': since 1940.

all-set   Ready; arranged in order; comfortable: coll.

all Sir Garnet   See *Sir Garnet*.

all the go   Thoroughly satisfactory; fashionable.

all up (with)   Of things, projects: fruitless, ruined. Of persons: bankrupt, doomed to die, as in Dickens's 'all up with Squeers'.

all wool & a yard wide   Utterly good and honest (person). Ex drapery.

almond rocks   Socks: rhyming s.

also ran, an   A nonentity: mostly Australian. Ex horse-racing.

Altmark, the   'A ship or a Shore Establishment in which discipline is exceptionally severe': naval: 1942 +. Granville, 'From the German Prison Ship of that name.'

altogether, the   The nude: coll.

amen wallah A chaplain.

ammo Ammunition (n. and adj.): military. Hence, *ammos*, ammunition boots, the ordinary Army boots.

anchor 'A parachutist who waits overlong before jumping' (Jackson): R.A.F.

anchor, swallow the To settle down on shore, esp. if one is still active: nautical.

and how! 'Rather!': an American c.p. anglicized by 1933.

and one, or simply **one, for the road** A C. 20 (orig. commercial travellers') c.p. applied to the last of several drinks. I.e., to keep one warm on the journey.

Andrew, the The Royal Navy: naval.

Andrew Millar (usually **the Andrew**) The Royal Navy: naval: mid-C. 19–20; ob. Bowen.

angel In theatrical s., any outsider that finances the production of a play.

Annie Laurie A lorry: rhyming s. (of an unusual kind).

Anna Maria A fire: rhyming s.

Annie's room (up in) A military c.p. reply to a query concerning someone's whereabouts: military; 1914–18.

anno domini Late middle, or old, age; the passage of the years (however young one is after early adulthood): coll.

Anthony Eden A black felt hat in the upper Civil Service style: coll. Of the kind favoured by the Rt Hon. Anthony Eden.

ants in one's pants (male or female), **have.** To be excited, restless; to be extremely, or even excessively, active and energetic: an Americanism adopted in England in 1938, but not gen. until 1942.

any, I'm not taking, or having Not for me!; 'not for Joe!': c.p. Hence in ordinary constructions.

any more for any more? Anyone want more food?: Services', esp. Army, c.p. (indeed, a consecrated and deeply revered phrase).

any racket A penny faggot: rhyming s., ca. 1855–1910.

any road (See *road, any*.)

anything, like, adv. Very; much: coll.

apple fritter A bitter (ale): rhyming s.

apples & pears Stairs; rhyming s.

apple-sauce Impudence: mostly lower middle class. An elaboration of synonymous *sauce*.

appro, on A coll. abbr. of *on approbation* or *approval*.

April fools Tools: rhyming s.—Stools: mostly public-house rhyming s. (Football) pools: rhyming s.: since *ca.* 1930.

are you happy in your work? Ironic c.p. to someone engaged in a dangerous, difficult or dirty job: Services, esp. R.A.F.: since ca. 1940.

argy-bargy To bandy words. Ex *argu*ment pronounced *argy*ment.

arrival The landing of an aircraft; esp., a poor landing: R.A.F.

artful dodger A lodger: rhyming s.

as ever is A c.p., emphasizing the preceding statement, as in 'This very Whitsuntide as ever is'.

as large as life & twice as natural A c.p. Ex waxworks?

ashcan A depth charge: orig. its container (ex its appearance): naval.

ask yourself! Be reasonable! Australian c.p.

aspi or **aspy** An aspidistra: non-aristocratic.

attaboy! Go it!: U.S. (−1917); anglicized in 1918. Probably from *that's the boy!* Hence, an approbatory exclamation.

aunt! my; my sainted aunt! A mild exclamation: coll.

Aussie, occ. **Aussey** Australia; (an) Australian: coll.

Aussie rules Australian football: Australian coll.

awful, adj. An intensive. Apparently C. 18 Scottish, then U.S. and, ca. 1840, adopted in England. Lamb, 1834, 'She is indeed, as the Americans would express it, something awful.' Coll., as is the adv. *awful(ly)* = very.

B

---

baa-lamb A tram: rhyming s.

babbling brook A criminal: Australian rhyming s. (on S.E. *crook*). As adj., unwell: Australian rhyming s. on Australian s. *crook*.

baby A girl; sweetheart: U.S., adopted ca. 1930.

baby-snatcher One who marries a person much younger: jocular coll.

bach, occ. **batch,** v. To live by oneself, doing one's own work; orig. like a bachelor. Ex U.S.; anglicized ca. 1890. Cf. the n.

back-chat Impudence; verbal recalcitrance.

back-room boy Usually pl., *boys*, inventors and theoretical technicians, working for one of the combatant Services: journalistic j. (1941) >, in 1943, a gen. coll.; in 1943–5, mostly Services'. They worked out of the limelight and often literally in backrooms or back-washes.

backsheesh, -shish; baksheesh, ba(c)kshee See *bakshee* (the latest form).

bacon, save one's To escape narrowly: coll.

bad, not Rather or (patronizingly) quite good: upper (hence, middle) classes' coll.

bad hat A rascal.

bad lot A person of indifferent morals: coll.

bad with, get in To get into bad odour with (e.g. the police): coll.

bag To obtain for oneself, esp. anything advantageous; to catch, take, or steal: coll.

bag, in the (Of a situation, a plan, etc.) well in hand; fully arranged; a virtual certainty: Services'. Ex game shooting. Be (put) in the bag, to be taken prisoner: Army.

bag of tricks, the, or **the whole b. of t.** Every expedient: coll. Ex the fable of the Fox and the Cat.

bags   Trousers. (By 1960, slightly archaic.)

bags, rough as   Extremely uncouth: Australian.

bags of   Much, plenty; many. E.g., 'bags of time'.

bail up   To demand money from: Australian. Ex earlier lit. use: (of a bushranger) to hold up.

Bajan (pron. Bay'jun)   A Barbadian: B.W.I. coll. For *'Badian*, aphetic for *Barbadian*.

bakey   A baked potato: (low) coll.

bakshee, backshee; ba(c)ksheesh; buckshee, bucksheesh, buckshish   A tip; gratuity. Hence, adj.: free, costing nothing: 1914–18. Popularized by the British Army in India and Egypt, esp. in G.W. Ex the Persian word for a present.

bald-headed, go (at) it   To act impetuously. Originally U.S.; anglicized ca. 1900.

ball and chain   A wife: Canadian. From U.S.A.; convicts' gyves.

bale up   See *bail up*.

bally, adj.   A euphemism for *bloody*. Since ca. 1945, archaic.

ballyhooly   'Advance publicity of a vulgar or misleading kind' (H. G. Le Mesurier): from ca. 1910; coll. by 1935; archaic by 1940. *Ballyhooly truth*, a ca. 1880–5 music-hall tag, perhaps ex *whole bloody truth*.

balmy   Just a little mad. Perhaps ex S.E. *balmy*, soft; but see also *barmy*.

bamboozle   To hoax, deceive, impose upon; to mystify. Etymology still a mystery.

banana boat   An invasion barge; an aircraft carrier.

band of hope   Soap: rhyming s.

bandstand   A cruet: Army and R.A.F. Ex the 'ironwork' surrounding one. 'The circular gun platform in small escort vessels' (Granville): naval.

bang to rights   Applied, predicatively, to a 'fair cop', a justified charge, a perfect case against somebody: underworld; London's East End; police. An elaboration, an intensive, of '(caught) *to rights*' or *in flagrante delicto*.

bang-up   First-rate, smart.

banger   A sausage: nautical, esp. naval.

banjo   In Australia, a shovel.

barge in, v.i.   To intrude; to interfere, esp. if rudely or clumsily.

barge into   To collide with; encounter, esp. if unexpectedly.

barge-pole, wouldn't touch with (the end of) a   One person thus indicates that he will have nothing to do with either another person or, it may be, a project: coll.

bark, v.t.   To scrape the skin off.—V.i. To cough.

bark up the wrong tree   To be at fault; to follow a false scent: coll.

barmy Very eccentric; mad. Ex *barmy*, full of barm, i.e. yeast. Cf. *balmy*.

barney A jollification, esp. if rowdy; an outing. Hence, a quarrel; a flight: grafters'.

baron 'Anything free in the Navy is said to be "on the Baron" or "Harry Freemans" ' (Granville): jocular.

barracking Banter, chaff; noisy jeering at cricket or football teams that offend the spectators: Australian. *To barrack* = to jeer at, interrupt clamorously; *barrack for*, however, has always meant to support enthusiastically. A *barracker* is a noisy interrupter. Origin obscure and bitterly disputed.

base wallah A soldier employed behind the lines; esp. at a Base: military coll.

bash, have a To make an attempt.

basher A Physical Training Instructor: Services'. *Basher* is very common for mechanics, as in *compass basher, instrument basher*: R.A.F. Indeed, *basher* has often, since 1941, meant little more than 'fellow', 'chap'.

basinful, a Of trouble, hardship, labour, etc. Hence, *get one's basinful*, to receive a severe—esp., a fatal—wound: 1914–18; 1939–45.

basinful of that, I'll have a A c.p. aimed at anyone using a long or a learned word.

basket Used jocularly as a euphemism for *bastard*.

bat A prostitute favouring the night.—Pace, as in *at a fair bat.*— A batman: military.—A drinking bout; esp. *go on the bat*, on the spree.

bat out of hell, go like a To go, esp. fly, extremely fast.

bath bun A son: rhyming s.

bats, adj. Very eccentric; mad.

bats Deck-landing officer in an aircraft carrier: naval. Ex the bats he carries.

bats in the belfry, have To be very eccentric; mad, to any degree: late C. 19–20.

batt A battalion.

battle, v.i. To 'get by' on one's wits: v.t., to obtain, esp. if deviously, the use of: Australian c.> by 1940, low s. Hence, *battler*, one who 'gets by', on odd jobs and alone; a tramp; a hawker. Both v. and n. occur in Kylie Tennant's fine novel, *The Battlers*, 1941.

batty, adj. Mad. Ex *bats in the belfry*.

bawl out To upbraid vigorously: Canadian coll. adopted from U.S. Hence a *bawling-out*.

bay window A protuberant belly.

S.S.D.—B

be good! A c.p. 'au revoir'. Often **be good and, if you can't be good, be careful!**

be your age! Stop being childish!; Use your intelligence!: a c.p. adopted from U.S.A.

beak A magistrate, as in *up before the beak*, on trial by a magistrate. Hence, in schools (esp. Eton and Marlborough), an assistant master.—The nose.

beam ends, on one's Short of money: coll. Ex a vessel in imminent danger of capsizing.

beam, off the; on the beam Failing to understand; fully understanding: R.A.F. (since ca. 1938); by 1943 also civilian. Ex that wireless beam which, in bad visibility, guided one to the airfield.

bean To hit (someone) on the head.

bean, not have a Esp. *I haven't a bean*, I'm penniless.

beanfeast A jollification.

beano Orig. an annual feast: printers'. Hence, a jollification.

beans, full of Energetic; in high spirits.

bear 'In Stock Exchange slang, bulls are speculators for a rise, bears for a fall.'

beat A newspaper 'scoop': journalistic.

beat Exhausted: coll. Often *dead beat*. Baffled, defeated: coll.

beat it To run away; to depart. Ex U.S.

beat up, n. Ground strafing; hence a lively visit to 'the local' or a good party in the Mess: R.A.F. Ex:—

beat up, v. To stunt-fly, at low level, about (a place): R.A.F. Ex U.S.

beaut A beauty: Australian. Hence, also an adj., as in 'It's a beaut day'.

bed-sitter A bed-sitting room.

beef To complain. Ex U.S.

been & gone & done it, I (etc.) **have** or **he** (etc.) **has** A jocularly coll. emphasized form of *I have* (etc.) *done it*, with esp. reference to marriage. Ex illiterate speech (*gorn and done it*): cf. P. G. Wodehouse, *Tales of Austin's*, 1903, 'Captain Kettle had, in the expressive language of the man in the street, been and gone and done it'.

been robbing a bank? often preceded by **have you** A jocular c.p., addressed to someone flush with money.

beer up A drinking bout: Australian coll.

bees & honey Money: rhyming s.

beetle off To depart. As a beetle flies.

before you came up Before you enlisted: military: 1914–1918.

beggar A man, chap, fellow: coll.

beggar for work, a A constant hard worker: coll.

behind The posterior: coll.

behind the eight-ball   In an extremely difficult position; at a grave disadvantage: Canadian: adopted from U.S. Ex snooker.

bellows; illiterately, **bellers**   The lungs.

belly-ache   To grumble, complain, esp. querulously or unreasonably.

belt   A hit, blow, punch. 'He caught me an awful belt on the ear.'

bend   An appointment; a rendezvous: Anglo-Irish.

bender   A drinking spree; esp., **(go) on a bender.**

bends, the   Diver's paralysis or, more accurately, cramp: pearl fishers'.

Benghazi cooker   Sand saturated with oil, a paste of sand and oil, within a tin or can or metal drum; used as a field cooker in North Africa: 1940–3.

berk   A fool. Originally an underworld term. Don't ask what the origin is—somebody might tell you.

better than a dig in the eye with a blunt stick or **than a kick in the pants**   Very much better than nothing or than a setback.

bevie, bevvy   Beer; loosely, any drink: military and theatrical.

bi   Biology; also as in *bi lab*: medical students'.

bible-banger   A pious, esp. if ranting, person.

bible-punching   A sermon; religious talk.

biblio   A bibliographical note (esp. on the reverse of the title-page) in a book: book-world coll.

bicarb   Bicarbonate of soda: coll.

biccy or **bikky**   Biscuit: nursery coll.

biddy   A chicken: coll. A young woman (ex *Bridget*). Cf. the American s. *chick*, a girl. Any woman.

biff   A punch; to punch.

big bad wolf   A threatening or sinister person: coll. Ex a popular song.

big eats   A good meal: Services'.

big noise   An important person.

big shot   Orig. a gang-leader: hence, any important male. Ex U.S.A.

big way, in a   Very much: coll. 'I've had him in a big way'— I've no more use for him.

bigger they are, the harder they fall, the; occasionally **the taller they are, the further they fall**   A c.p. of defiance and fearlessness towards one's superiors. It probably originated in the boxing-booths.

big wig   A person of high rank or position: coll. (The earliest of the 'big' men.)

bike   Bicycle: coll.

billed, ppl adj.   Detailed (esp. in orders) for a piece of work; briefed: R.A.F. Ex the theatrical *billed (to appear).*

billet   A job: coll.

Bill(y)   Shakespeare; esp. *spout Bill(y).*

billy   In Australia and derivatively in New Zealand, a can that serves the bushman as both kettle and tea-pot; at first, *billy-can.* Ex Aboriginal *billa*, water.

billy-cock   A low-crowned, wide-brimmed felt hat: coll. Origin disputed.

billy-o (or **oh**) or occ. **billy-ho, like**   With great vigour or speed: coll.

bind   A depressing, boring or very dull person, task or duty: Royal Air Force. Ex:

bind, v.   To weary, bore a person; (of things) to be tedious. R.A.F. Perhaps ex constipation.

binder   One who grumbles and moans more than is held permissible: R.A.F.

binding, adj.   Given to 'moaning'; boring; tedious: R.A.F.

binge   A drinking bout: Oxford University; hence among Army officers, 1914–19; then fairly general.

bint   A girl or woman: military; by 1945, slightly archaic. Ex Arabic.

bird   Rare except as *do bird*, to 'do time', and *in bird*, in prison. Ex *bird-lime*. As *the bird*, a hissing of an actor: theatrical. Ex the hissing of a goose.—A man, a chap; as in 'a strange bird'.

bird, give (one) or, hence, **get the**   To dismiss (a person); to be so treated. Ex the theatre.

bird-lime   Time: rhyming s.

birds, that's (or it's) for the   Not for me; rubbish.

birl   A variant of *burl.*

biscuit, take the   To excel slightly ironic: late C. 19–20.

bish   A bishop: general s. A chaplain: naval.

bit   In such phrases as *a bit of a fool*, rather a fool, the word is coll., as also in *a bit*, a little; *not a bit*, not at all: and *every bit*, entirely. Likewise when it = a short while, either as *for*, or *in*, *a bit* or simply as *a bit*, e.g. in 'Let's wait *a bit*'.

bit of all right, a (little)   Something excellent.

bit of jam   Something easy.

bit of no good, do a   To do harm: jocular coll.

bit of string with a hole in it, I've (or I've got) a   A facetious c.p., in reply to a request for something else.

bit on (have) a   (To lay) a stake: racing.

bit(-)player   A stage actor with a small part in pictures: theatrical and cinematic coll.

bitch To spoil or bungle: coll. Prob. a thinned form of the synonymous *botch.*

bite To 'take the bait', be deceived: coll.

bits Pleasant or pretty 'pieces' of scenery: photographers' and artists' coll.

bivvy A bivouac; a temporary shelter: military.

biz Business. Orig. U.S.; anglicized ca. 1880.

black A glaring error; esp. *put up a black*: R.A.F. officers', the R.A.F. other ranks saying, 'I've boobed'.

black maria A van for the conveyance of prisoners: orig. an underworld term.

black squad A stokehold crew: nautical coll.

black velvet Stout and champagne mixed: public-house s., mostly Anglo-Irish, C. 20.

blah, n. and adj. Nonsense; silly or empty (talk); deliberately wordy, insincere, window-dressing (matter): esp. among publishers and journalists. From U.S.

blame Fault: proletarian coll.

blarney Honeyed flattery or cajolery: coll. Ex a stone in the wall of Castle Blarney, Ireland, the kissing of which is reputed to ensure the gift of cajolery and unblushing effrontery. Cf.:

blarney, v.i. and v.t. To cajole; flatter grossly: coll. Ex the n.

blazes, how or **what** or **who the?!** An intensive coll. interrogation; e.g. in Dickens, 1838, 'What the blazes is in the wind now?' (O.E.D.).

blazes, like Vehemently or vigorously.

bleeder A fellow, a man: mainly Cockney. Like the next, slightly old-fashioned by ca. 1955.

bleeding A coll. intensive adj. of little meaning: its import is emotional, not mental.

blether, occ. **blather** Vapid or noisy talk; voluble nonsense: coll. Also as v.

blew To cause to disappear; spend, waste (money).

blighter A contemptible person (rarely of a woman). Hence, a chap, a fellow.

Blighty England; home: military. Ex Hindustani *bilayati*, foreign, esp. European.—Hence, a wound taking one home. Adj , as in *Blighty leave*, furlough to England. Very much less used in W.W. II than in W.W. I.

blim(e)y Abbr. of *Gorblimy!*: mostly Cockney.

blimp A small, dirigible airship, non-rigid: military: 1915: s. > coll. > j. Invented by Horace Shortt. Ex *limp*. Hence, *blimp*, an old-fashioned, unprogressive man.

blind, v. To curse.

blinded with science A c.p. applied to brawn defeated by brains: Australian and New Zealand.

blink, on the Out of order; esp. applied to mechanism: R.A.F. Adopted from U.S.A.

blinker A chap, fellow. Cf. *blighter, bleeder,* and *blinking.*

blithering (gen. with **idiot**) Volubly nonsensical; hence merely 'arrant': coll.

blitz A bombing by aircraft; hence, v., to aircraft-bomb (a place); esp. in *the London blitz* (Sept. 1940–May 1941). Ex Ger. *Blitz,* lightning, and *Blitzkrieg,* that lightning warfare which Germany conducted in April–June 1940.—Derivatively, a severe reprimand, to reprimand severely; that spring cleaning which takes place when important officials are expected: Services'.

blob A 'duck's egg': cricketers' coll. Ex the cipher 0.

block The head.

block-buster A heavy bomb of great penetrative power: R.A.F. and journalistic coll.: 1942–45.

block, lose (or **do in**) **the**; also **do one's block** To become angry or excited: Australian.

bloke A man; a chap, fellow (−1839). Until ca. 1860, c.; until ca. 1900, low. Perhaps ex Dutch *blok,* a fool.

blondie or **-y** A blonde girl: coll. Often in address.

blood A bloodthirsty 'thriller'.

bloody, adj. and adv. An intensive, otherwise meaningless. Ex the connotations of the S.E. adj. (See esp. 'The Word *Bloody*' in my *Here, There and Everywhere.*)

bloody-minded Obstructive, deliberately 'difficult', pig-headed, vindictive: coll. Hence, 'rebellious'.

bloomer A mistake. Perhaps a 'blend' of *blooming error.*

blooming A mildly intensive adj. and adv.

blotto Drunk. By 1955, slightly archaic. Of a drunken man, P. G. Wodehouse once said that 'He was oiled, boiled, fried, plastered, whiffled, sozzled, and blotto'. Ex the porousness of blotting paper.

blow To open (a safe) by the use of explosive: originally underworld.

blow in To arrive; enter (v.i.): coll. Ex U.S.

blow off steam To work, talk, swear, hard, as a 'safety-valve': coll.

blow one's top To explode with anger: adopted, ca. 1943, ex U.S. servicemen.

blow-out A heavy meal.

blow sky high To scold, or blame, most vehemently.

blow the gaff To reveal a secret.

blow up A disclosure. A scolding. A quarrel (temporary). By 1960, all three senses just a shade old-fashioned.

blower A telephone. Promoted from the underworld.

bludge To ask for, to 'scrounge'; to *bludge on*, to impose or sponge on: Australian. Hence, *bludger*.

blue, adj. Obscene. Gloomy, low-spirited.

blue, n. A learned or literary woman: coll. Short for *blue stocking*. Ex the blue stockings that such women are reputed to have worn in C. 18.

blue, n. A summons; a mistake, a loss: Australian.—A brawl: Australian.

blue, in the Gone astray, gone wrong; military. Perhaps 'gone off into the blue haze of the horizon'.—Hence, in a deserted place difficult of access: coll.

blue moon, once in a Extremely seldom: coll.

blue murder, like With great rapidity: coll. Cf. *yell blue murder*, to yell as if being murdered.

blues, the Despondency; low spirits.—The police. By 1960, ob.

bluey A bushman's, esp. a sundowner's, bundle, usually wrapped in a blue blanket: Australian. As in *hump bluey*, or *hump one's bluey*, to go on tramp.

bo-peep sleep: rhyming s.

boat A racing car: racing motorists'. Punning *motorboat*.—A submarine (usually pl): naval.—A builder's cradle: builders' jocular.

boat, push out the To pay for a round of drinks: naval.

bob A shilling. Origin obscure: many guesses; no certainty.

bob a nob Almost a c.p.: a shilling a head.

Bob's your uncle Everything is perfect: c.p. 'You go and ask for the job—and he remembers your name—and Bob's your uncle.' Origin unknown.

Bobby A policeman. Ex Mr, later Sir, *Robert* Peel (cf. *peeler*), mainly responsible for the Metropolitan Police Act of 1828.

boche, n. & adj. German, esp. a German soldier: since 1914; not much used by the British soldiers. Direct ex Fr. slang.

boco, boko The nose. By 1945, slightly ob. Perhaps ex *beak*.

bod A body, i.e. a real person, a person actually available: Services'.

boffins, the The inventors working for the advancement of aviation: R.A.F.; hence general Services'. A fanciful name of the Lewis Carroll type, yet with a glance at 'those who *baffle* the enemy'.

bog in, v.i. To eat (heartily); to work energetically: Australian.

bog-house; now usually *the bogs* A privy.

boloney; incorrectly **baloney** Nonsense; 'eye-wash'. Ex U.S. word; anglicized by 1931. Apparently ex *Boloney*, '*Bologna* sausage'.

Bolshie, Bolshyie (All senses are coll.) A Bolshevik. Hence, any revolutionary. Hence, an unconventional person. Also adj.

bomb In address, a bombardier: military.

bomb-happy With nerves gone, through exposure to bombing: Army: 1940–5.

bone, v. To seize, arrest; steal, make off with. Promoted from the underworld.

bone-orchard A cemetery.

boner A bad mistake; esp. *make*, or *pull*, a boner.

bonkers Slightly drunk, light-headed: naval.—Hence, crazy; naval > gen.

bonza, occ. **bonser** or **bonzer;** loosely, *bonzo* Excellent, delightful: Australian: C. 20. Perhaps ex *bonanza*. Also n.

booai or **booay** (pron. *boo-eye*) Remote rural districts: New Zealand. Ex Maori.

boob, n. A booby, a fool, a 'soft' fellow; hence, loosely, a fellow: U.S., anglicized in 1918.

boob To blunder: Army & Air Force.

boodle Bribe(ry), illicit spoils, political perquisites, profits quietly appropriated, party funds,—all these are *boodle*. Orig. U.S. Hence, money in general. Prob. ex Dutch *boedel*, estates, effects.

book A newspaper, a magazine: illiterate coll.

booky, often **bookie** A bookmaker: sporting coll.

boomps-a-daisy! Domestic and nursery c.p. to a child that has bumped its head or falls over.

boot To kick, e.g. 'I booted him good and hard': coll. Hence (gen. *boot out*), to dismiss, get rid of. To kick (the ball) exceedingly hard: football coll.

boot, give or **get, the** To dismiss; be dismissed: coll.

boot hill A graveyard: Canadian miners'.

boot, put in the 'To kick a prostrate foe' (C. J. Dennis): mostly Australian.

boots up, hang one's, or **hang up one's boots** To give up playing football; footballers' coll.

booze, boose, bouze, bouse, bowze or **bowze** Drink, liquor: c. until C. 19, then low s.; in C. 20, coll. Hence, drinking-bout: now coll. Ex:

booze, etc., v. To drink, esp. heavily; tipple: now coll. Perhaps ex Dutch *buizen* (low Ger. *busen*), to drink to excess.

booze, on the On a prolonged drinking bout: by 1910, coll.

boozer, etc. A drunkard; a public-house.

boozy Drunken, esp. if mildly; showing the marks of drink.

borak at, poke To jeer at: Australian. Ex a New South Wales Aborigine word.

borrow   To steal: jocularly coll.: from ca. 1880.

born yesterday, not   Esp. 'I wasn't born yesterday' (not a fool): c.p.

bosh   Trash; nonsense: coll. Ex Turkish (for 'empty', 'worthless'); popularized by Morier's *Ayesha* and later novels.—Hence, as interjection: nonsense!

boss   A master, owner, manager; leader: orig. U.S.; anglicized ca. 1850: coll. In England the term has a jocular undertone; in Australia and New Zealand, it lacks that undertone. Ex Dutch *baas*, master.

bossy, adj.   Over-fond of giving orders: coll.

bot, v.   To borrow money; (usually *bot on*) to sponge on (others): Australian and New Zealand. Cf. *bot-fly*, a sponger.

bot-fly   A troublesome, interfering person: Australian. Often abbr. to *bot*. Ex the bot-fly, which in hot weather greatly troubles horses.

bottle, n.   A share of money: showmen's.—A reprimand, a dressing-down; especially, *get a bottle*, to be reprimanded: naval.

bottle of Scotch   A watch: rhyming s.

bottle-washer   Often *head cook and b.w.* A factotum: jocular coll.

bounce, v.i.   (Of a cheque) to be returned, as worthless, by the bank on which it has been drawn; adopted, ca. 1938, from U.S.A. V.t., to attack (suddenly, unexpectedly): Air Force. To dismiss (a person), reject (a play): adopted, ca. 1940, from U.S.A.

bouncer   A 'chucker-out': public-houses' coll.

bounder   A vulgar though usually well-dressed man, an un-welcome pretender to Society, a vulgarly irrepressible person within Society: coll. Since ca. 1918, slightly old-fashioned; by 1960, archaic and reminiscent (or allusive) and jocular. Lit. one who bounds exuberantly about.

bow & arrow   A sparrow: rhyming s.

bow window   A big belly.

bow-wow   A dog: jocular and nursery coll.

bowl over   To dumbfound: coll. Ex skittles. Another variant (Dickens's) is *bowl down*, 1865.

bowler, be given—get—one's   To be demobilized: military. A civilian bowler in exchange for one's 'battle-bowler'.

bowler-hatted, be   To be returned to civil life: Services'.

box clever   To use one's head, be a 'shrewdy'.

box of toys   Noise: rhyming s.

box on   To keep fighting: hence, to continue doing anything important or strenuous: Australian.

boy, old (with **the**)   One's father; one's business chief, 'governor': coll.

boys; always the boys The lively young fellows of any locality: coll. Cf. *lads of the village.*

brain-wave A sudden, esp. if a brilliant, idea: coll. Ex telepathy.

brains The paste with which a sub-editor sticks his scissors-cuttings together: printers' (−1887); slightly ob.

brass Money.

brass, the (top) Officers; (*top*) high-ranking: Services'.

brassed off Disgruntled, fed up: Services'; Royal Naval since ca. 1927, general since ca. 1939. Perhaps ex brass-polishing in ships.

brass-hat A high-ranked officer: military and naval. 1893, Kipling. Ex gilt on his cap.

bread & butter letter A letter thanking one's recent hostess. Often abbr. to *bread and butter.*

bread & jam A tram: rhyming s.

bread basket The stomach.

break (gen. **bad break**) A mistake, blunder, *faux pas*: coll. Ex U.S. By itself, *break* usually means a piece of good luck.

break, v. (Usually in the present perfect tense; applied only to events that are exciting or important.) To happen: journalists' coll.; adopted ca. 1930 ex U.S.

breed A half-breed: Canadian coll.

breeze A disturbance, row, quarrel, tiff: coll.

breeze in To arrive unexpectedly.

breeze up, have the To 'have the wind up', which it deliberately varies: military. By 1960, archaic.

brekker Breakfast.

brew up, v.i. To make tea: Army. Hence, to catch fire. 'Tank brewed up and his driver's killed.'

brick A loyal, dependable person (orig. only of men); 'a good fellow': prob. ex the solidity of a brick.

brick, drop a Make a *faux pas*, esp. of tact or speech: now coll.

bricks Heavy shells: naval. In the Army, any shells. By meiosis.

bricky A bricklayer or his assistant: coll.

bride A girl; esp. one's best girl: c. until ca. 1930, then Cockneys' and Forces' s.

brief A ticket of any kind. A letter.—A furlough-pass: military. A bank- or currency-note: bank-clerks', mostly Anglo-Irish.

bright specimen, a A silly, foolish, rash, stupid, bungling person: coll.

briney or **briny, the** The sea: coll.

bring home the bacon To succeed in a given undertaking: by 1950, coll.

Briton, a A good fellow; a staunch friend: coll.

Brock's benefit In the Navy, 'any pyrotechnic display of gunfire' (Granville); esp. 1939–45.—'Bomber slang for a particularly large display of enemy searchlights, flares and ack-ack fire.'

broke to the wide Penniless: coll.

broke to the world Penniless: coll.

brolly An umbrella: coll.

brolly A parachute: R.A.F., esp. pilots'; *brolly hop*, a parachute jump from an aircraft.

brown A halfpenny: a 'copper'.

brown job, the The Army; *a brown job*, a soldier: R.A.F., hence also naval. From the colour of the uniform.

browned off (Extremely) disgruntled; depressed; disgusted: Regular Army since ca. 1915; adopted by the R.A.F. ca. 1929. Prob. ex cookery. Cf. *brassed off* and *cheesed off*.

brownie, browny The polar bear: nautical coll.—An Australian coll.: 'Cake made of flour, fat and sugar, commonly known as "Browny" ' (E. D. Cleland, *The White Kangaroo*, 1890).—A trout: anglers' coll.

bruiser A prize-fighter; coll. Hence, any person fond of fighting with the fists; a chucker-out: coll.—A reckless rider: hunting.

brum A counterfeit coin.—Abbr. *Brummagem*, q.v. Almost anything, but esp. jewellery, that is counterfeit or worthless.—(**Brum**) A native of *Brummagem*, Birmingham; Birmingham itself.

Brummagem Counterfeit money, esp. of copper. Made at Birmingham. Ex the local spelling, phonetic for the local pronunciation. Brummagem = Bromwicham (after Bromwich) = a corruption of Brimidgeham, the old form of *Birmingham*.

Brummagem, adj. The C. 20 connotation is that of shoddiness or of showy inferiority: as such, it is coll. See the n.

brunch Breakfast and lunch in one: coll.

brutal & licentious soldiery, the An Army officers' derisive c.p. dating from the Boer War (1899–1901). Perhaps ex some politician's speech.

bubble & squeak A Greek: rhyming s.

bubbly, often the bubbly Champagne.

Buck House Buckingham Palace: Society and Service officers'.

buck up To become energetic, cheerful. Also, to encourage, cheer up, or refresh ('A spot of b. and s. bucked him up no end'); and as v.i., to be encouraged; esp. in *buck up*.

Buckley's (chance) A forlorn hope: Australian coll. 'Buckley was a declared outlaw whose chance of escape was made hopeless' (Jice Doone). There have been many other explanations.

bucko (pl. **-oes**) A swashbuckling, domineering, or blustering man; occ. as term of address.

buddy   An American term of address (lit. brother): partially anglicized by 1918; very common by 1960.

buffer   A man; in C. 19 often, in C. 20 esp., in *old buffer*. Origin obscure.

bugs   Bacteria; bacteriology: medical students'.

bug-house   Mad; very eccentric: U.S.; anglicized, as rather low s., by late 1936.

bull, n.   Empty talk; blarney; deceptive talk.

bull-dog   A university (Oxford or Cambridge) proctor's assistant: coll.

bull's wool   Nonsense; meaningless talk; ballyhoo: New Zealand and Australia.

bullet, get & give the   To be dismissed and to dismiss, resp. Ex the effectiveness of a bullet.

bullocky   A bullock-driver: Australian coll.

bullocky's joy   Treacle; golden syrup: Australian.

bum, n.   A tramp; a beggar; a worthless loafer. Adopted ex U.S., which derives it ex earlier *bummer*, itself perhaps ex Ger. *bummler*, a tramp, a loafer.

bum fodder   Toilet paper: since ca. 1659; often, in C. 19–20, abbr. to:

bumf   A schoolboys' and soldiers' abbr. of *bum-fodder*, toilet paper. Hence, paper. In W.W. I and II, chiefly among officers: 'orders, instructions, memoranda, etc., especially if of a routine nature, e.g. "snowed under with bumf from the Division" ', B. & P.

bump off   To kill, destroy, criminally: an Americanism, anglicized by 1933.

bumper   A crowded house: theatrical. Anything very large: coll.

bumping, n.   Obstructing a bill: Parliamentary.

bun or **cake** or **biscuit, take the**   To obtain first honours; 'beat the band'.

bunce   Sheer, or almost sheer, profit; something for nothing.

bunch   A group or gang of persons: coll.

bundle, drop one's or **the**   To surrender; abandon hope; become frightened: Australian. Prob. abbr. *drop one's bundle and run.*

bundook, occ. **bandook**   A rifle; earlier, a musket; earlier still, cross-bow. Ultimately ex the Arabic *banadik*, Venice, where cross-bows were made. The Regular Army stationed in India used the term as early as C. 18, and in W.W. I it > fairly common; by 1940, archaic.

bung, v.   Often as *bung over*, to pass, hand (over), give; to send (a person, e.g. into the Navy; or a thing, e.g. a letter to the post): coll.

bung-ho!   Au revoir; by 1945, ob.—A toast to a friend.

bungs A ship's cooper.

bunk Nonsense. Ex *bunkum*.

bunk, v. To decamp. 'I'll bunk my class.'

bunk, do a To depart hastily, from ca. 1865.

bunk up, n.; less gen. **bunk-up, v.t.** Assistance, to assist, in climbing: Cockneys'. ' "Can you give us a bunk-up?" "Yus, I'll bunk you up, Bill." '

bunkered, be To be in a situation difficult of escape: coll. Ex golf. Cf. *stymied*.

bunny A rabbit: coll. Hence, an occ. variant of *rabbit*, a very poor player of any given game.

burg A town; a city: coll; U.S. partly anglicized (thanks to the 'talkies') by 1932.

burgoo, burgue Oatmeal porridge. An old military word. Ex *burghul*, Turkish for wheat porridge.

burl esp. in *give it a burl*. To give something a chance; make an attempt: Australian. Perversion of *hurl*?

burnt offering Food, esp. meat, that has been allowed to burn: jocular coll.

Burton-on-Trent The rent one pays: rhyming s. Often abbr. to *Burton*.

bus Abbr. *business*. (Pronounced *biz*.) An aeroplane. A motor-car.

bus, miss the To lose one's opportunity: coll.

bushed, be To be lost in the bush; hence to be lost, at a loss: Australian coll.

bush telegram, or **telegraph** An unfounded report or rumour: Australian coll.

business end, the The commercial part of a firm's activities: coll. The part that matters: coll. E.g., the business end of a sword.

business, quite a (Something) unexpectedly difficult to do, obtain, etc.: coll.

busk To perform in the street: grafters'.

busker A man that sings or performs in public-house or street.

bust, n. A spree or drinking-bout: esp. as *go on the bust*, orig. U.S., acclimatized ca. 1880.

busted, or **gone bust** Ruined: coll.

busy, occ. **busy fellow** A detective: c. and low s.

busy, get To become active: coll: U.S., anglicized by 1910.

butcher A medical officer: servicemen's jocular.

butcher's (hook) A look: rhyming s. (adj.) Angry: Australian rhyming s.

butter Fulsome flattery, unctuous praise, 'soft soap': coll. Hence, also v.

butter-fingers One who lets things, esp. a ball, slip from his grasp: coll.

buttinski An inquisitive person. Ex an American pun on *butt in*.

button B Penniless: very short of money.

buttons A page: coll. Ex numerous jacket-buttons.

buy, v. To incur, receive, be 'landed with' (something un-pleasant) with one's eyes open or very credulously: C. 20. Cf. *ask for it.*

buy it, I'll Tell me the answer or catch: c.p.

buy it Usually *He bought it* (or *He bought a packet*), he was shot down: R.A.F. In the other Services: to become a casualty.

buzz Often *buzz off.* To depart: esp. to depart quickly.

bye! or **'bye!** also **bye-bye!** Goodbye: coll.

bye-byes, go to To go to sleep.

C

cabbage   A bomb: R.A.F.

cabbie, cabby   A cab-driver: coll. Hence, a taxicab driver.

caboodle, the whole   The whole lot (persons or things): coll: orig.
U.S., anglicized ca. 1895. Prob. via U.S. *the whole kit and boodle*
(*kit and* being slurred to *ca*), ex English *kit* and U.S. *boodle*, a crowd.

cackle   The patter of clowns; the dialogue of a play.

cackle! cut the   'Shut up!' Occ. in other moods, esp. in *cut the
cackle and come to the 'osses*, which, however, = to get down to
business.

cackle-berry   (Gen. pl.) An egg: Canadian.

cactus, in the   In an awkward situation: Australian and New
Zealand.

cad   A man devoid of fine instincts or delicate feelings: coll.
Ex the obsolete *caddie*, a cadet.

cadge   An act or the practice of begging; esp. *on the cadge*.

cadge, v.   To go about begging; to beg, obtain by begging: coll.
Perhaps imm. ex Dutch, ultimately ex Fr. *cage*, a wicker basket
carried on back of cadger (pedlar) or his pony.

cadger   A beggar: coll. Hence, a genteel, despicable 'sponger':
coll.

cagey   Cautious; suspicious of others; unforthcoming, reserved.
Ex animals in cages.

cady, occ. cady or kadi   A hat. *Walford's Antiquarian*, April,
1887: 'Sixpence I gave for my cady, A penny I gave for my stick.'
Perhaps ex Yiddish.

caff   A café: low coll.

cage   A prison compound: military.

Cain, raise   To make a disturbance: coll. Orig. U.S., anglicized
ca. 1870.   App. euphemistic for *raise the devil*.

21

Cain & Abel A table: rhyming s.

cake, take the To carry off the honours; be the best.

cake-walk A raid or attack that turns out to be unexpectedly easy: military.

cakes, like hot Very quickly, promptly; esp. *sell* or *go like . . .*: coll. Orig. U.S.

call down To reprimand: coll.

call it a day To state one's decision to go no further, do no more; rest content, e.g. with one's gain or loss.

cam A camisole. Also *cami, cammy*.

camp To sleep or rest in an unusual place or at an unusual time; Australian coll.

camp, adj. Objectionable; (slightly) disreputable; effeminate. Origin unknown.

can do I can (do it); can you (do it)?: 'pidgin'. Hence, all right!: military and naval.

can I do you now, sir? A c.p. adopted from 'Itma' and dating since 1940. In that B.B.C. radio programme, the 'gag' was spoken by 'Mrs Mopp' (Dorothy Summers) to Tommy Handley.

canal boat, the The 'tote' (totalisator): rhyming s.

cane To damage considerably, to shell heavily: military. Hence, to treat badly, e.g. a motor-car.

canned Tipsy.

canoe, paddle one's own To be independent: coll. Orig. U.S., anglicized ca. 1875.

canoodle, v.t. and i. Fondle; bill and coo: coll. Orig. U.S., thoroughly anglicized by G. A. Sala in 1864. By 1930 ob.; by 1945, decidedly archaic.

canteen medal A beer stain on one's tunic; good-conduct medal: military.

Canuck, occ. Canack, Kanuck A Canadian: in England, from ca. 1915. Orig. a Canadian and American term for a French Canadian, which, inside Canada, it still remains. Etymology obscure. Hence, a Canadian horse (or pony): coll.

cap (Gen. in pl.) Abbr. *capital letter*: coll.—(Only in vocative.) Captain: coll. Ware, 1909, 'Common in America—gaining ground in England'.

Cape of Good Hope Soap: rhyming s.

Cape smoke 'A brandy manufactured in nearly all the vine-growing districts of the Colony' (Pettman): South African coll.

caper A dodge, device, performance: coll. *The London Herald*, March 23, 1867, ' "He'll get five years penal for this little caper," said the policeman'.

cap'n Captain: coll.

Captain Kettle   To settle (vigorously), v.t.: rhyming s. Ex the famous character of fiction: Cutcliffe Hyne's stories were published over the years 1898–1938.

caput   (Also *kaput, kapout.*) Finished; no more: military. Little used in W.W. II. Ex Ger. *kaputt*, done for, ruined.

card   A 'character', an odd fellow. Note *The Card*, a novel (1911) by Arnold Bennett.

card, one's best   One's best plan or action: coll.

career boy   One who, in a combatant Service, puts self-success before the nation's welfare: R.A.F. s. (1942) >, by 1944, all three Services' coll.

carney, carny   Seductive flattery; suave hypocrisy: coll.

carn(e)y, v.   To coax, wheedle insinuatingly: coll. and dial.

carn(e)y   Sly, artful: low and military.

carneying, ppl. adj.   Wheedling, insinuating, seductively flattering, suavely hypocritical: coll. Perhaps ex L. *carno, carnis*, flesh, via It. *carne* and after *blarney.*

carpet-biter; carpet-biting   One (usually male) who gets into a fearful rage; a distressing exhibition of uncontrollable rage: coll.: since ca. 1940. Ex the stories of Hitler biting carpets in his insane rages.

carpet, walk the (now rare); **be on the carpet**   To be reprimanded: coll. Ex 'servants . . . summoned into the "parlour" for a wigging', W.

carrots   Red hair, hence, a nickname: coll.

carry on   To behave conspicuously: frolic; flirt: coll. To endure hardship; show quiet and constant fortitude: a coll. popularized by W.W. I.

carry the can   To be reprimanded: naval. As *carry the can back* it means, since ca. 1920 in the R.A.F.: to be made the scapegoat; to do the dirty work while another person gets the credit.

carry the torch for (somebody; hence for a cause)   To be in love with, to be devoted to. Adopted, ex U.S., ca. 1943.

cart, in the   In the wrong; in a 'fix'. Esp. as *put in the cart*, to deceive, trick, embarrass, incommode seriously, as a jockey his owner.

carve up   To swindle an accomplice out of his share. Hence, a *carve-up* is any swindle. The amount of money left by a will.

case   An eccentric person, a 'character', a 'cure'. Orig., U.S. anglicized ca. 1850; by 1950, ob.—The certainty to fall in love; a falling-in-love, as 'It's a case with them'.

cases, get down to   To 'get down to brass tacks'; talk seriously.

caser   The sum of five shillings: orig. c. In C. 20, racing. Ex Yiddish.

S.S.D.—C

cash in To succeed, esp. financially: coll.

cash (or **hand in**, or **pass in**) **one's checks** To die: orig. U.S.A., anglicized ca. 1875. *Checks* = counters in the game of poker. Cf. *peg out*.

cat, v. To vomit: low coll.; in C. 20, mainly dial.

cat, sick as a Vomiting; very sick indeed: coll.

cat-nap A short sleep had while sitting: coll.

catch A person matrimonially desirable: coll.

catch (a) cold To get into trouble, esp. by being too impetuous. Services.

catch bending To catch (a person) at a disadvantage: jocular coll.

catch it To be scolded, reprimanded, castigated: coll.

catch on To 'take', be a success: coll.—To understand, grasp the meaning or significance, apprehend: coll., orig. U.S.

cats and dogs, rain To rain hard: coll.

cat's pyjamas, the Anything very good, attractive, etc.: American, anglicized by 1923 but † by 1933. Cf.:

cat's whiskers, the A variant of the preceding; virtually † by 1945.

caught with one's pants, or **trousers, down** Taken unawares: unready.

cauli Cauliflower: coll.

caulk or **caulking** A (short) sleep: nautical.

caulk, v. To sleep, esp. if surreptitiously: nautical.

caution A person or a thing wonderful, unusual or, esp., odd, eccentric: coll.: orig. U.S. One with whom caution should be employed.

cave! Schoolboys': ? first at Eton College for 'beware!' Direct ex the L. word.

cave-man A 'he-man', a rough and virile fellow: coll. Hence *caveman stuff*, rough treatment.

celebrate, v.i. To drink in honour of an event or person; hence, to drink joyously: coll.

century £100: the turf.

cert Abbr. *certainty*.

cert or **certif** Certificate.

c'est la guerre! A military c.p. by way of excuse or apology: 1915–18. Ex the Fr. explanation ('It's the war, don't you know!') of any deficiency.

chaff, n and v. Banter, ridicule; humbug: coll. Prob. ex *chafe*, to gall, fret, irritate.

chair, the The electric chair (for criminals): coll.: U.S., anglicized by 1930.

chair-borne divisions, the   Those members of the Force who work in offices: R.A.F. Ironically ex *Airborne Divisions*.

chalk, by a long   By much: coll. Ex 'the use of chalk in scoring points in games' (W).

chalk farm   An arm: rhyming s.

champ   A champion: coll.

champion   Excellent: coll. Esp. as 'That's champion!'

chance it   To take one's chances: coll.

chance one's arm   To take a risk in the hope of achieving something worthwhile. Prob. ex boxing.

chancer   A liar; too confident of his ability: coll.

change out of, get no   To receive no satisfaction from; fail to earn from: coll.

changes, ring the   To change a better article for a worse; esp., bad money for good: c. >, ca. 1830. In C. 20, it also = to adopt different disguises in rapid succession and with baffling effect.

chap   A 'customer', a fellow: coll. Abbr. *chapman*; ex the early sense, a buyer, a customer.

char   Abbr. *charwoman*: coll.—Tea (the drink).

char, chare, v.   To come in to do the cleaning work in a house, shop, office, or institution: coll. Ex Chinese.

chara   Charabanc.

character   An eccentric or odd person, esp. if humorous or witty or original: coll.

character   A character part: theatrical coll. Whereas the R.A.F. speaks of *types* and the Navy and the Army imitate, the Royal Navy speaks of *characters* and the other two Services imitate. Indeed, since ca. 1945, the term has become increasingly popular everywhere and means simply 'fellows' or 'guys'.

Charles James   A theatre box: theatrical rhyming s. On Charles James Fox. Hence *Charley*.

Charley James (2)   A fox: hunting s.

Charley Howard   A coward: rhyming s.

Charley Mason   A basin: rhyming s.

Charley Prescot   A waistcoat: rhyming s.

charming wife   A knife: rhyming s.

chase   To stand nearby and keep urging (someone) to get on with a piece of work: Service coll.

chaser   A drink taken immediately after another of a different sort: coll.

chat   In Parlary, a thing, an object; *any*thing.

chat, v.   (More frequent as v.i. than as v.t.) To search for lice: military. Vbl. n., *chatting*.—To address tentatively; to 'word': Australian.

chat, n. A louse: See next.

chatt In C. 20 gen. *chat*, before W.W. I rare in singular. A louse. Prob. ex *chattels* = live stock (q.v.) or chattels = movable property.

chatty Lousy. Ex *chatt*.

chauff To act as chauffeur to.

chav(v)y A child: Parlary. Ex Romany *chavo* or *chavi*.

chaw the fat A naval variant of *chew the fat*.

cheap, on the Cheaply; economically. Coll.; from the late 1850's. Hotten, 1st ed.

cheaps, the A cheap edition; cheap editions: publishers', book-sellers', and bookbinders' coll.

check To reprimand, to take to task, during the exercise of one's duty: Services'. Proleptic: it should check the recipient's evil ways.

cheek Insolence to an elder or superior; audacity, effrontery, assurance: coll.

cheek, v. To address saucily: coll.

cheekiness Impudence; audacity; tendency to 'give cheek': coll.

cheeky Saucy, impudent, insolent: coll.

cheerio or **cheero!** A parting word of encouragement; in drinking, a toast: coll. The former is the more familiar.

cheers! Often *three cheers*. A coll. expression of deep satisfaction or friendly approval.

cheese, hard In comment or exclamation: bad luck!: coll.; by 1945, slightly archaic.

cheese, the The fashion; the best; 'the correct thing'. By 1920, ob.; by 1960, virtually †. Prob. ex the Urdu *chiz*, a thing; cf. 'that's the thing'.

cheesed(-)off Disgruntled: Liverpool boys' (−1914); Liverpool troops' (1914–18); common in all Services since ca. 1935; but since 1940, esp. R.A.F. Professor Douglas Hamer derives it ex the Liverpool boys' *cheese off!*, run away and don't be a nuisance.

chemmy The game of *chemin de fer*: coll.

cherry hog A dog: rhyming s. In greyhound racing, *the cherries* = the dogs.

cherry-ogs Greyhound racing: rhyming s. (on *dogs*): since ca. 1920. Often shortened to *the cherries*.

cherry-ripe A pipe: rhyming s. Nonsense: rhyming s. (on *tripe*).

chest, get it off one's 'To deliver a speech; express one's feelings' (C. J. Dennis): coll.

chestnut A stale story or outworn jest: coll. Ex U.S. *roast chestnuts* (well-cooked).

chesty Weak in the chest: coll.

chew the fat or **rag** To grumble; to argue endlessly; to spin a yarn: mostly Army and Navy.

chi-chi, n. and adj. Half-caste (girl, rarely boy): Indian Army and Anglo-Indian coll. Ex Hindustani.—Unnecessary fuss, affected protests or manners: Society coll. Adopted from Fr. coll., itself either choice or derived from sense 1.—Hence, excessive red-tape: Army officers'.

chic Skill, dexterity, esp. in the arts: style; elegance; coll. Ex the Fr.

chic, adj. Elegant, stylish: s.> coll. Ex the n.

chicken, no Elderly: coll.

chicken-feed Small change: Canadian (and U.S.), hence also English and Australian. Hence, a pittance (financial) or a bare minimum (of food).

chief, as *the chief* The Chief Engineer: nautical coll. A Petty Officer, etc.: naval.—**(chief)** A—gen. jocular—form of address: coll.

chiefie A Flight-Sergeant: R.A.F.: since April 1918. Ex the days when, in the Royal Naval Air Service, the corresponding man held the rank of *Chief* Petty Officer (3rd class).

chiike, occ. **chy-ack** (or **chiack**) and **chi-hike** A street (orig. costers') salute; a word of praise heartily spoken. Echoic. Whence, in Australia, a jeering call, a piece of 'cheek'.

chiike, chy-ack, v. To hail; praise noisily: esp. Cockney coll. Among tailors: to chaff ruthlessly. Whence, in Australia, to 'cheek', of which it is a corruption.

child, this Oneself; I, me: coll.; orig. U.S., anglicized ca. 1890. Early in C. 20, there was a c.p.: *not for this child.* By 1945, archaic.

chimp A coll. abbr. of *chimpanzee*: among the keepers at the Zoo.

chin, v. To talk, esp. if loquaciously or argumentatively.

chin-wag Talk, chatter: *Punch,* in 1879: 'I'd just like to have a bit of chin-wag with you on the quiet.' By 1950, ob.

china: chiner (Often *old china.*) A pal, a mate: abbr. *china plate,* rhyming s.

chinaman A left-hand bowler's leg-break: cricketers'. Ex the manner of Chinese script, right to left.

Chink A Chinese: mainly Australian.

chip, v. To 'cheek', interrupt with (gen. deliberate) impertinence: Australian and New Zealand.

chip in, v.i. To join in an undertaking; contribute a share; interpose smartly in a conversation, discussion, or speech: orig. U.S. anglicized ca. 1890.—Hence, to interfere: C. 20.

chip on one's shoulder, have a To bear a grudge against the world: coll. Originally, U.S. lumbermen's; from chips falling onto the shoulders of men working beneath or very near a tree that is being felled.

chips A carpenter (esp. in Army and Navy). Money; esp., *be in the chips*.

chirpy Cheerful; lively: coll.

chisel To cheat: coll. Hence the old conundrum, 'Why is a carpenter like a swindler?—Because he chisels a deal.'

chit, give (someone) **a good—a bad** To speak well, or badly, of someone: Army.

chiv, chive, chivey A knife. Ex Romany; orig., an underworld term.

chiv(e)y, chivy, v. To chase around, as in H. Kingsley's 'The dog . . . used to chivy the cats'. Prob. ex S.E. *Chivy Chase.*

chivvy, v. To keep (someone) up to the mark by word and gesture: Army.

choc (Gen. in pl.) Abbr. *chocolate*: coll.

choice! you pays (yer or) your money and you takes (yer or) your A C. 20 c.p. = you take whatever you choose. Ex the cry of showmen.

chocker, adj. Disgruntled, 'fed up': naval lower-deck. Ex. S.E. *chockful.*

choke off To reprimand or 'tell off' or retort successfully upon: military coll.

choker A high all-round collar. A garotter: coll.

chokey, choky A lock-up; a prison. Ex Hindustani *chauki*, lit. a four-sided place or building. Hence, imprisonment. A detention-cell, occ. a guard-room: military.

choom Properly, but less gen., *chum*. A term of address much used by the Australian and New Zealand soldiers to an unknown English (not Welsh, Scottish or Irish) soldier.

choosey Fastidious; given to picking and choosing: coll.

chop A wood-chopping contest: Australian and New Zealand coll.

chop-chop! Quickly; immediately: pidgin. Prob. ex Cantonese.

chow-chow Food of any kind; now *chow*. Ex 'pidgin', where, lit., a mixture.

Christian A 'decent fellow'; coll. As adj. civilized, respectable: coll.

Christmas-tree order, in In heavy marching order: military.

chronic Unpleasant; objectionable; unfair; 'rotten'.

chronic, something Badly, severely, most objectionably: proletarian.

chuck, n. Food of any kind, but esp. bread or meat (−1850): orig. c., but popularized in 1914–18. Perhaps such food as one can chuck about without spoiling it.

chuck, v.   To abandon, dismiss; (v.i.) give up, often varied to *chuck up.*   Whence *chuck it!* = drop it! stop (talking, etc.).

chuck, get or **give the**   To be dismissed, to dismiss: low coll.— Hence, of a proposal for marriage or a courtship, as in Dorothy Sayers, *Clouds of Witness,* 1926, 'I got the chuck from Barbara and didn't feel much like bothering about other people's heart-to-hearts.'

chuck a dummy   A faint on parade: military, from ca. 1890.

chuck off   to employ sarcasm; **chuck off at,** to banter or chaff: Australian.

chuck one's hand in   To stop doing something. Ex cards.

chuck one's weight about   To 'show off'.

chuck out   To eject forcibly; to discard (thing or plan); coll.— Hence, jocularly, to cause to leave.

chucker-out   A man, often ex-pugilist, retained to eject persons from dances, meetings, taverns, brothels, etc.: coll.

chuff, n.   Food: Services, esp. Army.

chum   A friend; a (close) companion: now coll.—See *choom.* Perhaps by abbreviation and collision of *chamber-fellow* or *-mate.*

chum, long-eared; long-faced chum; long-haired chum   A mule; a horse; a girl: military.

chummy   A coll. diminutive of *chum* = friend, 'pal'.

chummy, adj.   Friendly, intimate; sociable: coll.

chummy ships   Ships whose crews are 'friends': nautical coll.

chump   The head; esp. in *off one's chump,* very eccentric; mad to almost any degree.

cig   A cigarette.

circs   Circumstances: trivial coll.

circumference   The waist of a large, fat person: coll.

circus   Any temporary group of persons that, housed together, are working at the same task, e.g. at an encyclopaedia: coll.

civies, civvies   Civilian clothes: servicemen's.

civvy, civy, adj.   Civilian, esp. with *life* or *clothes.* Also, a civilian: coll.

civvy street   The condition and status of a civilian; 'What did you do in Civvy Street?' was often heard, 1939–45, in the Services, where its use persists.

clam   One who says extremely little or is excessively secretive: coll.

Clara & Mona   The all-clear and air-raid warning sirens: 1939–45. Puns on clear and on moaning sound.

claret   Blood: in boxing circles; ob. Ex the colour.

classy   Stylish; fashionable; smart; well-turned-out: coll. Also *class.*

clean gone   Quite 'cracked'; mad: coll.

clean out To deprive of money, gen. illicitly.

clean round the bend See *round the bend*.

clean up To acquire (something) as profit or gain: coll.: U.S., anglicized by 1910.

clear, in the With no evidence against one; innocent, or app. so.

clear as mud Anything but clear; confused: coll.

clever 'At first a colloquial and local word', says the S.O.D.; it still is coll. if = 'cunning' or 'skilful' and applied to an animal or if = 'well', 'in good health or spirits'. *Not too clever*, indisposed in health; common in Australia and New Zealand.

clever boots Usually as comment: a clever, occ. a sly, person.

clever boys, the Servicemen (or others) with only theoretical knowledge; *the really clever boys*, those possessing academic knowledge. Services'.

clew-up, v.i. To join another ship; to finish a job. To meet an old messmate, as in 'I clewed up with old Dusty Miller in the Smoke': naval.

click A clique; a 'push' (Australian sense).

click, v. In 1914 +, orig. military, 'to do a drill movement with a click'; 'to click for a fatigue or a duty (i.e. to be put down for one)'; (of a man) 'to click with a member of the opposite sex', i.e. get off with one, also absolutely as in 'He's clicked'; hence, to be successful, to have a piece of very good luck (with variant 'he's clicked for something'; (of a woman) to 'meet' a man, usually as *click with* (a fellow). Ex the click one hears when a small mechanical object falls into position, or when a key is turned.

client A person, a fellow or chap: military, hence general. Suggested by *customer*.

clincher A conclusive statement or argument: coll.

cliner, occ. **clinah** A girl: Australian; by 1950, ob. Ex Yiddish: cf. *cobber*.

clink A prison; a lock-up; a detention cell. Echoic from the fetters.

clinking First-rate; remarkably good: coll.; esp. in racing and games. *The Sporting Times*, March 12, 1887, 'Prince Henry must be a clinking good horse.'

clippy A girl conductor on bus or tram.

clobber Clothes; among soldiers, one's full equipment. Chiefly Jewish, Cockney and C. 20 Australian. Prob. ex Yiddish *klbr*.

clock The face. Cf. *dial*.—A taxi-meter: taxi-drivers' coll.

clod A copper coin; esp. a penny and mostly in pl. Prob. ex both the colour and the weight.

clot A fool, a 'stupid'; an incompetent. By a pun on equivalent S.E. *clod*.

clothes(-)peg   An egg: rhyming s.

clue, have no   To be ignorant, have no information: mostly Army. Ex:

clueless   Ignorant; esp. in *clueless type* (opposite of *gen wallah*) and, in answer to a question, 'I'm clueless': R.A.F., since ca. 1940; hence also Army. Ex crime-detection.

co-ed   Co-educational: coll.

co-op   *Co-op store.* A co-operative store: coll.

coal & coke   Penniless: rhyming s. (on *broke*).

coal box   A German shell that, of low velocity, bursts with a dense cloud of black smoke; esp. a 5·9: military.

coaly, coaley, coalie   A coal-heaver or -porter: coll.

coat & badge   To cadge: military rhyming s.

cobber   A friend, comrade, companion: Australian. Ex Yiddish *chaber*, a comrade (cf. *cliner*). Dr Thomas Wood, *Cobbers*, 1934.

cobbo   A familiar form of *cobber*.

cobbon   See *cawbawn*.

cock & hen   A £10 note: the number 10; a pen (often *cockernen*): all, rhyming s.

cock-eye   A squinting-eye; *cock-eyed*, squinting: coll. Hence, *cock-eye* and *cock-eyed*, crooked; inaccurate. Lit., like a 'tilted' eye.— (Only *cock-eyed*.) Tipsy.

cock-linnet   A minute: rhyming s.

cock-sparrow   A barrow: rhyming s.

cockies' joy   Treacle: Australian: late C. 19–20. See *cocky, n.*

cockroach   A motor coach: rhyming s.: since ca. 1946.

cocky   Very pert: saucily impudent: over-confident: coll.—A low coll. form of address.—As n.: a small farmer: Aus.

codger, esp. with *old*   (Whimsically pejorative of) an old man: low coll.

coffee & cocoa   Often reduced to *cocoa*. To say so: rhyming s. The longer form is occasionally varied to *tea and cocoa*.

coffee-house, -houser, -housing   To gossip during a fox-hunt, esp. while the huntsmen wait for hounds to draw a covert; one who does this; the act of doing this: sporting. Hence applied to any gossiping done at work.

coffin-nail   A cigarette. Often as c.p., *another nail in one's coffin*. Cf. *gasper*.

coin money   To make money both easily and quickly: coll.

coke   Cocaine: c. and low; orig. U.S., anglicized ca. 1920. Esp. in Edgar Wallace's novels. Hence, *cokey*, a cocaine-addict.

coke   (A drink of) *Coca*-Cola: adopted, in 1944 or 1945, ex U.S.: s. until ca. 1950, then coll.

cold, have or **have got** (a person)   To have him at one's mercy.

cold, leave To fail to impress or convince or please: coll. 'My dear fellow, that leaves me cold.'

cold feet, get or **have (got)** To become, to be, discouraged, afraid: coll.

cold-meat ticket An identity disc: military.

cold shivers, the A fit of trembling: coll.

coll College: schoolboys' and undergraduates'.

collar, v. To appropriate; steal.

colleckers, collekers Terminal examinations with interviews: Oxford. Ex *collections*.

collect, v. To retrieve (objects) from a place; hence, to call for a person and then proceed with him: coll. V.i. and v.t., to receive (something as) one's deserts: Australian.—To receive one's salary or wages: coll.

collect a gong To be awarded a decoration: Army and Air Force officers'.

college A prison.

college chum A prisoner (orig. of Newgate, the *City College*).

colly-wobbles A stomach-ache: coll. Ex *colic*.

Colney Hatch A match: rhyming s.

Colonel, the The *Colonel Bogey* of golf: golfing coll. Personification of *bogey*, bugbear (of golfers).

colour, off Debilitated; indisposed: coll.

colour of a person's money, see the To see his money: esp., to be paid: coll.

com A commercial traveller; a comedian. (Both slightly ob.)— A commission (monetary).—A Communist: Aus.

comb cut, have one's To be humiliated; hence, down on one's luck. Coll. soon > S.E.; from ca. 1570. Cf. Scott's 'All the Counts in Cumberland shall not cut my comb'. But *be comb-cut*, to be mortified or disgraced, has always been coll. (−1860); ob. Ex cock-fighting.

comb one's head To scold: C. 18–19. A C. 19–20 variant, esp. as to rebuke, is *comb one's hair*; ob. With the addition of *with a joint* or *three-legged stool*, it means—as sometimes it does in the shorter form—to beat, thrash. Shakespeare, 1596, 'Her care should be, To combe your noddle with a three-legg'd stoole'.

combie (Pron. *com-bee*) Abbr. *combination-room*; at Cambridge University, from ca. 1860; ob. A woman's combination(s): from ca. 1870: women's, nursery, and shop.

combine A combination of persons, esp. in commerce: orig. (ca. 1887) U.S., anglicized ca. 1910: coll. till ca. 1930, when it > S.E.

combined chat A bed-sitting room: theatrical (−1935). Prob. ex underworld *chat*, a house, orig. a thing.

comboman   A mostly Central Australian name for a white man who associates with native women. See esp. Conrad Sayce's novel, *Comboman*, 1934. I.e., a 'combination' man.

come   To play a trick (v.t. with *over*): coll.—To act the part of, as in *come the old soldier*, q.v.

come across   To be agreeable, compliant; v.t. with *with*, to give, yield; lend. Ex U.S.

come again!   Repeat, please!

come-back, make (occ. **stage**) **a**   To succeed after (long) retirement: (orig. sporting) coll.

come clean   To confess. Ex U.S.

come down, v.   To give or lend money (or an equivalent). v.t., *come down with*: coll.

come down (up)on (a person) **like a ton of bricks**   To scold, blame, reprimand severely: coll.

come good   To make money; be in credit or in form; to be succeeding: Australian.

come it strong   To go to extremes; exaggerate; to lie: coll.

come off the grass!   Not so much 'side'! Don't exaggerate, or tell lies! Ex U.S.; anglicized ca. 1890. Often abbr. to *come off it!* or even *come off!*

come over   With *faint, ill, queer, sick*, etc., to become suddenly faint, etc.: coll.

come the old soldier (v.t. with *over*)   To bluff; to wheedle, to shirk; to domineer: orig. military.

come to a sticky end   To die murdered; to go to gaol.

come to that!   Since you mention it!: coll. 'Come to that, it was nothing special!'

come undone, unput, unstuck   To fall to pieces, lit. and fig.; to experience disaster: coll. (orig. naval and military).

comether on, put the   To coax, wheedle: Anglo-Irish coll. Ex *come hither*.

comfy   Comfortable: coll. (orig. Society). Prob. influenced by *cosy*.

comic, n.   A comic periodical; a music hall comedian: coll.

commem   Commemoration Day or Week: universities' coll.

commercial traveller   A person with bags under his eyes. Ex a music-hall joke.

commie   A communist.

commish   *Commission*, a percentage on sales.

common   Common sense.

comp   A compositor; to compose (type): printers' coll.

compo   A monthly advance of wages: nautical coll.

con   A *con*vict: low.

con-game, -man A confidence trick, trickster. Orig., an American underworld term.

conchy, or **conchie,** occ. **conshie** or **-y** (Pron. *ko'nshee.*) Abbr. *conscientious objector,* i.e. to military service.

confab A talk together, or a discussion, esp. if familiar: coll. Ex *confabulation.*

confounded Inopportune; unpleasant, odious. This coll., like *awful, beastly, terrible,* is a mere counter of speech, a thought-substitute.

congrats, congratters Congratulations, esp. as an exclamation.

conk The nose; esp., a large one: low. Prob. ex *conch,* L. *concha;* cf. L. *testa* (a pot, a shell) = head.

conk, v. esp. *conk out.* To fail, break down, mostly of an engine, a machine; aviation s. (1918) > by 1921, gen. coll.—Hence, to die.

conk, v. To hit: Australian. Echoic; imm. ex:—To punch (someone) on the nose: pugilistic, by 1950, ob.

conner Food: Regular Army's. Ex Hindustani.

conservatory Enclosed portion of an aircraft; sometimes the cockpit: R.A.F. Ex the 'glass-roofing'.

constitutional A walk taken for the good of one's constitution or health: coll.

contraption A contrivance or device; a small tool: coll. Perhaps ex *'contriv*ance' + 'inven*tion*'.

convey To steal. Shakespeare has 'Convey, the wise it call'. Orig. euphemistic; but in mid-C. 19–20 decidedly coll. in its facetiousness.

coo! Indicates astonishment or disbelief: coll. mostly proletarian. Prob. ex *good (gracious* or *Lord)!*: cf. the frequent *coo lummy!*

cooee, within Within easy reach: Australian coll.

cook To manipulate, tamper with; falsify: coll. (Of persons) to swelter in the heat: coll.; from ca. 1860.

cook one's goose To ruin; defeat; kill. Cf. *do brown* and *settle one's hash.*

cookie A heavy bomb: R.A.F. 1940–5.

cool, adj. (Of jazz music) good and modern; (of a singer) slow and husky: jazz lovers'.—Very pleasing or attractive or satisfactory: Canadian (esp. teenagers'): adopted, ca. 1955, from U.S.

cooler A prison; esp., *in the cooler*: orig. U.S.; anglicized ca. 1890.

coot A simpleton: orig. U.S.; anglicized ca. 1850. Gen. as *silly coot* or *old coot.* Ex the common coot's stupidity.—Hence, a person of no account: contemptuous Australian.

cop A policeman. Abbr. *copper.*—An arrest, as in *It's a (fair) cop* (spoken by the victim).

cop, v.   To catch, capture.—Hence to steal: low. In mid-C. 19–20, it also = to receive, be forced to endure, as in *cop it* (*hot*), to get into trouble,—*cop the bullet*, get the sack,—*cop the needle*, become angry. The C.20 *cop out* is a variant of *cop it hot*. Among servicemen, *cop it* = to die; *cop a packet* = to be wounded, esp. if severely.— To arrest, imprison: orig. an underworld term. The word derives Old Fr. *caper*, to seize.

cop, be no (or **not much**)   Of a task: to be difficult; of an object: valueless.

cope   To do one's duty satisfactorily: coll., orig. Services (esp. Army officers'), since 1935; adopted from Society s. Short for *cope with things, cope with it*, etc. 'Can you cope?' is perhaps the most frequent form.

copper   A policeman, i.e. one who 'cops' or captures, arrests. A penny or a halfpenny. In pl., coll. for halfpennies and pennies mixed. 'Still used of the bronze which has superseded the copper coinage' (O.E.D.).

copper's nark   A police spy or informer: c.; and low s. *Nark* = spy.

copy(-)cat   A person annoyingly given to imitation of others: coll.

copybook, blot one's   To spoil one's record: coll.

cords   A pair of corduroy trousers; clothes of corduroy: lower classes' s.; by 1945, gen. coll.

corker   Something that ends an argument or a course of action; anything astounding, esp. a great lie: coll.

corking   Unusually large, fine, good: coll. App. ex *corker*, q.v., on the model of other percussive adjj. (*whacking, whopping*, etc.).

corner-boy   A loafer: Anglo-Irish coll.

corns & bunions   Onions: rhyming s. also as in 'He knows his corns and bunions'.

corny   Old-fashioned and sentimental; over-sentimental; trite: adopted, 1943 or 1944, from U.S. servicemen. Ex U.S. *corn* (adopted ca. 1955), the sincerely and frankly sentimental, the trite but true and good, perhaps with a reference to the homely ways of those who live in the Corn Belt.

corp   Corporal: military coll. A corpse: nautical.

corporation   A prominent belly: coll. C. Brontë, *Shirley*, 'The dignity of an ample corporation'.

corpse, v.   To blunder and thus confuse other actors or spoil a scene; the blunderer is said to be 'corpsed': theatrical.

corpse-reviver   Any powerful, refreshing drink. Ex a specific U.S. mixed drink.

cosh   A life-preserver, i.e. a short thin but loaded bludgeon; occ. of a policeman's truncheon. Prob. ex Romany. Hence 'to *cosh*'.

cosy All very snug and profitable; remarkably convenient: coll.

cotton, v.i. With *to*, 'get on' well with (a person), take kindly to (an idea, a thing): coll.

cotton on, v.i.; v.t. with *to* To form, or have, a liking or fancy for a thing (plan, person): coll. Ex *cotton*. To understand.

cough up To pay, v.i. and t. To produce, hand over.

couldn't care less, I, or **he,** etc. A c.p. ('I'm quite indifferent') dating from 1940 and rampant ever since early 1948: originally, upper-middle class, but, by 1945, fairly general.

counter-jumper A shopman: coll.

county-court To sue a person in a county court: coll.

cove A man, a companion, chap, fellow.

cow Milk: Canadian and Australian.—(Always either *a cow* or, more strongly, *a fair cow*.) A despicable or objectionable person, a (most) unworthy act; an obnoxious thing: Australian and hence N.Z. Cows are awkward and 'awkward' creatures.

cow-cocky A dairy-farmer: Australia.

cowardy (occ. **cowardly**) **custard** A child's taunt: coll. A custard *quivers*.

cows-and-kisses Wife; the mistress of house; rhyming s. on 'missus'.

crab, v. To 'pull to pieces', criticize adversely: coll.

crack To break open, burgle. Esp. in *crack a crib*, to break into a house; by 1940 †. In cricket, to hit (the ball) hard; hence, to smite (a person).

crack, adj. First-class; excellent: coll.

crack, n. Esp. *have a crack at it*. An attempt. Orig. a Service term: 'have a *shot* at something'.—Short for *wisecrack*, a witticism: coll.

crack down on To suppress (lawless persons or acts); to reprimand: Services'.

crack hardy To endure patiently, suppress pain or emotion: Australian.

crack up To praise highly: coll.—V.i., to be exhausted; break down, whether physically or mentally: coll.

cracked Crazy: coll.

cracker A very fast pace: coll.

crackers, adj. Crazy; mad. Cf. *cracked*.

cracking, adj. Very fast, as 'a cracking pace': coll.

cracking, get See *get cracking*.

cracksman A house-breaker. Orig. an underworld term. Cf. *crack*, v.

crafty Skilful, clever, well judged; well planned; well timed; sly ('Just time for a crafty one'—a drink): Services', esp. R.A.F. coll.

cram, v. To ply, hence to deceive, with lies.—To prepare oneself or another hastily, gen. for an examination: coll.—To urge on a horse with spur or knee and with hand or reins: sporting.

crammer One who prepares students, pupils, for examination: coll.

crank A person odd, eccentric, very 'faddy', mildly monomaniacal: orig. U.S., anglicized ca. 1890; in C. 20, coll.

crash-lob; force-lob, v.i. To make a forced landing: R.A.F. and coll., resp. Here, *lob* (ex cricket) = to arrive, to land.

crash the swede To get one's head down on the pillow: naval (lower-deck).

crashing bore A very tedious or tiresome person or, occ., thing: coll. Anthony Berkeley, *Panic Party*, 1934, 'It's a crashing bore . . . to think of those dim cads knocking us for six like this, but . . . it's no use getting strenuous about it'. Ex aviation.

crawl with To be alive, or filled with: military coll. >, by 1920, gen. coll. On *be lousy with*.

crawler A contemptible sycophant: coll.

crawling Verminous: Army and working-class's coll. Short for *crawling with lice*.

crawly Having, or like, the feeling of insects a-crawl on one's skin: coll.

crazy Very eager (*for* or *about*, or *to do*, something): coll.

crease To kill (a person): orig. an underworld expression. Proleptic.

create, v.i. To make a fuss, a 'row'. Ex *create a disturbance* or *fuss*.

creep, n. An objectionable or unpleasant person; a dull, insignificant, unwanted person: adopted, ca. 1944, ex U.S.

creeper A sycophant. Cf. *crawler*.

creeps, the A thrill resulting from an undefined dread: coll. Hence the adj. *creepy*.

crib, n. A plagiarism: from ca. 1830; coll.—A literal translation illicitly used by students or pupils: coll.

crib, v. To pilfer; take furtively; to plagiarize: coll.—To use a 'crib'; to cheat in an examination: coll.—To grumble: military. Ex S.E. *crib-biter*.

croak Means both to die and to kill; it was, until ca. 1920, an underworld term.

croc A file of schoolgirls walking in pairs: mostly school s. Ex *crocodile*, itself orig. university s., now coll.—Also, of course, the crocodile itself: coll.

crock A disabled person: coll. Ex the Scottish *crock*, a broken-down horse.

crock up To get disabled; break down; fall ill. Ex preceding.

crocodile See *croc*.

crocus A surgeon or a doctor (esp. a quack). Short for *crocus metallorum*, itself of obscure origin.—Hence among grafters, also a herbalist, a miracle-worker. See esp. Philip Allingham, *Cheapjack*, 1934, and Neil Bell, *Crocus*, a novel of the fairs, 1936.

cronk (Of a horse) made to appear ill in order to cheat its backers: racing s. > gen. Ex Ger. *krank*, sick, ill.—Hence, unsound; dishonestly come by. Both senses are Australian. Cf. *crook*, adj.

crook Ill: Australian. Prob. ex *cronk*, via *crooked*.—Also see:

crook Spurious: Australian.

crook, go To give way to anger: to express annoyance: Australian. Prob. ex first *crook*.

cropper, esp. **come**, or *go*, **a cropper** A heavy fall, fig. and lit. Ex hunting.

cross To play false to; to cheat.

cross as the devil A variant, or perhaps rather an intensive, of:

cross as two sticks, as Very peevish or annoyed: coll. Perhaps ex their rasping together, but prob. ex two sticks set athwart.

cross-patch A peevish child or young woman: coll.

crow In the underworld with corresponding v., a confederate on watch.

crowd, v. To verge on: Canadian coll.: adopted, ex U.S. 'He must be crowding forty.'

crown To hit (a person) on the *crown*: orig. low.

cruel the pitch To frustrate schemes. Ex cricket.

crummy Lousy; hence dirty, untidy.

crump A 'coal-box', i.e. a 5·9 German shell or shell-burst; occ. of heavier guns: military: 1914–1918. Hence, to shell with heavy guns.

crump dump, the The Ruhr: R.A.F.: late 1940–early 1945. Ex the numerous bombs the R.A.F. dumped there.

crumpet The head: ob. by 1935.

crush A large social gathering, esp. if crowded: hence (in the Army) a military unit; ob. by 1939.—Hence a set, a group: coll. as in *Shakespeare—and That Crush*, by Richard Dark and Thomas Derrick, 1931.—An infatuation; a strong liking or 'fancy' for a person: U.S., anglicized in or by 1927. Esp. *have a crush on*.

crusher A policeman.—Hence, a ship's corporal: naval.

crust Impudence, 'cheek'; by 1945, ob. Perhaps ex face as hard as a crust.

crypto A 'secret' Communist; a sympathizer with Communism. Short for *crypto-Communist*.

cuckoo, adj. Mad, senseless, distraught; U.S., anglicized in early 1920's; by 1960, slightly archaic.

cuddy A nickname for a donkey: coll. ? ex *Cuthbert*.

cuff, on the On credit. Ex pencilling the debt on one's cuff.

cully A man, companion, mate, partner; orig., low s.; by 1960, rare except among Cockneys.

cup o(f) tea, one's What truly suits one; even one's ideal: coll.

cuppa A cup of tea; esp., a *nice cuppa*: Australian; by 1950, fairly gen.—and coll. By abbreviation and ex the Australian addiction to 'nice cups of tea'.

cure An eccentric, an odd person; hence, a very amusing one: coll. Perhaps abbr. *curiosity* or, more prob., *curious fellow*.

curl, make (a person's) hair To cause one to shudder: coll.

curl up To fall silent, 'shut up'.—(Sporting.) To collapse: coll.

currant bun The sun: rhyming s.

cushy Of a job, task, or post; easy, safe; (of a wound) not dangerous: military. Either ex Hindustani *khush*, pleasure, or Romany *kushto*, good.

cuss A person; esp. a man: coll. From U.S.; anglicized ca. 1880. Ex *customer*.

cussedness Cantankerousness (persons); contrariness (things): coll. From U.S.; anglicized ca. 1880. Ex *customer*.

custom, it's an old (orig. **Southern**) In 1935 this, in the *Southern form*, > a c.p.; it is a line from a popular song. By the end of the year, other words had begun to be substituted for *Southern*. In *The Evening News* of Jan. 4, 1936, we read of the man who, on being upbraided by his wife for kissing a girl in a square in London, W.2, explained that 'It's an old Bayswater custom'.

customer A man; chap, fellow: coll. Cf. *chap, merchant, artist*.

cut A refusal to recognize, or to associate with, a person: coll. A share: Australian and New Zealand coll.

cut, v. To ignore or avoid (a person); abandon (a thing, a habit): coll.—To move quickly; run: coll.

cut a rug To 'jive', or 'jitterbug'; dance addicts': adopted from U.S. soldiers in 1943.

cut & run Depart promptly; decamp hurriedly: coll.

cut it To run, move quickly: C. 19–20; coll. Interjection: cease! or be quiet! Also as *cut!, cut that!*, in C. 20 *cut it out!*

cut no ice; esp. that cuts no ice! That makes no difference, has no effect, is of no importance: orig. U.S.; anglicized ca. 1913.

cut the rough (stuff) To cease doing or saying something obnoxious: Australian and New Zealand coll.

cut throat A game of bridge with three players only: coll.—An open razor (not a safety): coll.

cut up To leave a fortune by will, v.i. (v.t. with *for*); usually with *big, large, fat, rich* or *well*. Disraeli, in *The Young Duke*, ' "You

S.S.D.—D

think him very rich?" "Oh, he will cut up very large", said the Baron.' This 'likens the defunct to a joint' (of meat), W.

cut up nasty, rough, rusty, ugly To be or become quarrelsome, dangerous: coll. In a race, cut up *rough*, *badly*, etc. signifies to behave badly.

cute Clever, smart; quaint; attractive. coll.: orig. U.S. Ex S.E. *acute*.

cuts & scratches Matches (ignition): rhyming s.

D

D.T.'s A coll. abbr. of *delirium tremens*.

dabs (Extremely rare in the singular.) Finger-prints: c. >, by 1945, s.

dachsie (or -sy) A dachshund: domestic coll.

daddy of them all, the The most notable; (of things) the largest: Australian coll.

daffy, adj. Slightly mad; soft in the head: dial > s. Ex Northern dial. *daff*, a simpleton.

daftie A daft person: coll. Ex *daft*.

dag A 'hard case'; a wag; a 'character': Australia, thence New Zealand.

dago One of Latin race, but rarely of a Frenchman: coll. In C. 17, *Diego* (James) was a nickname for a Spaniard.

daily Daily bread: coll.

daily dozen, one's or **the** Physical exercises, on rising in the morning: coll.

daisy roots Boots: rhyming s.

damage Expense; cost: coll.

dammit, as (e.g. **quick** or **soon**) **as** Exceedingly (quick, soon); coll. I.e. as saying *damn it!* Cf.:

dammit, (as) near as Very nearly indeed: coll.

dander Anger; a ruffled temper: coll.: orig. U.S.

dandy Anything first-rate; also adj.: orig. U.S., anglicized ca. 1905.

daps Slippers: Regular Army's: late C. 19–20.

Darby & Joan A telephone: rhyming s.: very late C. 19–20.

dark, keep it Say nothing about it; mostly in the imperative: coll.

dark horse A horse whose form is unknown to the backers but

41

which is supposed to have a good chance: sporting.—Variant: *dark
'un*. Hence a candidate or competitor of whom little is known:
coll.

darky, darkey A negro: coll.: orig. U.S.; anglicized not later
than 1840.

dart In Australia, an idea, plan, scheme, ambition. Ex the idea of
a 'darting' or sudden thought.—*The Old Dart*, Britain: Australian.

darl (Only in address and endearment.) Darling: Australian coll.

dash An attempt, esp. in *have a dash at*: coll.

dash Dash-board of a motor-car: motorists' coll.

dash off; dash out To depart with a dash; come out with a dash:
coll.

date An appointment esp. with a member of the opposite sex:
coll. Ex U.S. Hence also as v.

date up (Gen. in passive.) To fill the time of (a person) with
appointments: coll.

davy An affidavit.

David (or Davy)! send it down; often **send it down, David, send it
down!** A military c.p. apropos of a shower, esp. if likely to cause
a parade to be postponed. (Wales has a notoriously wet climate:
David the Welsh patron saint.) New Zealanders and Australians
say *send her down, Hughie!*

Davy Jones'(s), later **Davy's, Locker** The sea, esp. as an ocean
grave: nautical.

day, that'll be the It is not very likely to happen: c.p.: from late
1918. Satirical on *der Tag*?

dazzle with science To out-box; fig., to defeat by sheer brains:
coll.

dazzler A showy person, esp. a woman; a brilliant act: coll.

dead! and (s)he never called me 'mother'! A c.p., satiric of melodrama, whence, in point of fact, the phrase is drawn.

dead beat A worthless idler, esp. if a sponger as well: orig. U.S.,
anglicized ca. 1900. In Australian s., a man down on his luck or
stony-broke.—Meat: rhyming s.—Adj., completely exhausted: coll.

dead broke Penniless; occ., bankrupt or ruined: coll.; from ca.
1850.

dead from the neck up Brainless; very dull.

dead give-away A notable indication, or revelation, of guilt or
defect.

dead head One who travels free, hence eats free, or, esp., goes
free to a place of entertainment: coll.; orig. U.S.

dead horse Work to be done but already paid for, work in
redemption of a debt; hence, distasteful work: coll.

dead loss A person, place or thing that is decidedly 'dud' (dull;

inefficient; without amenities): R.A.F. Ex a 'plane no longer serviceable.

dead loss   (Of a job, or a course of action) lacking prospects; unpromising; utterly useless.

dead marine   An empty bottle at or after a carouse; orig. nautical.

dead set   A persistent and pointed effort, attempt: esp. such an attack.

dead to rights   In the (criminal) act: c. and low: late C. 19–20. James Spenser, *Limey Breaks In*, 1934, 'I had been caught "dead to rights", as the crooks say.' Cf. *bang to rights*.

deader   A corpse. *Be a deader* also = to be (very recently) dead.

deadly   Excessive; unpleasant; very dull (esp. of places): coll. Adv., excessively: very coll.

deaner, occ. denar, deener, or **dener**   A shilling: orig. tramps' c.; in C.20, racing and low. Common in Australia. Prob. ex Fr. *denier* or Lingua Franca *dinarly*.

deb   A *debutante* in society: coll.

debs   Debenture stock: Stock Exchange.

deck   A landing-ground; *the deck*, the ground: R.A.F.

deep   Exceedingly sly or artful: coll.

deevie, -vy; dev(e)y   Delightful, charming: 1900–ca. 1907, H. A. Vachell speaking of it in 1909 as †. Ex *divine*.

definitely!; oh, definitely   Yes!; certainly: coll. Notably Maurice Lincoln's novel, *Oh! Definitely!*, 1933.

dekho; gen. dekko, n. (esp. **take a dekko**) and v.   To see; to, or a, glance. Ex Romany *dik*, to look, to see.

demob   To demobilize: 1919. (Gen. in passive.) Hence also as n., thence as adj.

Derby Kelly   Belly: rhyming s. Often abbr. to **Derby Kell**.

Derry & Toms   An aerial bomb: rhyming s. (esp. Londoners'): 1940–5.

derry on, have a   To have a 'down' on: Australian. Perhaps ex the comic-song refrain *hey derry down derry*.

det   A detonator.

deuce, go to the   To degenerate; to fall into ruin: coll.; by 1940, ob.

deuce to pay, the   Unpleasant consequences or an awkward situation to be faced: coll.

devastating   Has, from ca. 1924, been Society s., as in 'Quite too devastating, darling'; by 1945, fairly gen.; E. F. Benson, *Travail of Gold*, 1933, 'The banal epithets of priceless and devastating just fitted her.'

devil! how or **what** or **when** or **where** or **who the**   An exclamation indicative of annoyance, wonder, etc.: coll.

devil-dodger A clergyman, esp. if a ranter: coll. A very religious person.

dial The face: orig. low; by 1950, ob. Cf. *clock.*

dib(b)s Money; by 1940, ob.; by 1960, almost †.

dicey Risky; dangerous: R.A.F.; 1940 +; by 1946, common among civilians.

dicing, n. Operational flying: R.A.F.: 1940-45. Cynically and refreshingly jocular, in derision of the journalistic *dicing with death.*

dickey, dicky A small bird: mostly children's coll. Abbr. *dickey-bird.*—A ship's officer in commission, esp. as *second dickey,* second mate: nautical.

dickey, dicky, adj. In bad health, feeling very ill; inferior; insecure; queer: low at first.

dickey-, gen. **dicky-bird** A small bird: coll.

dick(e)y bird (often **dickey**) A word: rhyming s.

dick(e)y dirt A shirt: rhyming s.

dicken or **dickin!** A term signifying disgust or disbelief (C. J. Dennis): Australian. Sometimes *dickin on!,* stop that, it's too much to believe, it's disgusting. Ex *the dickens!*

dickory dock A clock: rhyming s.

diddle To swindle.

diddler A sly cheat, a mean swindler; a very artful dodger; coll. See preceding.

diddlum buck The game of crown and anchor: military. Cf. the grafters' adj. *diddlum,* dishonest: ex *'to diddle 'em'.*

diff A difference; coll.

dig Dignity: 'elegant' lower middle-class.—Abbr. digger, 2, but not heard of before 1915.

dig, v. To live, lodge. Ex *diggings,* q.v.

dig, v. To become aware of; look at and enjoy; to enjoy; to look at and understand; to understand and enjoy: dance-fanatics': adopted, ca. 1945, ex U.S.

dig in, v.i. To eat heartily.

dig in (and) **fill your boots!** Eat as much as you like!: naval.

dig (oneself) in To secure one's position: coll.: from 1915. Ex trench-warfare.

dig up To look for, to obtain, with connotation of effort or difficulty: coll.; orig. U.S. Ex mining.

digger The guard-room: military; by 1939, slightly ob.—2. A common form of address—orig., on the gold-fields—in Australia and New Zealand since ca. 1855, and—3. common in W.W. I. In 1914-17, a self-name of the Australian soldier and the New Zealand soldier. Prob. revived, ex sense 2, by those who 'shovelled Gallipoli into sandbags'.

diggings Quarters, lodgings, apartment: coll.; orig. U.S., anglicized in late 1850's. (In S.E., *diggings*, gold-fields, and *digger*, a miner, date from the 1530's.)

digs Abbr. *diggings*.

dilly, adj. Delightful: ca. 1905–25. Cf. *deevie*.—Foolish; half-witted: Australian. Prob. ex Somersetshire *dilly*, queer, cranky.

dilly-bag A wallet; a civilian haversack; small shopping-bag, general-utility purse-bag: Australian coll. Ex Aboriginal *dilli*, a basket.

dim Unimportant, undistinguished; colourless, insipid. (Persons only.) Oxford University; then general. Evelyn Waugh, *Decline and Fall*, 1928, 'Who's that dear, dim, drunk little man?'

dim type A stupid fellow (or girl): R.A.F. and W.A.A.F.

dingbat An officer's servant: Australian army. Apparently ex *dingo + batman*.

dingbats Eccentric; slightly mad: Australian. Prob. ex:—*the dingbats*. Delirium tremens: Australians' and New Zealanders': C. 20; by 1940, ob.

dingo, n. A coward; a mean-spirited or treacherous person; Australian—rather, allusive coll. than s.

dingo on, v. To betray (someone); to fail (him): Australian.

dingus What-do-you-call-it; what's-his-name: South African s. verging on coll. Ex Dutch *ding*, a thing: cf. therefore, *thingummy*.

dinkum Honest; true, genuine; thorough, complete: Australian. Prob. ex synonymous *fair dinkum*, itself ex Lincolnshire dial. *fair dinkum*, fair play.

dinkum oil, the The truth: Australian.

Dinny Hayes, let loose; Dinny Hayes-er To punch; a punch, esp. a mighty punch: Australian. Ex a noted pugilist.

dirty look A look of contempt or strong dislike, as in 'He gave me a dirty look': coll.

dip, v. To pawn: coll. Ex the S.E. sense, to mortgage, esp. lands. To lose (e.g. a good-conduct badge), forgo (one's rank): naval.

dip, n. Diphtheria; a patient suffering from, a case of, diphtheria: medical, esp. nurses'. 'It's dip, you know.'—(*the dip*). The assistant purser: nautical, esp. ship's stewards'.

dippy Extremely eccentric or foolish. Perhaps ex:

dipso, n. Cf. *dipsomaniac*, or confirmed drunkard: coll.

dire Unpleasant; objectionable; inferior.

dirt Anti-aircraft fire: R.A.F. Bad weather: Coastal Command, R.A.F. Scandal: adopted ca. 1932 from the U.S.A.

dirt, put in the; do dirt on To act unfairly (towards someone); mostly Australian.

dirt? what's the What's the scandal, hence the news?: orig. Society: from ca. 1932.

dirty money Extra pay for very dirty work: Labour coll.

dish, n. A girl; (young) woman: adopted, ca. 1936, from U.S.A. Shakespeare adumbrates the term.

dish To cheat; baffle completely; ruin: coll.

dish out To distribute (food) equally or decorations indiscriminately: military coll.: 1914.

ditch To land (an aircraft) on the sea.

ditch, the The sea; *The D.*, both the Atlantic and the English Channel: coll.

dither, v.i. To be very nervous on a given occasion; to hesitate bewilderedly: coll.

dithers Trepidation; (an access of) nervous shiverings: coll. (Hence adj., *dithering*.) Perhaps ultimately ex *shiver*, via *didder*.

dive A place of low resort, esp. a drinking-den: coll.: orig. U.S., anglicized ca. 1905.

div(v)y A division: military. A share; a dividend: coll. Also as v.i. and v.t., with variant *divvy up*.

dizzy Scatter-brained; wild; foolish.

do Action, deed; (a) success, as C. 17–18 S.E., but from ca. 1820, coll., in *make a do*—a success—*of it.*—An entertainment, a social function. C. 20.

do, v. To swindle, cheat; from ca. 1640, hence, to deceive, trick, without illegal connotations.—To punish, defeat heavily; in underworld, to murder.—Visit; go over, as a tourist: coll. Shirley Brooks, 1858, *The Gordian Knot*, 'I did Egypt, as they say, about two years back.' With *the amiable, polite, heavy, grand, genteel*, etc., *do* is coll., the exemplar being Dickens's *do the amiable.*—To please, meet the requirements of (a person).

do as you like A bicycle: rhyming s. (on *bike*): late C. 19–20.

do for To ruin, destroy; wear out (person or thing) entirely: coll. To attend to or on, as a landlady for a lodger: coll.—To kill: low s.

do gooder An inveterate busybody, intent on reforming everybody's soul but his own: Canadian coll.

do in To kill; to defeat; (recklessly, utterly) to despatch, dispose of; to spoil completely; to exhaust (a person).

do me goods 'Woods' (Woodbine cigarettes): rhyming s.

do one's bit To serve in Army, Navy or Air Force: coll.

do one's stuff To perform one's social task: ex U.S.A., ca. 1931.

do the lot To lose all one's money: coll.

do proud To flatter, act hospitably or generously towards: coll.

do the trick To gain one's object; (of something) to do what is required of it: coll.

do time   To serve a prison sentence: coll.

do with, (I) could   I would very much like to have: coll. By meiosis.

doc   A coll. abbr. of *doctor*, in address and narrative.—Hence, any sick-bay rating, esp. in address: naval.

dock   Hospital, chiefly *in dock*: orig. nautical.

Doctor Crippen   Dripping (the culinary n.): rhyming s. C. 20.

Doctor Livingstone, I presume   This c.p., adopted from H. M. Stanley's greeting, 1871, in the African jungle, was originally (ca. 1900) a skit on Englishmen's proverbial punctiliousness, no matter what the circumstances; but, by ca. 1920, it was extended to almost any chance, or unexpected, meeting.

dodge   A shrewd and artful expedient; an ingenious contrivance: coll.

dodge the column   To shirk one's duty: military,—esp. in the Boer War and in W.W. I.

dodgy   Difficult or complicated or tricky; risky; likely to become dangerous, esp. of a situation, a transaction, a concerted action.

doer   A 'character'; an eccentric or very humorous fellow: Australian.

dog   Abbr. *dog-watch*: nautical. See *dog, put on*. A cigarette-end: low. Short for *dog-end*.

dog, put on   To put on 'side': coll.; by 1960, ob.

dog-collar   A 'stand-up' stiff collar, esp. a clergyman's reversed collar: coll.

dog-collar   Broad necklace, usually of small pearls, worn tightly round the neck: Society.

doggo, lie   To make no move(ment) and say nothing; to bide one's time. Prob., 'like a cunning dog'.

doggie (or -y) day   New Year's Day: Post Offices'. Ex the dog-licences renewable then.

doggy, adj.   Stylish: smart appearance; 'just a little too gay and dashing' (Denis Mackail, 1934).

dogs   Feet: adopted ca. 1935, from U.S.A.

dog's body   Any junior officer, R.A., esp. a midshipman: hence, pejoratively, of any male.

dog's dinner, like a   Stylishly: low coll.

dogun or **d-**   A Catholic; Canadian. Possibly ex that very Irish surname, *Duggan*.

doing!, nothing   'Certainly not!': coll.

doings, the   The thing (*any* thing); esp. what is at the moment needed or otherwise relevant: coll.

doll up, v.i. and reflexive   To dress oneself very smartly: mostly Australian. Whence *dolled-up*, dressed 'to death'.

Dolly (Varden)   A garden: rhyming s.

dona, donah (mostly in sense 2) A woman; esp. the lady of the house: Cockney and Parlary. Ex It.—2. Hence, in Australia, a girl, a sweetheart: by 1945, ob.

done, it isn't It is bad form: an upper-class c.p. Hence, *the done* (correct) *thing*.

done-for Exhausted; cheated; ruined: coll.

done to the wide: done to the world Utterly exhausted, defeated, or baffled; ruined; coll.

dong To strike: to punch; New Zealanders' and Australians'. Perhaps ex the *dong* emitted by a bell when struck.

donkey's years A long time. Suggested by the sound of *donkey's ears* when illiterately pronounced and by the length of a donkey's ears.

don't make a fuss A bus: rhyming s.

don't make me laugh, I've got a split lip A c.p.: ob. by 1945.

dooda or **dooda(h), all of a** Excited: from late 1914. Ex the choice refrain *doo-da, doo-da, doo-da day*; prob. on *all of a dither*.

doodah A thingummy.

doodlebug A small, cheap car: motorists'; ca. 1933-40.

doodlebug Hence, a utility truck or light motor-van: Army; 1939–45.—A German flying-bomb (V.1): since mid-June 1944–5, then historical.

dooks The hands. Usually *dukes*, q.v.

doolally (or **doolali**) **tap** Off one's head: military. Ex *Deolali*, a sanatorium in Bombay, and Hindustani *tap*, fever. Often abbr. to *doolally*.

door to door Four; occasionally, where the context is clear, 24 or 34 or 44 or . . .: rhyming s.

doorstep A (gen. thick) slice of bread and butter.

dope Information: coll.; ex U.S.—A fool, a bungler: military > gen.

dope out To discover, ascertain, comprehend, work out: coll. —orig. U.S. Ex *dope*.

dopy, adj. Dull, lethargic, half asleep (lit. and fig.): coll. Ex U.S. Hence also n., with variant *dopey*.

dorm, dormie A dormitory: schools'.

doss A, and to, sleep; lodging, to lodge; a bed: all implying extreme cheapness and roughness. Ultimately ex L. *dorsum*, the back.

doss-house A very cheap lodging-house.

dot, v. To strike; esp. *dot* (a person) *one*.

dot, on the (Constructed with *be*.) Right on the spot; right on time: coll. (English and Canadian). 'On the dot of nine.'

dot, the year A date long ago: coll. Lit., 'the year 0'. 'Ganpat', *Out of Evil*, 1933. 'He's been in every frontier show (skirmish) since the year dot'.

dotty   Idiotic; (a little) mad.

double-take, esp. **do a**   A second look, takèn because one doesn't credit the first: Orig., film-producers' j.

dough   Money: U.S. then (ca. 1880) Australia, then—ca. 1895—Britain.

douse, dowse   To put, esp. down or (of a candle, lamp, etc.) out: low coll. esp. in *douse the glim*, put out the light.

down, v.   To trick; circumvent: coll.

down on, get   To remove; appropriate; steal: Australian and New Zealand low s.

down on or **upon, be**   To be aware of, alertly equal to; to pound upon, treat harshly: coll.

down south, esp. with **go** or **put**   (Of money) to go or be put into one's pocket, hence to be banked.

down the drain   Lost; wasted: coll.

down the drains   Brains: rhyming s.

drag, n.   A street or a road: mostly Cockney.—Three months' imprisonment: c.; by 1940, ob.

drag, n.   A quick draw at a cigarette: Cockneys' and Services'.

drag, n.   A vehicle: East End Londoners'.

draw it mild!   An expressive of derision; incredulity; supplication: coll.

draw out   To cause to talk; elicit information from: coll. Ex *drawing a badger.*

dreadful, adj.   Very bad, objectionable: coll.

dress down   To beat, thrash; hence, scold severely: coll.

drill, the, occ. **the right drill**   The correct way to do anything: Army—by 1942, also R.A.F.: coll. (Mostly officers'.)—One who knows his drill *must* be good.

drink, the   The sea; The English Channel: mostly Air Force.

drink, the   Water: London Fire Brigade.

drip   A simpleton, a 'stupid', a bore. To complain, to 'grouse': naval. 'Sloppy' sentiment; a person 'sloppily sentimental.

drip   Nonsense.

drop   A tip; a bribe.

drop   To get rid of (a person).

drongo   A lazy (and undesirable) person: Australian.

drop it!   Stop! Esp., stop talking or fooling.

drop off   is coll. for *drop off to sleep.*

drop on   To reprimand, to reprove.

drop on, have the   'To forestall, gain advantage over', orig. and esp. 'by covering with a revolver': (U.S. and) Australian.

drown   To put too much water into whisky or brandy: jocular coll. 'Don't drown it!'

drum In c., a road, highway, street. Ex Romany *drom*, a road. Hence a house, lodging, flat: c. and low s.

drum, v. To ring or knock at (a house) to ascertain whether it is occupied: c. and low s.

drum, v. To inform, tell; to 'put wise', to warn, tip off: (low) Australian. Also n.: *the drum*, correct information.

drum up To make tea, esp. by the roadside: tramps' c. also, by 1914, military s. Ex Romany *drom*, highway.

drunk A drinking bout; a drunkard: coll.

dry, the Desert; waterless country; the dry season: Australian coll.

dry up, v. Cease talking: mostly in the imperative.

dub up To 'fork out'; pay: s. verging on coll.

Duchess of Teck A cheque: rhyming s. Often shortened to *duchess*.

duck, v. To avoid; to neglect to attend (e.g. a meeting): coll.

duck & dive To hide: rhyming s.

duck, make a To score 0 at cricket. Short for *duck's egg*.

ducks or **ducky** A coll. endearment, mostly feminine.

dud A person without ability or spirit: orig. Scottish; resuscitated in 1914–18, from sense 'unexploding shell, hence any very inferior or unsuitable object'. Hence also adj., as in 'a dud show', a poor entertainment. Perhaps ultimately ex Dutch *dood*, dead.

duds Clothes. Orig. in underworld.

duff gen Unconfirmed and improbable report; unreliable news: R.A.F.

duffer A person of no ability; a dolt: coll. Ex the underworld.

dug-out An over-age officer back in service: military. Because *dug-out* of his retirement.

Duke of Kent Rent: rhyming s.

Duke of York To talk; to walk; cork; chalk: rhyming s.

Duke of Yorks Forks: rhyming s. Hence, fingers; hence hands; hence *dukes*, q.v.

dukes Often pronounced *dooks*. Hands; fists. Ex preceding.

dumb Stupid; dull; silent: S.E. ca. 1530–1650; revived in U.S. but as s. influenced by Ger. *dumm*; anglicized, as s., ca. 1920.

dummy A deaf-mute: coll. Ex *dumb*, prob. via *dumby*. Hence, a person notably deficient in ability or brightness: coll.

dummy run A practice evolution: naval coll.

dump In 1915, orig. military, a place where war material is stored, hence a refuse heap, itself ex *dump*, v.—Hence, a hotel, or residence.

dump, v. To put, set, place, no matter how.

dumps, the A fit of melancholy; low spirits: coll.

Dunlop (tire) A liar: rhyming s.

dunnage Clothes; baggage: nautical coll.

dunnaken or **-kin; dunneken** or **-kin; dunnyken** or **-kin; dunagan, -egan.** A privy: orig. c.; now low coll.

duration, for the; rarely **the duration** For a very long time indeed: military. One enlists for *the duration of hostilities*.

dust A disturbance, 'row', esp. in *kick up a dust*, cause a 'shindy': coll.: by 1960, slightly ob.

dust-bin Gun position on the underside: R.A.F. It receives the *dirt*; also, pre-war bombers had belly turret-shaped like a dust-bin. Bridge in a motor torpedo (or gun) boat: naval.

dust-up A variant of *dust*.

dusting A thrashing; (nautical) rough weather.

dusty, dustie A dustman: Cockney coll.

dusty, not so Good (cf. *not so* or *too bad*): coll.

Dutch; esp. **my old Dutch** A wife: mostly Cockney. Albert Chevalier explained it by the resemblance of 'the wife's face to that of an *old Dutch clock*': cf. *dial*, q.v.

Dutch pegs Legs: rhyming s.

Dutchie A Dutchman; occ. a German: allusive and nick-nominal coll.

Dutchman if I do!, I'm a Certainly not!: coll. Older is *I'm a Dutchman*, i.e. I'm somebody else.

duty dog Duty Officer; loosely, Orderly Officer: Services'.

duty stooge Duty Corporal; Duty Airman: R.A.F.

dying duck in a thunderstorm, look like a To have a ludicrously forlorn and helpless appearance: coll., orig. rural.

E

---

eager beaver   One who pitches right in, sometimes to the dismay of colleagues: Canadian: ex U.S.

ear bashing   Conversation; talking, esp. fluently and at length: Australian soldiers': 1939–45.

ear-biter; ear-biting   A persistent borrower; borrowing.

earthly, no; not an earthly   No chance whatsoever: coll.

easy, n.   A short rest, esp. as *take an easy*: coll.

easy, adj.   Esp. in 'I'm easy'—I don't mind one way or the other: R.A.F. coll.

easy to look at; easy on the eye   (Esp. of women) good-looking.

eat   To enjoy enthusiastically: theatrical.

eats   Food: coll.

eating irons   Knife, fork and spoon: Services coll. Weapons with which to attack the meal.

ed (or ed.), the   The editor: journalists' and authors' coll.

edge on, have the   To have a slight advantage over: orig. U.S.

edgy   Irritable; nervous: coll. Ex *nerves on edge*.

effort   'Something accomplished involving concentration or special activity': coll., esp. in *that's a pretty good effort*.

egg   A person: coll., esp. in *good egg* and, as exclamation, *good egg!*, and *a bad egg*, a person that disappoints expectation. An aerial bomb; a submarine mine.

egg-head   A scholar; an erudite person; anyone interested in intellectual matters: ex U.S. Ex the high brow and the general shape of the scholar's head—in the popular misconception.

egg-whisk   A helicopter: mostly naval.

eggs are, be, or **is eggs, as sure as**   Undoubtedly; certainly: coll. Influenced by *X is X*, the logician's statement of identity.

eight, one over the   One drink too many; hence, slightly drunk.

eighteen pence   Common sense: ryhming s.

ekker   An exercise (scholastic task): Public Schools' and universities' (orig. Oxford).

elementary, my dear Watson!   An educated c.p. dating from ca. 1900. Ex Sherlock Holmes's frequent remark to touchstone Watson.

elephant's trunk   Drunk: rhyming s. Often abbr. to *elephant's* or *elephants*.

elevenses   Morning tea: C. 20 coll. ex C. 19–20 dial.

end, at a loose   With nothing particular to do: coll.

end, go (in) off the deep   To get very excited or passionate: military > gen. by 1921. Ex leaping into the water at the deep end of a swimming-bath.

end, no, adv.   Immensely; *no end of,* a great number or quantity of. Hence, *no end of a fellow,* 'one of the best'.

enemy, the   Time; clock, watch: coll.; esp. as *how goes . . .?*

enough on one's plate, have   To have as much work as one can manage: orig. Forces'. Ex the lit. domestic sense.

Epsom races   A pair of braces: rhyming s.

erk   An *air*craftman; esp. an A.C.2.; hence, a recruit: R.A.F.

even Stephen (or **Steven**)   Share and share alike: Canada and Australia. Ex U.S. By reduplication of *even.*

ever?, did you   (Self-contained.) Have you ever seen, or heard, such a thing?: coll.

ever is (or **was), as**   A coll. tag, orig. intensive, as in 'Bad riding as ever was', 1708. Now approximately = 'mark you' (parenthetic).

ever so   Ever so much, as in *thanks ever so!*: coll, mostly proletarian.

every which way   In every manner or direction: jocular coll., orig. U.S.; anglicized ca. 1910. Perhaps ex confusion caused by *every way (in) which.*

everything in the garden's lovely!   All goes well!: a C. 20 c.p.; by 1950, slightly ob.

everything (or **everything's) under control**   A Services c.p., applied to a situation where things are 'ticking over' nicely.

ex, his   His Excellence: coll.

exactly!   Certainly! excellent!: coll.

exam   Examination: coll.

exes   Expenses: coll.

expecting, adj.   Pregnant: coll.

eyeful? got your or **had an**   Have you had a good look?

eyes peeled or **skinned, keep one's (best)**   To be wary: coll.: U.S., anglicized in late C. 19.

eye-wash Something done, not for utility but for effect: coll.: orig. military.

Eyeties Italians: orig. military. Ex the illiterate pronunciation *Ey(e)talian*.

F

fabulous A verbal counter for 'very, or merely, agreeable' or 'unusual' or '(very) interesting' or . . . : coll. In 1962 it was often supplanted by the shortening, *fab*, esp. among teenagers.

face-ache A jocular term of address; by 1945, ob.

face-fungus Moustaches; esp. beard; or both: jocular.

face, put on a To change one's expression, usually to severity: coll. Cf. *what a face*: how severe or disapproving you look!: coll.

facer A sudden check or obstacle: coll. Hence, a problem: coll.

fag A cigarette: o rig., an inferior cigarette (only from ca. 1914, any cigarette). Abbr. *fag-end*.

faintest, the The east idea; as in 'I haven't the faintest': coll. I.e. *the faintest* (remotest) *idea*.

fair Complete, thorough; completely, thoroughly: coll. 'A fair cop'; 'fair done up' (completely exhausted).

fair doo's or **doos** or **does** or **do's** A fair deal; justice; a just proportion: military >, by 1920, gen.

fair enough As a question it = 'Satisfied? Convinced? Agreeable to you?'; as a comment it = 'That sounds plausible, or reasonable, enough' or 'I'll accept your statement': Services' (esp. R.A.F.) coll.

fairish Fairly large: coll. As adv.; in a pleasant manner; to a fair degree: coll.

fake An action, esp. if illegal; a dodge; a sham; anything used in illicit deception or manufacture. Ex the underworld. Ex:

fake, v. To do anything, esp. if illegally or with merely apparent skill; to cheat, deceive; tamper with; forge; 'dope' (a horse). This underworld term prob. derives ex Ger. *fegen*.

fall down (on) To make a bad mistake (in or at): coll. U.S., anglicized ca. 1910.

fall for To be greatly attracted by (esp. a member of the other sex): U.S., anglicized ca. 1920. Hence, to be deceived by (a trick).

fall (or **lean**) **over backwards** To go beyond the normal and the expected in order to show how honourably disinterested or how honest or upright one is: 'He'll fall over backwards, just to prove that his friendship in no way influences him in your favour.'

famous Excellent; 'capital': coll.

famous last words A catch-phrase rejoinder to such fatuous statements as 'Flak's not really dangerous' (Air Force); hence in the other Services and, since ca. 1945, among civilians. A jocular reference to History's 'famous last words'.

famously Excellently: coll.

fan An enthusiastic, orig. of sport: ex U.S.; anglicized ca. 1914. Abbr. *fanatic*.

fan An aircraft propeller: R.A.F.—(Also *whizzer*.) A ship's propeller: naval.

fanny One's posterior; adopted, ca. 1939, ex U.S.—Talk; esp., sales-talk; deceptive eloquence.

Fanny Adams Tinned mutton: naval >, ca. 1900, also military. Ex Fanny Adams, a girl that, ca. 1812, was murdered and whose body, cut into pieces, 'was thrown into the river at Alton in Hampshire' (O.E.D. Sup.). Cf. *Harriet Lane*.—2. *Fanny Adams* or nothing at all: military; by 1939, rather ob.

fancy, v. To have a (too) high opinion of oneself, of another, or of a thing: coll. In the imperative, either as one word (*fancy!*) or two words (*fancy that!*) or preceding a phrase (e.g. 'Fancy you being in plus fours!'), it expresses surprise: coll.

fantastic Unusual; very good. For exaggeration, cf. *fabulous*. It was, orig., literary and cultured; but in 1963 it was widespread, even among children.

fast one, bowl a Since ca. 1939, usually *pull a*. To 'pull a trick' of some sort. Ex fast bowling at cricket.

fat, n. A good part: theatrical.—In journalism, a notable piece of exclusive news.—In the underworld, a piece of luck, a successful coup.

fat-head A fool: coll. Hence the adj. *fat-headed*.

father & mother of a hiding (thrashing, beating, etc.**)** or, esp., **of a row** A tremendous or extremely vigorous thrashing or quarrel: Anglo-Irish coll. An elaboration of:

father of a ——, the A severe; esp. *father of a hiding* (or *licking*), a very severe thrashing: coll.

fatty A jocular epithet, endearment, or nickname for a fat person: coll.

fearful, fearfully Adj., adv.: a coll. intensive (cf. *awful, terrible*). 'I say, you're looking most fearfully fit.'

feather & flip A bed; sleep: rhyming s. on *kip*. Often shortened to *feather*.

fed to the back teeth   An intensive variant of:

fed-up   Bored; disgusted; (*with*) tired of: orig. military; possibly ex the Boers.

feed   A meal. Ex the stables.

feed, v.   In the theatre, to supply (the principal comedian) with cues.

feel like   To have an inclination for a thing or—esp. in form *feel like doing*—to do something: coll. A 1933–4 trade-slogan ran: 'A. I feel like a Guinness.—B. I jolly well wish you were!'

feel like death warmed up   To feel very ill—half dead, in fact: (until ca. 1940, proletarian) coll.: cf. S.E. *to look like a living corpse.*

feel one's own man   To feel (quite) oneself, i.e. fit or normal: coll.

feel the draught   To be financially inconvenienced.

feloosh   Money: coll. among soldiers with service where Arabic is spoken. Direct ex Arabic.

fence   A receiver of stolen goods: c.; then low s.; then, in C. 20, gen. s.; now almost coll. Cf. the v.

fence, v.i.   To receive stolen goods: c. > s. Both n. and v. derive ex S.E. *fence = defence.*

fence, sit (up)on the   To be waiting to see who wins: orig. U.S. political s., anglicized ca. 1870; now coll.

ferret   A German security guard: prisoners-of-war in Germany: 1940–5. Ex his sharp eyes and the colour of his overalls.

fetch . . . a crack   To strike (a person): coll.

fib   A trifling falsehood; a lie: coll.

fib   To tell a (trivial) lie: coll. Hence, *fibber.*

fiddle, v.   To cheat. C. 17–20; S.E. until ca. 1800; then low s. Hence, to make a living from small jobs done on the street.

fiddle, v.t. and v.i., hence, n.   To obtain or to sell illicitly or by a trick; practise something illicit. Fringe of the underworld stuff and word.

fiddle, n.   A swindle.

fiddler   A sharper or a cheat: low. Ex *fiddle,* v. Hence, a 'wangler', a constant schemer or contriver.

fierce   Objectionable, unpleasant; difficult: coll. (ex U.S.) Exceptional in some way: U.S., anglicized ca. 1910. A. E. W. Mason, *The Dean's Elbow*, 1930, ' "Such a one!" "A regular comic." "Fierce, I call him." '

fifty-fifty, adv.   Equally: coll., orig. U.S.; anglicized ca. 1914. I.e. on a basis of 50% each. Hence, adj.

fig, in full   In full dress: s. > coll.; by 1945, rather ob.

fighting cats (Army) or **galloping horses** (R.A.F.)   The coat of arms on a Warrant Officer's lower sleeve; hence, a Warrant Officer.

filbert   A very fashionable man about town: Society: ca. 1900–20.

Popularized by the song about 'Gilbert the filbert, Colonel of the Nuts'.

filthily Very; as in 'filthily rich'.

filthy A pejorative and intensive adj., applied e.g. to an entertainment, holiday, present, etc. (now coll.). Cf. *foul*. It occurs in Devonshire dial. as early as 1733 for 'excessive'.

filthy, the Money. Ex 'filthy lucre'.

fin An arm; a hand: nautical > gen.; by 1950, archaic.

financial In funds: Australia.

find A person worth knowing, a thing worth having: coll.

find, v. To steal: military. Cf. *win* and *make*.

find something To obtain a job: coll.

fine and large, all very A c.p., expressing admiration or incredulity or derision. Popularized by a music-hall song much in vogue 1886–8.

finee, occ. finnee 'Done for'; no more (of supplies): military since late 1914; by 1960, ob. Ex Fr. *fini*.

finger & thumb Rum: rhyming s.

finish The 'end' of a person by death; social, professional, physical ruin: coll.

finisher Something constituting, a person administering, the final or decisive blow: coll.

fire, v. To dismiss: orig. U.S.; anglicized ca. 1905.

first A first-class degree: coll. Likewise *second, third, fourth*.

first(-)class Exceedingly good; (adv.) very well: coll.

first(-)rate, adv. Excellently: coll.

first thing Early in the morning or the day: coll. 'The boss wasn't here first thing.'

fish A man; usually derogatory—always in such combinations as *cool fish, odd f.* (prob. influenced by *odd fellow*), *queer f.* (after *queer bird*), *shy f.*: coll. Orig. presumably an angler's term.

fish, pretty, nice kettle of A quandary: coll.

fisherman's (daughter) Water: rhyming s.

fishy Morally or financially dubious; equivocal, unsound. Whence *fishiness*.—'Seedy', indisposed: ex and esp. in *have a fishy*, i.e. a glazed, *eye*: coll.

fit? are you Are you ready?: R.A.F. coll. Perhaps elliptical for 'Are you ready and fit?'

fit to be tied 'Hopping mad'—furiously angry: Canadian: adopted ex U.S. Cf. the Australian *ropeable*.

fit(-)up A stage easily fitted up; hence, a small theatrical company: theatrical coll. Hence, *fit-up towns*.

fits, beat (in)to; fits, give To 'beat hollow': coll.

five by two A Jew: rhyming s. Also *four-by-two* and *buckle-my-shoe*.

fives, bunch of   A fist.

fizz   Champagne.

fizzer   Any first-rate thing or, occ., person: coll. A very fast ball: cricketers' coll. A charge-sheet: military.

flabagast, gen. **flabbergast**   To astound; utterly to nonplus or confuse (a person): coll. Ex *flap* (or *flabby*) + *aghast.*

flak-happy   Not caring; reckless: R.A.F. Contrast the Army's *bomb-happy.*

flag, show the   Put in an appearance, just to show that one is there: business and professional men's coll.

flaming, adj. & adv.   'Bloody': euphemistic coll., as in 'a *flaming* nuisance'. Cf. *ruddy.*

flannel, n. & v.   (To speak or make) sweet things or small gifts to one's superiors in order to ask favours later; to flatter, flattery: Services'.

flannel-mouth, n. & adj.   (A) well-spoken (person, esp. if a man): Canadian.

flannel through, v.i.   To bluff one's way through (an awkward situation): naval.

flap, in a   Excited: naval.

flapper   In society s. of early C. 20, 'a very immoral young girl in her early "teens" ' (Ware). But W.W. I firmly established the meaning (already pretty gen. by 1905), *any* young girl with her hair not yet put up (or, in the late 1920's and the early 30's, not yet cut short); by 1939, ob.

flapper-bracket   A motor bicycle seat at the back for the spatial transference of a youthful female; by 1945, ob.

flare-up   A sudden quarrel, commotion, or fight: coll. Hence, v.

flash, v.   To show; esp. excessively, vulgarly, or with unnecessary 'pomp' or pretence: coll.—Showy, vulgar by ostentation. (Orig. underworld.)

flat   A fool; an easy dupe. (*the flat*) The season of horse-racing on the flat. Sporting coll.

flat, adj.   Penniless; short of money.

flat broke   Penniless: coll.

flat foot   A policeman; orig. lower classes. Hence, *flattie.*

flat top   An aircraft carrier: naval.

flea-bag   A bed: low: ca. 1835–1915. From ca. 1909, an officer's sleeping-bag.

flea-pit   A second-rate, dirty cinema. A flat (apartment): from ca. 1919; ob. by 1939–42.

flicks, the   The films; the moving pictures; (*go to the flicks*) a cinema: ob. by 1945. Ex the flickering of the pictured screen; imm. ex: 2. (*flick*). A moving picture; the performance at a cinema; † by 1939.

flies on a person, there are no   He is wide-awake; esp. very able or capable.

flies won't get at it, where the   (Of drink) down one's throat: coll.

flimsy   A banknote.

flimsy   An important message that, written on rice paper, can, if one is captured, be swallowed without ill effects: Services' s. > coll.

flipper   The hand: nautical, soon > gen.

flit, do a moonlight   To quit one's flat or house, or one's lodgings, by night and without paying the rent or (board and) lodging: coll.

flivver   A cheap small motor-car; ob. by 1946.

floater   A mistake, a faux pas; a moment of embarrassment: university s. (ca. 1910) >, by 1929, gen. middle-class; by 1960, ob. A penny that does not spin: two-up players'.

flog   To sell illicitly, orig. Army stores.

floor, on the   Penniless. (Orig., underworld.) Ex boxing.

floosie (or **-y**)   A girl (as companion): naval: ca. 1940. Adopted from U.S.

flop   (Of a book, play, plan) to fail: s. now verging on coll.

flounder   Short for *flounder and dab*—a taxicab.

flowers!, say it with   A c.p. (ex U.S.) = send flowers!; also, say it nicely!

flowery dell   A (prison-) cell: rhyming s.

'flu, flu   Influenza: coll., often with *the*.

fluence (or **'fluence**), **the**   Delicate or subtle influence: Australians' and New Zealanders'.

fluence on, put the   To persuade: mostly Australian and New Zealand from ca. 1910. Ex hypnotism.

fluff   Short change given by clerks: railway s. 'Lines' imperfectly learned and delivered: theatrical. Both senses have corresponding verbs.

fluff, little bit of   A girl; ob. by 1945.

flummox, flummux   To perplex, abash, silence; victimize, 'best'; dodge, elude.—Hence, to confuse another player: theatrical. Both senses occur mostly as ppl. adj. *flummoxed*. The word is prob. echoic.

flutter, v.   To gamble: now coll.

flutter   A venture; a spree; a gamble: now coll. 'Fond of a little flut er.'

fly, adj.   Artful, knowing; shrewdly aware: orig. low; by 1960, slightly ob.

fly a kite   To raise money by means of accommodation bills.—In Anglo-Irish banks, it = to cash a cheque against non-existent funds. —To test public opinion by tentative measures: promoters' and copy-writers' coll.

fly by the seat of one's pants   To fly by instinct rather than by instruments.

fly off the handle   To lose one's temper: orig. U.S.; anglicized ca. 1860; in C. 20, coll.

foggiest (notion), have not the   To have no idea: coll.

fold up, v.i.   (Of an aircraft) to crash; (of a person) to go sick unexpectedly or without warning: Services, esp. R.A.F.; adopted from U.S.A.

follower   A female servant's sweetheart or suitor, esp. if he frequents the house: coll.

foot!, me or **my**   Rubbish! Hugh Walpole, *Vanessa*, 1933, ' "But, Rose, you're wrong . . ." "Wrong my foot! you can't kid me." '

foot & mouth disease   The tendency of golfers to talk at night of the day's exploits: jocular coll.

foot on the floor, put one's; with one's   To accelerate; by accelerating: motorists'.

foot-slogger   An infantryman: military coll.

footle, v.   To dawdle, potter, trifle about; act or talk foolishly; coll.: from ca. 1890; slightly ob.

footling   Insignificant; trivial; pettily fussy: coll. Ex S.E. *futile*.

foozle, v.   To miss; make a bad attempt at; bungle: coll.

foreigner   An article made in the firm's, or the Service's, time and with its materials.

for it, be   To be due for punishment; hence, in trouble: military s. > by 1919, gen. coll.

forget it!, (and) don't (you)   An admonitory c.p.: U.S. >, by 1900, anglicized.

fork out   Hand over (valuables or money); pay: s. > coll. by 1900. Ex *forks*

forks   The hands.

form   The height of one's attainment: Public Schools'. P. G. Wodehouse, 1902, 'He sneers at footer, and jeers at cricket. Croquet is his form, I should say'—(With *in*) high spirits; 'concert' pitch: coll.

form   Situation, position, as in 'What's the form?' or 'It took me a couple of days to find out the form at H.Q.'—to ascertain how things were done and what the people were like: Services officers', now general.

form? what's the   What's it like (at, e.g., a house-party)?: Society: from the middle 1920's.

forty winks   A nap, short sleep: coll.

foul   In C. 20 hyperbolical use is fairly to be described as s. > coll. of the *awful* and *terrible* kind. Cf. *filthy*.

four-by-two   An Army biscuit: military. Ex *four-by-two*, a rifle pull-through (of that size in inches).—A Jew: rhyming s.

four-letter man A very objectionable fellow: by 1960, just slightly ob.

fourth of July A tie: rhyming s.

fox To puzzle (a person)—e.g., with a flow of technicalities or of other erudition: Services' coll.

'fraid Afraid: coll.

frame, v. To work up and present an unjustified case against: orig. U.S.; anglicized ca. 1924.—To effect a pre-arranged conspiracy, a faked result: U.S., anglicized ca. 1924. Hence, as corresponding nouns (variant *frame-up*).

France & Spain Rain: rhyming s.

frat, v. To fraternize: Armed Forces': since May 1945. By back formation.

fraud An impostor, humbug, hypocrite: coll. Often jocular.

Fray Bentos Very well, esp. in reply to inquiries about one's health: jocular military: 1915–18. Ex the well-known brand of bully beef, with a pun on *très bien*.

free gratis, for nothing; f., g., and for nothing Costing nothing: coll., orig. low.

Freeman's!, it's Harry There's nothing to pay: naval.

freeze on to Cling to, hold fast: coll.

French! pardon (or excuse) the, or my Please excuse the, or my, strong language.

Frenchy A Frenchman: coll.

Friday while Week-end leave: naval coll.

fridge, occ. frige A refrigerator.

frightful An intensive adj.: coll. Cf. *awful, terrible*.

frightfully An intensive adv.: coll.

frightfulness Anything, esp. behaviour, that is objectionable: jocular coll.

frisk To search the person; examine carefully for police evidence: c. >, by 1920, low s.

Fritz A German; esp. a German soldier: 1914 +, but, in 1917–18, less common than *Jerry*.

frog & toad A (main) road: rhyming s.

froggie or froggy; also frog A Frenchman. All the *frog* terms for a Frenchman refer to the eating of *frogs*.

frog's march (esp. with give the), occ. frog-march The carrying by four persons, of a drunken man face downwards, e.g. to the police-station. Hence also as v.

frost An utter failure or complete disappointment, whether thing, event, or person: theatrical s. > gen. coll.

froust, frowst A stink; stuffiness (in a room): coll.

frousty, frowsty Unpleasant-smelling; fuggy: coll. when not dial.

fruit salad   A large collection—three or more rows—of medal ribbons: Services'. As worn on the left breast, where they made a colourful display.

fruity   Very rich or strong (e.g. language); very attractive or suggestive (e.g. story): coll.

fudge   'Late News' column: journalists'. Often the type is blurred, the ink not having had time to dry.

fug   A stuffy atmosphere. Prob. ex S.E. *fog*. Hence, the adj., *fuggy*.

full   Tipsy: coll.

full of emptiness   Empty: jocular coll.

full of oneself   Conceited; somewhat ludicrously arrogant: coll.

full up   (Constructed with *of*) sated; weary; disgusted: Australian and, later, New Zealand: by 1950, ob.

fun   Difficult work; exciting or dangerous events: military, esp. in W.W. I & II. Ironic.

fun (at), poke   To ridicule, make a butt (of): coll.

fun & games   A (very) agreeable time: middle-class coll.

fun, have   Mostly as vbl. n., *having fun* (a being engaged in) a raid, an attack: Army officers'.

funeral, it's his, my, your, etc.   Or negatively. It's his (not his, etc.) business affair, concern, duty: c.p.: orig., negative only and U.S.; anglicized, mainly in the affirmative form, ca. 1880.

funk   (A state of) fear, great nervousness, cowardice; a coward: schoolboys'. Flemish *fonck*. Hence as v.

funk-hole   Any place of refuge, esp. a dug-out: military. Hence, a safe job. Common in W.W. I; uncommon in W.W. II.

funnies   Comic magazines or newspapers: Canadian; ca. 1950, gen.

funny, adj.   Strange, odd, queer: coll.

funny, feel   To feel ill.

funny bone   The extremity—at the elbow—of the *humerus*, the 'funniness' being caused by the ulnar nerve: coll. By a pun on *humerus*, but greatly influenced by *funny feeling*.

funny business   A shady transaction, dubious dealing; monkeying about: s. >, ca. 1930, coll. Ex a clown's *funny business*.

funny for words, too   Extremely funny: coll. Prob. suggested by *too funny for anything*, which was orig. U.S.

Furphy   A false report, an absurd story: Australian military: since early 1915. Ex *Furphy*, the contractor supplying rubbish-carts to the camps at Melbourne.

Furphy king   A soldier making a habit of circulating rumours: Australian military: 1915–18.

fuss pot, fuss-pot   A very fussy person: coll.

future at all, no; no future in it, or **in that**   Of these catch-phrases

(Services', esp. R.A.F.), the former implies danger in the sortie concerned, whereas the latter either does the same or merely hints that the job concerned is a thankless one.

fuzzy Tipsy: coll. Hence, incoherent, temporarily 'dense', bewildered: coll.

G

gab, v.   To talk fluently, very well; or too much: (low) coll.

gab, gift of the   'A facility of speech, nimble-tongued eloquence' (Grose): coll.

gabber   A prater, ceaseless talker: coll.

gaff   A fair; a cheap music-hall or theatre.

gaff, blow the   To inform; divulge a secret: low.

gaffer, the   The foreman: navvies'.—The steward of a race-course: the turf.—'A market-master or fair-ground superintendent': grafters'. (Philip Allingham.)

gag   A joke; invention; hoax: imposition; humbug; false rumour: low s. >, ca. 1880, coll. Interpolated words, esp. jokes or c.p. comments: theatrical. An excuse; a 'dodge'.

gaga   Incorrectly *ga-ga*. Senile; fatuous. Adopted ex Fr. s., itself prob. echoic of idiotic laughter.

gall   Effrontery; impudence: more gen. in U.S., where app. it arose, than in England.

gallery, play to the   Orig. theatrical, then sporting, then gen.: to act as to capture popular applause: coll.

galoot, occ. **galloot**   A man, chap, fellow; gen. a pejorative, implying stupidity or boorishness or moral toughness. Ex the † nautical s. sense, 'a young or inexperienced marine', itself ex that, slightly earlier, underworld sense, 'a soldier', prob. ex Dutch *gelubt,* a eunuch.

gam   With variant *gamb,* a leg, nearly always in pl.: c. > low s. Ex Northern Fr. *gambe* or else ex It. *gamba.*

game   A 'lark' or source of amusement: coll.

gammon   Nonsense, humbug; a ridiculous story; deceitful talk; deceit: to tell deceitful or extravagant stories to: low s. > (low) coll. Origin unknown.

65

gammy, adj. and n.   (A) lame or maimed (person): low. Prob. ex S.E. *game,* lame.

Gamp Ex Mrs Sarah Gamp in Dickens's *Martin Chuzzlewit,* 1843. An umbrella, esp. a large one loosely tied: coll.

gander, n. and v.   To look through the mail or over another's shoulder at a letter or a newspaper: Services, esp. R.A.F. Adopted ex U.S. (cf. Am. *rubberneck*); the gander is a long-necked bird.

Garbo, do a To avoid Press reporters and photographers and other publicity: journalists' and publicity men's, also film-world's: since ca. 1925. Ex Greta Garbo's often-expressed wish 'to be alone'.

garden or **garden-path, lead up the** To blarney (a person), humbug, entice, mislead. Ex gently suasive courtship.

gardening Patting the pitch, picking up loose bits of turf: cricketers' jocular coll.

gargle A drink; to drink.

garn! 'Get away with you!': low coll.

gas Empty talk: bombast: U.S., anglicized ca. 1860.

gas, step on the To put on speed: U.S., anglicized ca. 1926. Ex motor-driving, *gas* being gasolene.

gas-bag A person of too many words; a boaster: coll. Ex *gas,* n.

gash, adj.   A shortening of *gashion*; often—'spare' or 'available': naval.

gash, the Waste food; an over-issue; anything surplus: Services', esp. Navy.

gashion Additional, free; often in pl. as n., 'extra of anything': naval.

gasper An inferior cigarette; hence, any cigarette. Ex its effect on one's 'wind'.

gassy Full of empty talk or boasts.

gat A revolver: Canadian, orig. U.S. (Ex *Gatling gun.*) Since ca. 1924, thanks to gangster novels and films, the word has > fairly well known in Britain; by 1964, however, slightly ob.

gate, on the Forbidden to leave barracks: military. On the danger list at a hospital: proletarian.

gate-crasher, -crashing One who attends, attendance at, a private party or entertainment without invitation: coll.: U.S., anglicized in late 1926.

gate, go through the To open the throttle full out; hence, fly at full speed: R.A.F.

'gator An alligator: Australian coll.

gay & frisky Whiskey: rhyming s.

gee A horse: coll. Orig. a child's word. In full, *gee-gee.*

geezer, occ. **geyser** (incorrectly); esp. **old geezer** A person: low coll. Albert Chevalier in his still-remembered *Knocked 'Em in the Old*

Kent Road, 1890, 'Nice old geezer with a nasty cough'. Ex † *guiser*, a mummer, via dial.

gefuffle   A to-do, a fuss; a 'flap': R.A.F. Partly echoic and prob. reminiscent of such terms as S.E. *fluster* and s. *waffle*; the *ge-* is intensive.

gen, the   Information: whether *pukka gen*, trustworthy, or *duff gen*, incorrect, or *phoney gen*, doubtful or unreliable: R.A.F., hence (post 1945) civilians'. Ex the consecrated phrase 'for the *general information* of all ranks' or '. . . of all concerned'.

gent   A gentleman; proletarian coll.

geog (pron. jog), **geom** (pron. jom)   Geography; Geometry: Public Schools'.

Geordie, geordie   A pitman; any Northumbrian: North Country coll. Prob. ex the Christian name there so pronounced.—Hence, also a North Country collier (boat): nautical.—The George Stephenson safety-lamp: miners'.

German bands   Hands: rhyming s.

gertcher   Get out of it, you!: coll. low, when not used allusively. Don't pull my leg!: Cockneys'. A corruption of *get out with yer!*

Gestapo, the   The Service police: R.A.F. and Army. Humorous on the name of the German Secret Police of the Third Reich.

get!   Abbr. *get out!*, go away! or clear out! Orig. U.S.; anglicized ca. 1900, but found in Australia ca. 1890. 'None of your damned impertinence. Get!'

get a load of that!   Just look at that!

get a load of this!   Listen to this!: adopted, ca. 1942, from U.S.A.

get, do a   To depart hastily: Australian.

get along with you!   Go away! Be quiet!: coll.

get at   To assail; strike.—To banter, chaff, take (or try to take) a rise out of.—To influence, bribe, corrupt a person; to 'nobble': coll.—To mean; intend to be understood: gen. as 'What are you getting at?' Coll.

get away with it   To succeed beyond expectation or rights: coll.

get cracking   To begin work; work hard: R.A.F. I.e. cracking on speed.

get cracking—get mobile—get skates on—get stuck into it—get weaving   To respond (immediately) to an order; to get a move on: Services': the 2nd, 3rd, 4th, general; the 1st, orig. Army and then gen.; the 5th, R.A.F. All usually in the imperative. Origins: whip-cracking at the mustering of cattle; *mobile* and *skates*, obvious refs. to speed (cf. a *mobile* column); *stuck*, perhaps ex dough-kneading, but prob. ex ditch-digging, road-making, mining; see *weaving*.

get down to it   To begin to work seriously: coll. To go to sleep; military.

get his   To receive a wound, an injury, esp. a fatal one: Army.

get in bad   To make (a person) disliked; v.i., to become disliked. Ex U.S. Construction: *with*.

get it in the neck   To be thrashed (lit. or fig.), to receive a shock, to be severely reprimanded.

get off, v.t.   To succeed in marrying one's daughters: coll. Hence, v.i., to get engaged or married: coll. Hence, to 'click' with a member of the opposite sex: coll.

get on   To agree well (with a person): coll. 'We got on like a house on fire.'—To become elderly: coll. Abbr. *getting on in years.*—To depart: coll. Cf. the S.E. *get along.*

get on to   To suspect; find out about.

get one's feet under the table   To establish friendly relations; esp. of servicemen in homes of residents local to barracks or camp.

get one's head down   To lie down and sleep.

get out!   Tell that to the marines!

get outside of   To eat or drink, esp. a considerable and specified amount: coll.

get some flying hours in   To get some sleep: R.A.F.

get that way   (Esp. *how do* or *did you get that way?*) To get into such or such a condition: coll.; orig. U.S., anglicized by 1930.

get (th)em   To tremble with fear: orig. military; ob. also, but always in form *has*, or *have, got 'em*, to have the 'd.t's'.

get weaving   See *weaving*.

get (a person) wrong, esp. in form have got (him) wrong   To misunderstand; have a wholly or mainly wrong opinion or impression of him.

ghastly   A vaguely pejorative, or a merely intensive, adj. or adv.: coll.

ghost of a chance, not the   No chance whatsoever: coll.

ghost walks, the; . . . does not walk   There is, is not, any money for salaries and wages: theatrical. Ex *Hamlet*, I. i.

Gib   Gibraltar.

giddy goat, play the   To play the fool; live a fast life: coll.

gift   Anything very easily obtained or won; an easy task: coll.

gig-lamps   Spectacles: by 1920, slightly ob.; by 1960, almost †.

gilt, n.   A gilt-edged security: financial.

gimmick   Any device or plan or trick calculated to ensure success. Ex U.S.

gin & It   Gin and Italian vermouth.

ginger-beer   An engineer: rhyming s.

ginger-pop   Ginger-beer: coll.

gink   A fellow: always pejorative: U.S., partly anglicized by 1920. Origin unknown.

gip   To cheat (a person): U.S., anglicized by 1930. Ex *Gipsy.*

gip (gyp, jip), give (a person)   To thrash, punish, manhandle, give a bad time: coll.

girl, old   A woman of any age whatsoever: pet or pejorative term, in reference or in address: coll.

give and take   A cake: rhyming s.

give (a person) **a piece of one's mind**   Frankly to impart one's ill opinion of him in gen. or in particular: coll.

give-away   A betrayal: coll.

give (one) **best**   To acknowledge a person's superiority; admit defeat: coll.

give it a rest!   Oh, stop talking!: coll. Ex U.S. *give us a rest.*

give the works   See *works . . .*

give what for, occ. **what's what**   (With dative.) To beat, thrash; scold, reprimand: coll.

glad eye, the   A come-hither look; esp. in *give the g.e.:* now coll. Ex † sense of *glad* (bright).

glad rags, one's   One's best clothes: coll.: U.S., anglicized ca. 1906; by 1945, slightly ob.

glass, v.   To hit with a tumbler or a wine-glass, esp. to cut a person with one; to slash with (a piece of) broken glass: low.

glass house   A guard-room; esp. detention-barracks: Regular Army. Ex *the Glass House:* the military prison at North Camp. It has a glass roof.

glass of beer   Ear: rhyming s.

glazier?, is, occ. **was, your father a**   A c.p. addressed to one who stands in the light.

glimmer, not a   Not (or none) at all: coll. Mostly in answer to some such question as 'Have (had) you any idea how to do this, or that this would happen?' Abbr. *not the glimmer of an idea.*

glory hole, the   The stewards' quarters: nautical.

glossies   Glossy-paper magazines: adopted ca. 1945, ex U.S.; by 1950, coll.

glutton   A boxer—hence, anyone—that takes a lot of punishment before he is 'satisfied': coll. Cf. the S.E. *glutton for work.*

go, n.   The fashion, esp. in *all the go:* coll. An affair, incident, occurrence, as in 'a rum go'.

go, v.   To deal with; to find acceptable.

go-ahead, adj.   Progressive; anxious to succeed—and usually succeeding: coll.

go & get your brains—or **head—examined!**   A c.p.—addressed to someone arguing foolishly.

go & take a running jump at yourself!   Go to blazes!: a c.p. expressive of scorn.

go back on, v.t.   To desert, turn against, or to fail, a person; break a promise: coll. Ex U.S. anglicized ca. 1895.

go over big   (Of a play, a book) to be very successful: U.S., anglicized ca. 1928.

go crook   To become angry, speak angrily: Australian.

go for   To attack: coll.

go-getter   A very enterprising person; a pusher: coll.: U.S., anglicized by 1925. Ex *go and get what one wants.*

go (or **get**) **into a flat spin**   To know not which way to turn, to become flustered: esp. in the Services and chiefly in the R.A.F. 'A flat spin is very much harder to recover from than a nose-down one' (Flying Officer Robert Hinde).

go it; often **go it strong**   To act vigorously or daringly; speak very strongly or frankly: coll.

go, man, go!   A jazz c.p.: adopted, ca. 1948, ex U.S.

go-off   (Time of) commencement: coll. Esp. in *at the first go-off,* at the very beginning.

go on   To talk volubly: coll. With *at,* to rail at: coll.

go on!   An exclamation of surprise, incredulity, or derision: coll.

go on about; be always on about   To complain of or about; (*be . . .*) to do this habitually: coll.

go places   To travel extensively, or merely to gad about: coll.; adopted, ca. 1938, from U.S.A.

go slumming   To mix with one's inferiors: jocular coll.

go the whole hog   To act thoroughgoingly: ex U.S.; anglicized ca. 1850.

go through on   To leave; give the slip to; deliberately see no more of (a person): Australian.

go to the top of the class!   A c.p. remark to one who has made a quick and accurate answer.

go west   To die: popularized in W.W. I; adumbrated in late C. 16, as in Greene, *Cony-Catching,* Part II, 1592, 'So long the foists (thieves) put their villanie in practise, that West-ward they goe, and there solemnly make a rehearsall sermon at tiborn'. The basic idea is that of the setting sun; pioneering in North America may have contributed.

goalie   A goal-keeper: Association football coll.

goat   A fool: coll.

goat, get someone's   To annoy him: U.S., anglicized by 1916; by 1950, slightly ob.

goat, play the   To play the fool: coll.

gods, the   (Those occupying) the gallery in a theatre: theatrical s. > gen. coll. Ex their elevation.

gold-digger   A female attaching herself to a man for (her) self and pelf: U.S., anglicized by 1930. Also *gold-digging*, the corresponding (not too) abstract n.

gollop, gollup   To gulp; swallow noisily and greedily: (low) coll.

golopshus, goloptious, galoptious   The best form is *goluptious*, for the term is a 'facetious perversion . . . of *voluptuous*; cf. rustic *boldacious*' (W), *delicious* being the 'suggester'.

gone for a burton   (Of persons) dead or presumed dead; hence, (of things) lost, missing and, occ. (of persons), absent: R.A.F. ' "He's had it" and "He's gone for a Burton" indicate that he's been killed' (Sgt.-Pilot F. Rhodes). Lit., for a glass of the excellent Burton ale, rather than for a suit made by Montague Burton.

gone on   Infatuated with: coll.

goner   One who is undone, ruined, or dead; that which is (almost or quite) finished, extinguished, or destroyed: orig. U.S.; anglicized ca. 1880.

gong   A medal; loosely, a decoration: military.

goo-goo eyes   Loving glances.

good, feel   To be jolly or 'in form': coll.: ex U.S.; anglicized ca. 1895.

good as they make 'em (as)   The best obtainable (things only): coll.

good for him (or **you**)!   Excellent work!; splendid news!: coll.

good hunting!   A c.p. popularized—perhaps generated—by Kipling's *Jungle Book*, 1894 (2nd, 1895).

good-looker   A pretty girl or handsome fellow: coll.; orig. U.S., anglicized ca. 1920.

good night!   A c.p. retort expressive of incredulity, comical despair, delight: ob. by 1945.

good sort, occ. **g. old s.**   A generous, a sympathetic, or a readily helpful person: coll.

goods, the   (Precisely) what is needed, esp. if of considerable worth or high merit. Gen. in *have the goods*, to be a very able person, and *deliver the goods*, to fulfil one's promise(s): coll.: anglicized, ca. 1908, from U.S.

goof   A person that is silly, 'soft', or stupid; hence adj. *goofy*. Ex dial. *gof, goff*, a fool.

goofy   Stupid; dull-witted and almost crazy; wildly crazy; excessively sentimental; *goofy about*, infatuated with.

goon   A stupid, sub-human fellow; hence (1940–5) a German guard; (post-1945) a brainless, strong-arm man, 'a great ape'. Ex U.S.: ? a blend of *goof* + *loon*.

goop, goopy   A fool, a fatuous person; foolish, fatuous. Perhaps a corruption of *goof*; cf. *looby, loopy*.

goose & duck   A truck: rhyming s.

gooseberry, play To act as propriety-third or chaperon: coll.

goosey, goosy, adj. With a goose-flesh feeling: coll.

goosgog A gooseberry: nursery and proletarian; ex dial.

gospel-shop (Methodist) chapel: coll.

got-up Dressed (ppl. adj.); esp. well-dressed, in the coll. variations: *got-up regardless* (abbr. *regardless of expense*)—*to kill*—*to the nines.*

government house The house of the owner or manager of an estate: a Dominions' jocular coll.

government stroke A slow lazy stroke, hence a lazy manner of working: Australian coll.

governor One's father: s. > coll. A term of address to a strange man: s. > coll. A superior; an employer: coll.

graft Work, labour: coll. Esp. in *hard graft,* (hard) work: in C. 20, mostly in the Army and in Australia and New Zealand. Hence, any kind of work, esp. if illicit: low coll. Cf. the U.S. (orig. s.) sense, illicit profit or commission, which itself prob. derives ex the Eng. term.

graft, v. To work; esp. to work hard: coll., mostly Australian and New Zealand.

grafter 'One who toils hard or willingly' (C. J. Dennis): coll. mostly Australian. Ex *graft,* v.

gram Gramophone. *The Gram,* the local grammar school: schoolboys'.

gran, grandma, granny, granty; grandpa Mostly in address: grandmother, grandfather: coll., esp. domestic.

grand, n. £1,000: adapted, ca. 1940, from U.S. *grand,* 1,000 dollars—a 'grand' sum.

Granny; also, **The Old Girl** *The Sydney Morning Herald*: Australian. Long established, very respectable.

grapevine, the A secret means employed by the chiefs of the underworld to ensure rapid and trustworthy transmission of important news: c. > low, and police, s.: adopted, ca. 1920, from U.S. where orig. *the grapevine telegraph.* Hence, that haphazard network of rumour-mongers in the Services, in factories, in offices, which, through Unit or Staff, transmits advance knowledge—often not inaccurate—of policy and of administrative decisions: s. that, by 1955, had > coll. Also, in this sense, *the bush telegraph,* a term that has radiated from Australia.

grass A police informer; to inform on (someone) to the police: underworld; but also police and low s. Short for *grasshopper,* rhyming s. for *copper,* policeman.

gravel-rash Abrasions resulting from a fall: coll. Perhaps jocular on *barber's rash.*

graveyard shift   A night shift: shipbuilders' and munition workers'. Cf. the Canadian rail-roadmen's *graveyard watch*: 12.01 a.m. to 8 a.m.

gravy   Perquisites: adopted, ca. 1943, from U.S.

grease   Butter: Australians' and New Zealanders' and *Conway* cadets'. If inferior, *axle-grease*.

grease-spot   The figurative condition to which one is reduced by great heat: coll.

greaser   A Mexican: orig. and mainly U.S.: anglicized ca. 1875, though used by Marryat much earlier.—A ship's engineer: naval.

great, adj.   Splendid; extremely pleasant; a gen. superlative: orig. U.S.; anglicized ca. 1895: coll.—In *run a great dog, filly*, etc., the sense is: the dog, etc., runs splendidly, runs a great race: sporting.

great big   A mere intensive of *big*: coll.

great I am, the   Used jocularly of oneself, pejoratively of others, it connotes excessive self-importance: coll. Ex the Biblical *I Am*.

great life if you don't weaken, it's a   A 1918 c.p., carried on into civilian life; ob. by 1945, yet still far from † even in 1960.

great smoke, the   London.

great stuff   Excellent; also as n.: coll.

greedy guts   A glutton: coll.

green in my eye?, do you see any   Do you think me a fool?

green fingers, have   To be a successful gardener; to succeed, as an amateur, with one's flowers and vegetables: coll. Popularized by the late Mr Middleton, B.B.C. broadcaster and newspaper writer on gardening.

greens   Green vegetables, e.g. and esp. cabbage and salads: coll.

grey mare   One's or the fare: rhyming s.

grey matter   Intelligence: jocular coll.

grid   A bicycle. Ex *grid*, a grid-iron.

grief, come to   To get into serious trouble; fail: coll. To fall from a horse: coll., mainly sporting.

griff   News, information. An abbr. of *griffin*.

griffin   A signal or warning; in *give* (ex *tip*) *the griffin*, to give a warning, and in *the straight griffin*, a straight tip.

grim   Unpleasant: a C. 20 (rare before 1918) middle- and upper-class coll. intensive.

grind   Hard work; routine.—Study, esp. for an examination: coll.

grip   A traveller's handbag: coll., ex U.S.; short for *gripsack*.

gripe, v.   To complain, as in 'What are you griping about?'; coll.

grit   Stamina; courage, esp. if enduring: orig. U.S.; anglicized as a coll. ca. 1860. Ex its hardness.

grizzle   To fret; complain whiningly or lachrymosely; hence, one who does this: coll.

groceries, the Bombs: R.A.F.: 1939–45. 'We delivered the groceries.'

groggy Unsteady on one's feet: pugilistic and gen. In poor health. Ex *grog*, orig. diluted rum, then any strong spirits.

ground floor, let in on the (Of the promoters) to allow to share on equal terms, in a financial speculation: orig. U.S.; anglicized ca. 1900: mainly financial and commercial. From the opp. angle, *get*, or *be let, in on the g.-f.*

Groupie A Group Captain: R.A.F. coll.

grouse To grumble; hence, a grumble: coll. Kipling, 1892, 'If you're cast for fatigue by a sergeant unkind, / Don't grouse like a woman, nor crack on, nor blind'. Hence *grouser* and *grousing*.

grouter, on a, or **the** Out of one's turn, interferingly; unfairly: Australian. Esp. *come in on a grouter*, e.g. to obtain something to which one is not entitled. Ex the game of two-up.

growing pains The difficulties and anxieties of getting settled down in life when one is young: coll. Ex. the lit. *growing pains*.

grub Food; provisions of food. Orig., and long, a very low word.

grub-stake, v.t. To give (an author) money to keep him going while he writes a book: publishers', hence also authors' coll. Hence also n. Ex gold-mining.

grub-stakes 'Grub' (food); food-supply.

grunter A pig: coll.

guard-rail critic One who tenders overmuch advice and no assistance: naval. He leans back against the rail while *you* work.

guess and by God (or euphemistically, **Godfrey**), **by** (Of steering) at hazard: naval coll.

guff Humbug; empty talk; foolish bluff; nonsense: coll.

guinea-pig A public-company director, one who merely attends board meetings.

guiver Flattery; artfulness: theatrical. Whence, in Australia, it is gen. s., with additional sense of nonsense, esp. if plausible; make-believe. Ex the † adj. *guiver*, smart, fashionable.

gum up the works To spoil or upset things.

gum tree, be up a To be in a predicament; be cornered: Australian coll. Cf. the much earlier U.S. sense, be on one's last legs, whence prob. the Australian. Perhaps ex an opossum being shot at.

gummie, gummy A gum-digger: New Zealand and Australian coll. A shark: Australian. Ex the lavish display of teeth.

gumption Commonsense; shrewdness: coll. Grose, his *Provincial Glossary*, 'Gawm to understand . . .' Hence, possibly, *gawmtion*, or *gumption*, understanding. Orig. Scottish. Sometimes shortened to *gump*.

gun A thief; a pickpocket: c. >, ca. 1880, low s. Abbr. *gon(n)oph*, *gon(n)ov* or *-of(ſ)*.—Hence, a 'rascal', 'beggar', as a vague pejorative more Australian than English; by 1940, ob.—Orig. and mainly U.S.; anglicized ca. 1900.

gunfire   Early-morning tea (or a cup of tea): military. Prob. ex the morning gun of a garrison town.

gup   Gossip, scandal; hence, silly talk: coll., orig. Anglo-Indian.

gurk, v.i.   To belch: coll. Hence, also n.

gush   Talk effusive and objectionably sentimental: coll. Also v., whence *gusher* and *gushing* and *gushy*.

guts   The stomach and intestines. Until ca. 1830, S.E.; then coll. Courage: coll. Cf. the exactly similar ascent of *pluck*.—The essentials: coll. 'Let's get at the guts of it.'

gutser   A heavy fall; hence used fig.: low coll.

gutsy   Energetic; spirited; courageous: coll.

guy   A man, fellow, chap: orig. U.S.: anglicized ca. 1910.— Prob. ult. ex *Guy* Fawkes but perhaps a mutilation of Yiddish *goy*, a Gentile.

guy, v.   To quiz, ridicule: coll.

guy, do a   To run away, escape: c. > gen. s. Referable to Guy Fawkes.

gym   Abbr. *gymnasium*: coll.

gyp   To cheat or swindle: Canadian, from U.S. Ex S.E. *Gypsy*.

gyppy or **gippy**   An Egyptian; a Gypsy. But *Gyppies* also = Egyptian cigarettes: coll.

gypsy's warning   Morning: rhyming s.

gyro   A gyroscope: coll.

H

---

habitual, n.   A confirmed criminal, drunkard, drug-taker: coll.

hacky   Of, or like, a hack (horse): coll. (Of a cough) hacking: coll.

hag   A matron: certain Public Schools'.

hail & rain   A train: rhyming s.

hair, get in one's   To annoy or irritate someone. Ex grit embedded in hair.

hair-do   Having one's hair dressed in a fashionable style: feminine coll.

hair on, hold or, more gen., **keep one's**   To keep one's temper; esp. in imperative.

hairs, get or **have by the short**   So to hold (lit. and fig.) that escape is painful or difficult: coll. Ex hair on nape of neck.

hairy, n.   A draught-horse; any rough-coated horse: military.

hairy, adj.   Ill-bred; bad-mannered.—Angry; (angry and) excited: Anglo-Irish.

half   A half-holiday; schools' coll. A child travelling half fare: coll.

half-baked   In C. 20, implies lack of intelligence (but not downright silliness) plus a lack of culture.

half-inch   To steal: c. and low s.; rhyming on *pinch*.

half-section, one's   One's friend: Services'.

half-seas over   Half or almost drunk: orig. nautical s. > gen. coll.

ham it   To be an inferior actor; esp. to act badly: adopted, ca. 1939, from U.S.A. Also adj. *hammy*: 'inferior'.

ham-fisted, -handed   Clumsy.

hammer   To declare (a member) a defaulter: Stock Exchange. Ex the hammer-taps preceding the head porter's formal proclamation.

hammer & tongs   Violently: coll.

76

Hampstead Heath   The teeth: rhyming s. Often abbr. to *Hampsteads*.

hand, get or **give a**   To be applauded or to applaud: theatrical.

hand it to   To admit the superiority of: coll., orig. U.S., anglicized ca. 1930.

handle   A title; mostly in form *handle to one's name*: coll. In C. 20, occ. loosely used to include Dr and even Mr.

hang   The general drift or tendency, gen. in *get the hang of*: coll., adopted ex U.S.

hang out, v.   To reside, live, lodge; be temporarily (at, e.g., a dug-out in the trenches): coll. Ex the ancient custom of hanging out signs.

hangover   A 'morning after the night before' feeling.

hankie, hanky; rarely **handky**   A handkerchief: nursery coll.

hanky-panky   Legerdemain; hence, almost imm., trickery. Also adj., as in *hanky-panky business* or *tricks*. An arbitrary word; perhaps ex '*hokey-pokey* by association with *sleight of hand*'.

happy, adj.   Slightly (and, properly used, cheerfully) drunk: coll.

hard   Hard labour.

hard, adj.   Intoxicating, spirituous: coll.: orig. U.S., anglicized in mid-1880's.

hard case   An incorrigible: orig. U.S.; anglicized ca. 1860. In Australia and New Zealand, a person morally tough but not necessarily incorrigible; also an amusing dare-devil: all coll.

hard cheese   Bad luck; orig. esp. at billiards. A humorous variant is *hard cheddar*.

hard doer   An irrepressible, devil-may-care, dryly amusing person: Australian.

hard-hitter   A bowler hat: Australian.

hard nut   Abbr. *hard nut to crack*: a dangerous foe; a 'hard case': coll.

hard-up, adj.   In want, gen. of money: coll. Hence, *hard up for*, sorely needing: coll.

hardware   'Ammunition in general and shells in particular. Jocular' (Ware): military and naval.

Harry Flakers   'Compietely flaked out after a party' (Granville); exhausted: naval. *Harry* is predominant in s. phrases.

Harry Flatters   A calm, *flat* sea: naval.

Harry Freeman's (or **Freemans**)   Free cigarettes. Often corrupted, esp. among Cockneys, to *Yenhams*.

Harry Tate   A plate: rhyming s.—State: rhyming s.

Harry Wragg   A cigarette: rhyming s. on *fag*.

hash, settle one's   To subdue, silence, defeat; kill: coll.

hash-up   A 'mess', a bungling; fiasco: coll.

hat, eat one's; esp. **I'll eat my hat, if . . .** A strong asseveration: coll.

hat, talk through one's To talk nonsense: coll., orig. U.S.; anglicized ca. 1900.

hate A bombardment: military. In 1915–18, the usual German night or morning bombardment. 'An allusion to the *Hymn of Hate*, perpetrated (Aug. 1914) by one Lissauer.' A (gen. morning) grumble.

hate (someone's) **guts** To hate someone intensely: adopted, ca. 1937, from U.S.A.

hatter A miner working alone: Australian s. >, by 1890, coll., with connotation, 'a man who has lived by himself until his brain has been turned'.

have A trick or imposture; a swindle.

have, v. To cheat; hence, to trick, deceive, humbug, fool.

have a good chit To be well spoken, or thought, of: Army (mostly officers'). Cf. *give* (someone) *a good chit*: to speak well of: Army officers'.

have for breakfast, occ. **before breakfast** (as an appetizer) A humorous way of implying that a man is easy to beat, as in 'Why! I have one like him every day before breakfast' or 'I could have *or* do with six like him for breakfast'.

have had it Esp. in *You've had it*, You won't get it, you're too late, etc.: Services' >, in 1944, fairly general civilian. Ironic—perhaps short for 'Somebody else has (or, may have) had it, so you certainly won't'.

have it, let one To strike hard; punish (lit. or fig.) severely: coll.

have it in for (someone) To bear a grudge against: coll.

have on To be prepared, or actually, to fight (someone): Australian.

have the goods on To have abundant evidence for the conviction of (a person).

haw-haw, adj. Affected in speech (rarely of women); rather obviously and consciously English upper-class: (mostly Colonial) coll.

hay-seed A countryman, esp. if very rustic: orig. U.S.; anglicized, as a coll., ca. 1905 in Britain, but ca. 1900 in Australia and New Zealand. Ex hay-seeds clinging to outer garments.

hay-wire; now **haywire** Beside oneself with anger; crazy, very eccentric: anglicized, ex U.S., in 1936. Hence:

haywire, go To go crazy: of mechanisms, to get (completely) out of order.

he-man A virile fellow; a 'cave-man'; one who 'treats 'em rough'. Whence, *he-man stuff*.

headache A problem; a worry ('That's *your* headache!'): coll. >, by 1947, familiar S.E.

head, (can) do on one's To do easily.

head, get or **have a big** To become or be conceited: coll.

head, have a To have a headache from drinking: coll. Often *have a (shocking) head on one.*

headlines, make the To get one's name into the headlines or on to the front page: journalistic.

head, off one's Out of one's mind; crazy: coll.

head cook & bottle washer One in authority; a foreman; a boss: coll.—Often applied to a person temporarily doing a general servant's work.

head off, eat one's or **its** To cost, in keep, more than one's or its worth: coll. Orig., of horses.

head-serang An overseer, master, one in authority: nautical s. > ca. 1900, gen. s. Ex Persian *sarhang*, an overseer.

head worker A schemer, a shirker, a malingerer: military coll.

heads, the Those in authority, the singular being *one of the heads*: coll.

heads I win, tails you lose A mock bet: also = I *cannot* fail!

healthy Large; excellent: coll.: 'A healthy cheque.'

heard, or **have you heard, the news? The squire—**or **the squire's daughter—has been foully—**or **most foully—murdered** A c.p. satirical of the late Victorian and the Edwardian melodrama.

heart, have a To have a weak heart: coll.

hearts of oak Penniless: (ironic) rhyming s. on *broke*.

heart throb One's girl friend; occ. one's boy friend. A glamorous film-star (either sex).

hearty Sporting and healthy, and brainless: orig., and still mainly, university coll. Hence, as n.

heavy father, do the To be excessively parental: coll. Ex theatre.

hectic Exciting; sensational: coll.

hedge (and ditch) A 'pitch' (stall; stand); cricket or football pitch: rhyming s.

hedge-hopping, n. Flying very low: Air Force.

heebie (or **-y)-jeebies, the** A fit of depression or irritation: U.S.; by 1928, anglicized. Ex a dance.

heel Ex U.S.A., ca. 1938. An objectionable fellow. You can't usually see your heel.

hefty Big and strong: coll.: orig. U.S.; anglicized ca. 1905. Hence also as intensive adv.

Heine, Heinie, occ. **Hiney** The Canadian (and later the U.S.) soldiers' name for 'Fritz' or 'Jerry', qq.v.: 1914–18 and 1939–45. Ex *Heinrich*, an extremely common Ger. Christian name.

helio, n. and v.   Heliograph; heliotrope: coll.

hell & high water, between In a great difficulty: nautical coll.

help yourself! Please yourself!: c.p.

hep In the know; having good taste: British jazz-lovers'. Ex Canadian jazz-musicians and -lovers, who adopted it ex U.S.

here goes! Now for it!; there's not much chance, but I'll try: coll.

het-up; often **all het-up** Excited; 'in a state': adopted, ca. 1935, from U.S.A. I.e. heated up.

hick A (simple) countryman: s. > coll.; now mostly U.S.

hide The human skin: s. >, ca. 1710, coll. Impudence; excessive self-assurance: Australian.

hidey hole A hiding-place: children's coll.

hiding A thrashing; hence also a heavy defeat: (low) coll. Cf. *hide*.

high, n.   A peak or record in, e.g., production or sales, the opposite being *low*: coll.

high & mighty Arrogant; imperious: coll.

high-hat To treat (a person) superciliously: an American coll., anglicized by 1930.

high-hat, adj. 'Superior'; supercilious.

high old Excellent; very merry, jolly, or joyous: coll.; esp. *a high old time.* Ex U.S.

high spots, hit the To go to excess (of dissipation, or merry-making); to attain a very high level: U.S., anglicized ca. 1927. Likewise *the high spot* (gen. pl.), the outstanding feature of something: anglicized ca. 1925.

high-tailing Running away without looking behind; bolting: Canadian coll. Ex U.S. Ex the flight of scared horses.

high-up High; fig., of high rank or position: dial. >, in late 1890's, coll. Hence, also n.

high-ups Persons with high rank; politicians enjoying their brief authority: coll.

highbrow A person affecting intellectual superiority: coll., orig. U.S.; anglicized ca. 1917. Cf. *lowbrow*, q.v.—Hence, as adj.

highty-tighty Peremptory, quarrelsome; uppish: coll. 'The earliest record upon the *hoyty-toyty* (1668) suggests the *high ropes* and *tight rope*, or simply a jingle upon *high*' (Weekley).

hike, n.   A long walk, esp. for exercise or pleasure. Ex the v.

hike, v.   To tramp, for pleasure or exercise: coll., ex dial. Becoming, except in dial., disused in England, *hike* went to U.S., whence it returned to gen. coll. usage in England, ca. 1925. To pull, to drag, esp. with considerable effort: coll., ex dial. Cf. *hoick*; prob. akin to S.E. *hoist*.

hiker; hiking   One who 'hikes' (*hike*, 1st sense); n. and adj. (connected with, characteristic of) the going for long walks. Both coll.

hipe   A rifle, esp. in *slope hipe*: military. *Rifle* being less easy to pronounce, *ripe* none too easy, and *slope* perhaps effecting the form.

Hippo, the   Any city's Hippodrome: coll.

hippo   Hippopotamus: coll.

hit it up; orig. hit things up   'To behave strenuously; riotously' (C. J. Dennis): Australian.

hit (someone) for six   To rout decisively in argument or business. Ex cricket.

hit the deck   To land; to crash-land: R.A.F. Hence, to sleep.

hit the hay   To go to bed: U.S. (orig. tramps')—anglicized ca. 1930.

hit the roof   To flare up, be or become extremely angry: coll.

hit where one lives   To appeal to, make a great impression on, a person: 1907, P. G. Wodehouse, 'This is just the sort of thing to get right at them. It'll hit them where they live.'

hitch, v.   To marry; esp. *get hitched*: orig. U.S.: anglicized ca. 1890.

hitch-hike   To obtain a free ride on a walking tour, or, esp. to obtain a series of free rides, going on, or returning from, leave: coll.: adopted, ca. 1936, from U.S.A.

hobo, pl. hoboes   A tramp; esp, one who occasionally works. Orig. U.S.; anglicized ca. 1905. A C. 20 tramp's distinction, made ca. 1925: 'Bums loafs and sits. Tramps loafs and walks. But a hobo moves and works, and he's clean.'

hock   To pawn; *in hock*, pawned. Ex U.S.

hog (pl. hog)   A shilling: orig. c.; now low s. Prob. ex the figure of a hog on a small silver coin.

hog, v.   To appropriate, esp. appropriate and eat or drink greedily: orig. U.S.; anglicized ca. 1912; now coll.

hog-wash   Worthless, cheap journalism: journalistic. Cf. *slush*.

hoick, v.   To raise, hoist, esp. with a jerk: coll. Prob. cf. S.E. *hoist.*—Hence, to force (an aeroplane) to mount steeply: coll. Hence, v.i., to climb steeply, jerk oneself up (and *out of*): coll.

hok(e)y-pok(e)y   A cheat, a swindle: low coll. Cheap ice-cream sold in the streets: low coll. Both of these senses are ex S.E. *hocus-pocus*.

hokum, occ. hocum   Anything designed to make a melodramatic or a sentimental appeal; bunkum: U.S., anglicized by 1936. Prob. ex *hocus*(*-pocus*) on *bunkum*.

hold   To be in funds: coll.; at first, Cockney; in C. 20, mostly Australian, as in *are you holding?*

hold it! Stay in precisely that position!: painters' s. > coll. ca. 1910 in the theatrical, and ca. 1925 in the cinematographic, world.

hold out on To keep something (esp. money or important information) back from (a person): orig. U.S.; anglicized ca. 1924.

hold your horses! Hold the job up until further notice! Services'. Ex a horse-drawn artillery order.

hole, better; gen. **better 'ole** A better, esp. a safer, place; notably *if you know of a better 'ole, go to it*, which > in 1915 (the year of Captain Bruce Bairnsfather's cartoon), a c.p. not yet †; Bairnsfather's play of the same title (staged in 1916) reinforced the cartoon.

holiday (Gen. pl.) A spot carelessly left untarred or unpainted: nautical coll. Hence, a gap 'left between slung hammocks or clothing hung up to dry' (Bowen): nautical.

holla, boys, holla; often shortened to **holla boys** A collar: rhyming s.

hols (Rarely *hol*, a single day's holiday.) Holidays: orig. and mainly schools'; C. 20.

holus-bolus, adv. All together; completely; hence, in confusion: orig. dial.; coll. from ca. 1860. O.E.D. suggests by facetious latinization of (*the*) *whole bolus* or as through Gr. *holos bōlos*, (the) entire lump.

holy Joe A pious person: coll. A parson, a chaplain: nautical. Hence, the shallow, circular-crowned hat worn by clergymen: ecclesiastical.

holy terror A very formidable person; a person of tiresome manner or exasperating habits: coll.

home, James! A c.p., dating from ca. 1870—if not earlier; *James* being the coachman, later the chauffeur. At first usually, and still occasionally, *home, James, and don't spare the horses.*

home on the pig's back Very successful; thoroughly (and easily): a c.p., mostly among New Zealanders and Australians.

home with the milk, come, or **get** To reach home in the early morning: coll.

homework Girls in gen.; one's girl in particular: Services'.

homy, occ. **homey** Home-like; unobtrusively comfortable: coll.

honest! It's true, on my word it is: coll.

honest-to-goodness, adj. and adv. Real(ly), genuine(ly), thorough-(ly): coll.; orig. U.S., anglicized 1921.

hoo-ha An argument, a 'row'; hence, an artillery demonstration: orig., military. Echoic.

hooch, hootch Alcoholic liquor, esp. spirits: U.S., anglicized by ca. 1918. Ex Alaska *hoochino*, a very strong drink, made by Alaskan natives.

hoodlum   Any, esp. if dangerous, rough: orig. and still mainly U.S.; anglicized ca. 1895. Origin unknown; cf. *hooligan*.

hooey   Nonsense; 'eyewash': adopted, ca. 1937, from U.S.A. Short for *ballyhooey*.

hoof   A human foot: low coll.

hoof it   To dance or to walk.

hoofer   A dancer: Canadian. A chorus girl: Australian.

hook, v.   To obtain, esp. in marriage: coll.: usually of a woman.

hook, n.   A shoplifter: c.: C. 20.—An anchor badge: naval.—An anchor; nautical.

hook, sling one's; also **hook it**   To run away; depart, secretly or hastily, or both: low.

Hooky Walker!   A phrase signifying that something either is not true or will not occur: (low) coll., from ca. 1810. Note also *Hook(e)y!* as in Bee, and *by hooky!*, as in Manchon.—2. Be off!: (low) coll. Now usually abbr. to *Walker!*. Both, ob. by 1920. Acc. to Bee, ex *John Walker*, a prevaricating hook-nosed spy.

hooligan   A lively rough, not necessarily nor usually criminal: s. till ca. 1910, then coll. Ex a 'joie-de-vivre' Irish family (the Houlihans) resident, in the middle 90's, in the Borough (London): see esp. Clarence Rook, *The Hooligan Nights*, 1899.

hoop, go through the   To have a bad time of it: coll. Ex circus tricks. Hence, to be up for punishment: military. Complement: *put through the hoops*.

hoot   Money; payment, wage; compensation: New Zealand and soon Australia. Ex Maori *utu* (money), often pronounced with clipped terminal.

hootch   See **hooch**.

hop   A dance: coll.

hop   A stage—the flying done in one day—of a long journey by air: coll.

hop, on the   (Esp. *catch on the hop*.) Unawares: (orig. low) coll. At a disadvantage: coll. (Adj.) On the go; unresting.

hop it   To depart quickly: coll., orig. Cockney.

hop off   To die; by 1945, ob.

hop out   A definite challenge to fight: mostly Australian.

hop the bags   To attack; 'go over the top': military: 1915–18. Ex sandbags forming the parapet of the trench.

hope (or **I hope**) **it keeps fine for you!**   A c.p., often ironic. *The Jesting Army*, 1930. A parting-phrase c.p., which may refer to prospects other than meteorological. *Hope you have a fine day for it.*

hopes!, some or **what**   A c.p. expressive of extreme scepticism.

horizontal champion   A sailor endowed with an immense capacity for sleep: naval.

horn in To interfere; v.t. with *on*: U.S., anglicized ca. 1930. Ex cattle.

horrible Excessive; immoderate: S.E. till ca. 1830, then coll. The same applies to the adv.

horrid Very bad or objectionable: coll. Esp. as a feminine term of strong aversion.

horrors (Gen. with *the*.) The first stage of *delirium tremens*: low coll.—Low spirits, a fit of horror: coll.

horse, eat like a To have a very large appetite; coll.

horse, strong as a (Of a person only) very strong: coll.

horse-sense Common sense, esp. if unrefined and somewhat earthy: orig. U.S.; anglicized ca. 1895 as a coll.

horse's neck A drink of ginger ale and brandy.

horsing around The playing of practical jokes: Canadian. Cf. the S.E. *horse play*.

hot, adj. (Of a horse) much betted-on. Esp. in *hot favourite*.— Exceedingly skilful. In C. 20 insurance s., applied to a very likely insurer, a promising 'prospect'. Ex *hot* in children's games. Excessive, extreme. (Of a Treasury bill) newly issued: coll.—But also: novel, new.

hot, adj. Stolen: adopted from U.S., where, orig., c.

hot, catch or **get it; give it hot** To be severely thrashed, defeated, or reprimanded; to thrash, defeat, reprimand severely: coll.

hot-foot (it) To hasten; run; to decamp speedily: adopted ca. 1917 from U.S.A.

hot, make it To ask too much; exaggerate grossly; in short, to behave as if one were ignorant of the limits and limitations imposed by the commonest decency: coll. Esp. in *don't make it too hot!* Prob. ex S.E. *make it hot*, i.e. uncomfortable, *for*.

hot, not so Bad; unattractive; inefficient; ineffective. Ex U.S.

hot air Boastful or exaggerated talk; talk for the sake of effect: coll. Ex U.S.

hot & strong, give it (to a person) 'To punish . . . severely, either physically or verbally' (Lyell): coll.

hot bricks, like a cat on, adj. and adv. Restive(ly); uncomfortable (or -ly): coll.

hot gospeller A fanatical preacher, or a preaching fanatic: coll.

hot on Unusually good or skilful at: coll. Variant, *hot at*.

hot stuff A person very excellent, skilful or energetic (*at*, e.g., a game): coll. A person, out of the ordinary in degree—dangerous— (mostly of women) sexually hot or lax: coll. A thing that is remarkable, behaviour that is either remarkable or censurable, a striking action: coll. Hence, as adj. or as an admiring exclamation: coll.

hot time (of it), give (a person) **a**   To make him thoroughly uncomfortable; to reprimand severely: coll. See also *hot, catch it*.

hot with   Spirits with hot water and sugar: coll. Contrast Fr. *café avec*.

house on fire, like a   Very quickly or energetically: coll.

houses, (as) safe as   Perfectly safe: coll. Perhaps, as Hotten suggests, the phrase arose 'when the railway bubbles began to burst and speculation again favoured houses'.

housey-housey!   The c.p. cry with which players of 'House' are summoned: coll., mostly military.

how   A howitzer: military coll.

how!, and   The U.S. variant, anglicized by 1933, of the English *rather!* By ellipsis, thus: '"That's pleasant."—"And *how* (pleasant)!"'

how come?   How does that come about? or Why is that?: adopted, ca. 1943, ex U.S. servicemen.

how-do-you-do, how-d'ye-do   A fuss, a noisy difficulty, a 'mess': low coll. Often preceded by *a pretty*.

how much?   What do you say, mean? A coll. request for an explanation: not quite extinct, though ob. so early as 1938.

howler   A glaring (and amusing) blunder: coll. Lit., either something that howls or cries for notice or perhaps, as W. proposes, by way of contracting *howling blunder*.

hubby   Husband: coll.

hubris   'Accomplished, distinguished insolence' (Ware): academic >, by 1890, coll.; slightly ob. Direct ex Gr. For status, cf. *nous*.

huddle, go into a   To go into secret or private conference; (of several people) to 'put their heads together': jocular coll.

Hue & Cry, The   *The Police Gazette*: mostly journalistic. Ex the wanted's.

hum   To stink: low: from ca. 1895. Ware states that 'this is an application from the humming of fermentation in an active manure heap'.

humbug, n.   An impostor, a 'fraud'; deception pretence, affectation: coll. Etymology obscure.

humbug, v.   Impose upon, hoax, delude; to cajole: coll. Hence the adj. and n. *humbugging*.

humbug!   Stuff and nonsense!: coll.

humbug about   To play the fool: coll.

hump, the   Temporary ill humour; a sulky fit; esp. in *get* or *have the hump*: Jerome K. Jerome, *Idle Thoughts*, 1886, 'He has got the blooming hump'.

humpey (or -y)   A hump-backed person.—A camel: Australian.

Hun   Jocular, or pejorative, for a very objectionable person: coll.: ca. 1914–1929. Ex the *Huns* or Germans.

hunch A suspicion; an intuition or premonition: orig. U.S.; anglicized by 1916, thanks to Canadian soldiers.

hung up, be To be held up, hence at a standstill: coll.

hunky-dory, everything's Predicatively, as in 'That's hunky-dory' —fine, just the thing: adopted ca. 1938 from U.S.A.

hurrah party Men going ashore on a spree: naval.

hurry-scorry The n. v., adj., adv. denoting or corresponding to 'a disorderly rushing-about, a confused crowding': coll.

husky, adj. Well-built and sturdy and rough: coll.: U.S., anglicized ca. 1918, though Canadianized by 1900.

I

I believe you, (but) thousands wouldn't   A c.p. tactfully implying that the addressee is a liar.

I couldn't care less   See *care less* . . .

I don't mind if I do   A c.p. (= Yes, please) that in 1945 > fairly widespread and in 1946 almost a public nuisance. A Tommy Handley 'gag' in 'Itma'.

I say!   A coll. exclamation, indicative of surprise.

I suppose   The nose: rhyming s.

icicle's chance in hades or **hell, not an**   Not the least chance: coll.

ickle   Little: nursery coll.

iddy (or **itty**) **umpty**   A signaller; hence a R.E. lineman repairing telephone and telegraph wires: military; ob. by 1945 † by 1960.

idea? what's the big   What folly have you in mind?: coll.; orig. U.S., anglicized ca. 1930.

iffy   Uncertain; unsound, risky: coll.—Addicted to excessive *if's* in conversation: coll.

Ikey   A Jew; hence a pawnbroker of any nationality.

ikey, adj.   Alert, wide-awake; artful: low; ob. Ex the preceding.

I'll bite; I'll buy it   'I'll bite' is often said and understood as 'I'll buy it', which leads to the further c.p. *No, I'm not selling—serious!*

I'll do (or **fix**) **you!**   A c.p. threat, 'I'll settle your hash'; often jocular.

I'll have a basinful of that!   A (mostly lower-classes' and lower-middle classes') c.p. directed at a long word or a new one.

I'll try anything once   A c.p., affected by the adventurous or the experimental; sometimes jocular.

I'm afloat   A boat, or a coat: rhyming s.

I'm so frisky   Whiskey: rhyming s.

I'm telling you   A c.p., indicative of emphasis.

immense, -ly   General superlatives: coll.

imposs or **impos**   Impossible: coll.

impot   In Australia and New Zealand, occ. *impo*. A schoolboys' abbr. of *imposition*.

improve, on the   Improving: coll., mostly Australian.

in-and-out   Stout (the drink): rhyming s.

in-laws   One's parents-in-law: coll.

in on   Participating in, admitted to a share of, some matter or affair of unusual interest or importance: coll. 'Am I to be in on this?'

incog   A coll. abbr. of *incognito*, n., adj., and adv.

indicated, ppl. adj.   (Always with v. *to be*.) Desirable; advisable: coll. 'A drink was indicated.'

info   Information: mostly Australian.

inner man, the   The stomach; one's appetite: jocular coll. Esp. in *satisfy the inner man*.

intense   Excited; excitable: Society coll.: from ca. 1920. Evelyn Waugh, *Vile Bodies*, 1930, ' "Darling, I *am* so glad about our getting married." "So am I. But don't let's get intense about it." ' By 1960 ob.

intercom   Inter-communication telephonic system of an aircraft: R.A.F.

into next week   Violently; fatally; into insensibility: coll. Esp. with *knock*.

intro   An introduction (to a person): coll.

invite   An invitation: S.E. until ca. 1830, then coll.

Irish as Paddy's (or Patrick's or Pat's) pig, as; or **(as) Irish as Paddy Murphy's pig**   Very Irish indeed: coll.

Irish up, get one's   To become angry. Cf. *paddy*.

iron (it) out   To put (it) right. To remove the creases by ironing.

irk, or **erk**   An air mechanic: Air Force. By concertina-ing.

Iron Duke   A lucky chance: rhyming on *fluke*.

issue, the (whole)   The complete set, number, amount; 'the lot': military: ca. 1914–39. Ex an *issue* or distribution of, e.g., cigarettes.

is there room for a small one?   A c.p. addressed to occupants of crowded vehicle.

itch & scratch   A match (ignition): rhyming s.

it's a piece of cake   See *piece of cake*.

It's That Man Again!   A c.p. dating from late 1939; during the bombing of Britain by the Luftwaffe, esp. in 1940–1, applied chiefly to bomb-damage, that man being Hitler. Ex Tommy Handley's scintillating B.B.C. radio programme 'Itma' (*It's That Man Again*).

ivories, tickle the   To play the piano.

J

Jack A sailor: coll. Ex earlier *sailor Jack, Jack the Sailor*. A policeman: Australian. Among Aus. and N.Z. soldiers, *the Jacks* = military policemen.

jack Money: low: adopted ex U.S.

Jack, on one's Alone; without assistance: low rhyming s. Ex *Jack Jones*.

Jack & Jill A till; a bill; a (small) hill: rhyming s.

Jack Dusty; Jack in the dust A ship's-steward's assistant: resp. nautical and naval.

Jack Jones Alone: (imperfect) rhyming s.

Jack Malone, on one's Alone: rhyming s. Often abbr. to *on one's Jack*, which also abbreviates the synonymous *on one's Jack Jones*.

Jack Randall A candle: rhyming s. (−1859). Ex a famous boxer.

Jack the Ripper A kipper: rhyming s.

jack up To abandon, 'chuck up'.

jackaroo, jackeroo A young Englishman learning sheep- or cattle-farming: Australian s. >, by 1900, coll. Either ex *Johnny Raw* after *kangaroo* or ex the Brisbane Aborigines' name (orig. for a garrulous bird) for a white man.

jacob A ladder: c. >, by 1900, low s. Perhaps, as Grose suggests, ex Jacob's dream.

jag (A bout of) intoxication; *on a jag*, on a drunken spree, and *have a jag on*, gen. supposed to be U.S., were orig. Eng. dial., whence U.S. and Eng. s. usage in late C. 19–20. Lit. sense, a load.

Jag A Jaguar motor-car: coll.

jake, adj. Honest, upright; equitable, correct; 'O.K.'; excellent: Colonial and U.S.: C. 20.

jake, adv. Well, profitably; honestly, genuinely: Colonial. Ex preceding.

jakes A privy: S.E. till ca. 1750, then coll. Prob. an abbr. of *Jack's place*. Cf. *John, the*.

jaloppy A cheap, or an old, motor-car: adopted, ca. 1950, ex U.S.

jam A difficulty, awkward mess: coll. Ex sense, 'crowd, crush'. Esp. in *get into a jam*.—A clear profit, a certainty of winning; orig. racing s. > coll.

jam-jar A tramcar; a motor car: rhyming s.

jam on it Something pleasant: naval and military.

jam tart Heart: rhyming s.

jamboree A frolic, a spree: coll.; orig. U.S.; anglicized ca. 1890. Origin unknown.

jammy Exceedingly lucky or profitable; hence, excellent, splendid.

Jane A woman; a girl. Cf. *Judy*.

jankers Defaulters; their punishment; punishment cells; defaulters' bugle-call: naval and military. Echoic. Whence, *jankers king*, a provost-sergeant, and *jankers man*, a defaulter.

jannock, jonnick, jonnock, jonnuk Honest, loyal, equitable; proper, customary; conclusive: dial. > fairly gen. coll.

Jap A Japanese: late C. 19–20 coll. Also adj.

java Coffee: Canadian: ex U.S.

jaw A talk, speech, lecture: low coll. To address abusively, scold or address severely: low coll.

jaw-breaker A word difficult of pronunciation: coll.

jaw-breakers Cheap, usually rather large, and either hard or sticky sweets.

jay-walker (Hence, *jay-walking*). One who crosses a street to the peril of the traffic: s., adopted in 1925 ex U.S.; by ca. 1934, coll.

jazzy Loud-coloured; 'flashy': since ca. 1935.

jemimas Elastic-sided boots: coll.

Jenny Lea or **Lee** Tea: rhyming s. Also *Rosy Lee* and *you and me*. A flea: rhyming s. One authority differentiates thus: Jenny Lea, tea; Jenny Lees, fleas.—A key.

Jenny Linda A window: rhyming s. On *winder*, the low coll. pronunciation; ex Jenny Lind, the famous mid-C. 19 singer.

jerk, n. A chap, fellow; usually with a pejorative tinge: adopted, in 1943, from American soldiers.

jerk in(to) it, put a To act smartly; to hurry. Ex physical training and prob. suggested by *jump to it*.

Jerry, occ. **Gerry,** n. and adj. German; esp. (of) a German soldier: 1914–18. Hence a German aircraft: 1915–18 and revived in 1939–45.

jerry A chamber-pot: low. Ex *jeroboam*.

jerry, v.i. and t. To recognize; discern, discover, detect; understand: low; from ca. 1870. Prob. ex † *jerrycummumble*, to shake, to tumble. Cf. *rumble*, itself prob. suggested by *tumble*, the latter prob. ex *jerrycummumble*.

jet   A jet-propelled aircraft: coll.

Jew   A ship's tailor: nautical, late C. 19–20. Hence *jewing*, tailoring, sewing.

jiffy   A moment.

jigger   A prison cell; a guardroom: military. The front line, esp. as a trench.

jigger, v.t. and i.   To shake or jerk often and rapidly: coll. Ex S.E. *jig*, v. of motion.—To circumvent, damage, ruin. Ex (exclamatory) *jiggered!*

jiggery-pokery   Humbug; underhand work: now coll. Ex Scottish *joukery-paukery*, ex *jouk*, a trick. Cf. *hanky-panky*.

jildi, jildy; jildo, occ. **jeldi** (-y); very often **jillo**   Adj. and adv., lively; look sharp!: Regular Army's. Ex Hindustani.

Jim Crow   A roof spotter of aircraft: civilian Services' 1939–45. Hence, one who keeps watch while, e.g., gambling is in progress: combatant Services'.

jim-jams, the   The fidgets; nervousness; the 'creeps': low spirits: coll.

Jimmy O'Goblin   A sovereign (coin): rhyming s., often shortened as *Jimmy*.

Jimmy the one   The First Lieutenant: naval.

Jimmy Woodser   A drink by oneself: Australian.

jinx   A bringer, a causer, of bad luck: adopted, ca. 1936, from U.S.A. Hence, bad luck, as in 'That's put a jinx on it'. More precisely: something that, midway between a devil *in* a thing and a curse *on* it, causes it to go repeatedly wrong, as in 'This machine—this undertaking—has a jinx on it'.

jipper, jippo   Gravy: nautical. In the British Army, *jippo* occ. = stew. Origin unknown.

jitters, the   A feeling, a bout, of (extreme) nervousness or of irritation, annoyance. Perhaps a perversion of S.E. *twitter*, a trembling.

jittery   On edge; very nervous: adopted, 1935, from U.S.A. Ex preceding.

joanna, occ. **johanna** or **-ner**   A piano: rhyming s.

job   A passenger: taxi-drivers'.—An aircraft: R.A.F. Ex a *job of work*. Hence, fig. as in *blonde job*, a beautiful girl.

Jock   A Scot; a Scottish soldier: coll.

Joe Blake   A cake; beefsteak: rhyming s. A snake: Australian rhyming s.

Joe Brown   (A) town: rhyming s.

Joe Hook, Rook, Savage, Skinner A crook—book—cabbage—dinner. All, rhyming s.

Joe Soap An unintelligent fellow that is 'over-willing', and therefore made a 'willing-horse': Services'. Rhyming on *dope*. Also as v.: 'He's always Joe Soaping for somebody.'

John A policeman: mostly Australian.

John, the The water-closet: upper and middle class. Less probably from Fr. don*jon*, a castle-keep, than a pun on dial. *Jack's house*.

Johnnie, Johnny A fellow, a chap; a sweetheart: coll.: ob. by 1940. A (fashionable) young man about town.—A penguin: nautical.—A policeman: low.

Johnny Armstrong Manual work, hand-power: jocular nautical from ca. 1920.

Johnnie Rutter Butter: rhyming s.

joint Any place or building: low: ex U.S.

joker A man, chap, fellow.

jolly, n. A Royal Marine: nautical. Bowen 'Taken from the old nickname of the City Trained Bands'.

jolly To rally, chaff; to treat (a person) pleasantly so that he stay in, or become of, a good humour; esp. with *up* or *along*.

jolly, adj. Excellent; fine; indicative of general approbation: coll. Extremely pleasant, agreeable, suitable, charming: coll. 'Healthy and well developed; well conditioned; plump' (S.O.D.): coll. and dial.

jolly, adv. Very; exceedingly: coll.

jolly well An intensive adverb: middle-class coll. 'You jolly well know I did!'

jonnick, jonnock, jonnuk See *jannock*

josh, v.t. and v.i. To banter; indulge in banter: U.S., anglicized by 1935, thanks to the 'talkies'.

joy Satisfaction; luck. Mostly in 'Any joy?' and 'No joy!': R.A.F. and naval.—Electrical current: R.A.F.

joy-ride A ride at high speed, esp. in a motor-car: orig. U.S.; anglicized ca. 1912 as a coll. Hence, v.i. and *joy-rider, -riding*.

joy-stick The control-lever of an aeroplane.

jube A coll. abbr. of *jujube* (the lozenge).

Judy A girl. Cf. *jane*.

jug A prison.

jug, v. To imprison; lock up: c.; by ca. 1860, low s.

juggins; occ. jug A fool: s. >, in C. 20, (low) coll. Prob. suggested by *muggins*.

juice Electricity; electrical current: electricians' >, ca. 1920, gen. s.

juicy Excellent: by 1945, ob. (Of stocks and shares) attractive in price: Stock Exchange.

juke-box   An automatic gramophone-record player: adopted, 1945, from U.S.A.

jump, be for the high   To be faced with a difficult or very unpleasant task: military; esp. to be on the crime-sheet, hence due for trial. Ex steeple-chasing.

jump out of one's skin   To be greatly startled: coll.

jump the gun   To be premature; to publish 'news'—prematurely: journalistic. Ex athletics.

jump the queue   To get ahead of one's turn: coll. Orig., cheat for a place in a queue.

jump to it   To bestir oneself: military.

jump (up)on   To criticize severely: coll.

jumped-up   Conceited, arrogant: coll.

jumps, the   Delirium tremens: ob.—The fidgets; a state of nerves: coll.

just one of those things, it's or **it was**   A c.p., applied to something there's no explaining, or to something that, although inexplicable, simply has to happen.

just the job   Precisely what I need or wish; exactly what one wants: c.p.

just what the doctor ordered   A c.p. of approval applied to anything particularly applicable or suitable or to anything very good or very pleasant: C. 20.

K

***

kaffir piano The marimba, a musical instrument: South African.

kamerad! Stop: that's enough; don't make it too hot!: military: 1915; ob. Ex the Ger. soldiers' cry (lit., 'comrade!') on surrendering.

kanga Abbr. *kangaroo*: Australian coll.

kangaroo A Jew: rhyming s. Often *kanga*.

kap(o)ut Finished, dead; no more: military: ob. by 1939, † by 1960. (Only predicatively.) Ex Ger. *kaputt*. Cf. Low Ger. *kaputt* (or *kapuut*) *gaan*, to die.

Kate & Sydney A steak-and-kidney pudding.

Kate Karney The Army: military rhyming s.

Kathleen Mavourneen system The hire-purchase system: Anglo-Irish. Ex the refrain of the song, 'It may be for years and it may be for ever'. Hence, *on the Kathleen Mavourneen*.

Keelie A (street) rough: Scots s. >, ca. 1870, coll. Ex *the Keelie Gang*, an Edinburgh band of young blackguards, ca. 1820. (O.E.D.).

keen as mustard Very keen: coll. A pun on *Keen's mustard*.

keep it clean! Don't be smutty!: c.p.: since the late 1920's.

keep one's eyes peeled, or **skinned** To maintain a sharp look-out: coll.: U.S., anglicized ca. 1860.

keep one's lip buttoned To maintain silence; to tell nothing: Cockneys'.

keep tabs on To observe (someone) long and closely: coll.: adopted ex Canada, which adopted it ex U.S.

keep (something) under one's hat To say nothing about.

Kelly's eye One, esp. a solitary one: mostly in house (the game): military. Anecdotal ex a one-eyed Kelly.

kerdoying, or **kerdoink** or **gerdoying!** Crash! Air Force interjection to indicate crash of aircraft, etc.

94

kibosh, v.   To spoil, ruin; check; bewilder; knock out (lit. and fig.). Also *put the kibosh on.* Origin disputed.

kick   A sixpence: slightly ob., except in *two and a kick*, half a crown. A pocket: c. and low s.—(Cf. *the boot.*) Dismissal from a job; esp. in *get the kick.* A complaint, a 'grouse'; a refusal: coll. Ex U.S.

kick off   A start: coll. Esp. *for a kick-off.* Ex football.

kick out of, get a   To find that something is exciting or absorbing: coll. Ex drug-addiction.

kid   A child, esp. if young. Ex the young of a goat. Chaff, leg-pulling; esp. in *no kid.* Ex *kid*, v., to wheedle, flatter; to chaff, quiz; hence v.i., to pretend to give the impression . . .; esp. *stop kidding!*, let's talk seriously. Hence, *kidder* and *kidding.*

kid brother or **sister**   One's (however slightly) younger brother or sister: coll. Ex U.S.A.

kiddy   A little child: coll.

killick   A petty officer's arm-badge: blue-jackets'. Ex the shape.

killing   Extremely funny: coll.

killing, make a   To win substantially from the bookmakers: Australian sporting. Also *make a kill*, current in England too.

kind of, adv.   In a way, somewhat; as it were: coll.: orig. U.S.; anglicized ca. 1845. Often—this is a sol.—spelt *kinda, kinder.*

kindness!, all done by   An ironical c.p.

king   A steward in charge of this or that on a modern liner: nautical. Thus, *the linen king, the crockery king, the silver king.*

king (death)   Breath: rhyming s.

king's proctor   A doctor: rhyming s.

kingdom come   The after-life: coll. Hence, *go, send, to k.c.*, to die or kill. Cf. *thy kingdom come* in the Lord's Prayer.

kip   A bed; a hammock: low; and nautical. A lodging or a lodging-house, a doss-house: low. Sleep: unrecorded before C. 20. To lodge; sleep: orig. c.

kip down   To go to bed; dispose oneself for sleep; a C. 20, mainly military, variant of *kip*, v.

kipper   To ruin the chances of (a person). Prob. ex *scupper* influenced by *cook one's hash.*

kisser   The mouth: pugilists' >, ca. 1900, gen. low s.

kit   A set, collection of things or (rarely in C. 20) persons, esp. in *the whole kit*: coll. Cf. the U.S. *whole kit and boodle.*

kite   An aircraft: Royal Air Force: since 1917.

kite, fly a   See *fly* . . .

kittens, having   Nervous, agitated; 'all hot and bothered'. Ex a cat's perturbation during this crisis.

Kiwi   A New Zealander: coll. Ex the national bird.

klip A diamond: South African diamond fields's >, by 1920, coll. Ex Cape Dutch *klip*, a rock, a pebble.

knapper The head: low. Because the 'receiver general'.

knees, on one's Exhausted: jocular coll.

'knife', before one can or **could say** Very quickly, swiftly, or suddenly: coll.

knobs on, with With embellishments; with interest, forcibly. Here *knob* = excrescence = ornament.

knock, n. An innings: cricketers' coll.

knock, v. To impress greatly, to 'fetch', to surprise. Cf. Chevalier's song title, 1892, *Knocked 'Em in the Old Kent Road.*

knock, v. (Also *knock back* or *knock over*.) To consume (a drink).

knock about, v.i. To wander or roam: coll. 1850. Mayhew, 'I've been knocking about on the streets'.

knock-about, adj. Noisy and rough (e.g. comedians): theatre.

knock back, v. To cost (a person) so-much. 'That knocked him back a fiver.'—To refuse, to reject: mostly Australian.

knock-down An introduction. To introduce (one person to another): Australian ex U.S.

knock 'em cold To amaze 'them'; to have a sensational success. Ex boxing.

knock into To encounter: coll.

knock it back (invariable) To eat; occ. to drink: mostly military.

knock off To complete or despatch easily or hastily: coll.

knock-out Applied in admiration, or by way of outraged propriety, to a person, esp. one who does outrageous things; also to an outstanding or outrageous thing. Chiefly *as a regular knock-out.* Perhaps ex boxing.

knock-out, v. To make (very) quickly or roughly: coll. Hence, to earn: Colonial.

knock out drops A liquid drug—butyl-chloride—put into liquor to facilitate robbing: U.S., anglicized ca. 1904.

knock the stuffing out of To confound, defeat utterly; render useless, valueless, or invalid: coll.

knock up To make (so many runs) by hitting: cricket coll.

knocked, wounded; **knocked cold,** killed: New Zealanders' and Australians', in 1914–18; less in 1939–45, diminishing afterwards.

knocker A person given to fault-finding: coll.' orig. U.S., partly anglicized by 1927. (*O.E.D., Supplement.*)—One who contracts debts without the intention to repay them: Glasgow (− 1934) >, by 1940, fairly gen.

knocker, on the On credit: Cockneys'.

know all the answers Applied to a person smart in repartee or in circumventing the cunning: coll., often ironic. Adopted ca. 1939, from the U.S.A.

know one thing and that ain't (or **isn't**) **two;** esp. **I know**   To know a thing for certain or emphatically: coll., esp. Cockneys'.

know one's onions   To be well informed or smart or very wide-awake: anglicized, ex U.S., ca. 1935.

know, in the   Possessing special knowledge: coll.

know-how   Skill; the knack of doing something: coll., adopted, ca. 1943, from U.S.; by 1953, S.E. Short for 'the *know how* to do it'.

know it!, not if I   Not if I can prevent it: coll.: 1874, Hardy. (O.E.D.).

know-it of know-all park   A know-all: coll.

knows, all one   (To) the best of one's ability; (to) the utmost: coll.

kosh   Variant of *cosh*.

Kraut   A German, esp. a German soldier: Army, most in Italy in 1944–5. Ex that favourite dish of the Germans: *sauerkraut*.

kudos   Glory, fame: university s. >, ca. 1890, gen. coll. From Gr. *kudos*.

kybosh, or **kyebosh**   See *kibosh*.

L

la-di-da, or **la-de-da;** also **lardy-dah** Affectedly smart of costume, voice, manners: coll. 'Its great vogue was due to a music-hall song of 1880.—*He wears a penny flower in his coat, La-di-da!*': W.

la-di-da A tram; a motor-car: rhyming s.

lab Laboratory: coll.

lad A dashing fellow: coll. Also *one of the lads.*

Lady Godiva Five pounds sterling. Rhyming on *fiver.*

lag A convict, is † except in *old lag,* itself by 1945 somewhat ob.: ex the underworld.

lagging A term of penal servitude. Ex the underworld.

lakes Short for *lakes of Killarney.* Mad: rhyming s. on *barmy.*

lam, on the On the run from justice. Ex U.S.

lambaste To beat, thrash: S.E. > dial., and increasingly low coll. Hence, *lambasting,* n.

lamps Eyes.

Lancashire lass: mostly in pl. A tumbler: rhyming s. (on *glass*).

lance-jack A lance-corporal: military coll.

land To deliver: orig. boxers'. 1888, J. Runciman, 'Their object is to land one cunning blow'. Earlier *lend,* playful for *give,* as W explains.

landowner, become a To die: esp. among soldiers in 1914–18.

lardy-dardy, adj. Affected of speech or manner: proletarian. Ex *la-di-da.*

lark A piece of merriment or mischief; a trick: coll. Ex the v. Hence, a line of business: grafters'.

lark, v. To play (esp. the fool); be mischievously merry; go on the 'spree': coll. Prob. related to † S.E., now dial., *lake,* to play.

larky Ready or inclined to play 'larks': coll.

larrup, or **larrop** To beat, thrash: coll. and dial.

Larry, (as) happy as   Very happy: Australian coll.

lashin(g)s   Mostly of drink, occ. of food, rarely of anything else. Plenty: coll., orig. Anglo-Irish. Lever, 1841, 'Lashings of drink'. Perhaps ex, or for, *lavishings* (W).

last   A person's most recent joke, witticism, etc.: coll. 'X's last is a scream.'

last thing   Late at night: coll. Short for *last thing at night*. Cf. *first thing*.

lat   A latrine: orig. military. Also *the lats*.

latest, the   The latest news: coll.

laugh & joke   A smoke: rhyming s.

laugh like a drain   To chuckle heartily.

laughing, be   To be comfortable, safe, fortunate: military coll., ob.

lav   Lavatory.

lawner   Refreshment served on the lawn to a hunt: middle and upper classes'. 'The Oxford-er.'

lawyer   An argumentative man, esp. one given to airing his grievances: military coll. In Australia, *bush lawyer*.

lay   An occupation, esp. if criminal; a 'line'; a trick: orig. c. >, ca. 1840, low s.

lay-about   A professional loafer: low.

lay into   To thrash: s. > coll. Cf. *pitch into*.

lay on   Esp. in 'It's all laid on'—planned, arranged, assured: Services'.

lay on air   To arrange for, obtain, provide, air support: Services'.

lazy   Is navally applied to a person or thing 'serving no particular purpose at the moment' (Granville).

lazy-bones   A very lazy person: coll.

lead on, Macduff!   A c.p. (late C. 19–20) based upon a frequent misquotation of 'Lay on, Macduff' in Shakespeare's *Macbeth* (V. vii. 62).

lead, swing the   To malinger, evade duty: orig. and mainly military, by folk-etymology corruption, of synonymous nautical *swing the leg*.

lead me to it!   That's easy!; with pleasure!: a c.p. of ca. 1910–40.

lead-swinger   A loafer or malingerer: military.

leaf   Furlough: naval and military.

lean over backwards   See *fall over backwards*.

left in the lurch   (A) church: rhyming s.

leary, leery   Artful; wide-awake; (suspiciously) alert: c. > low s. Prob. ex dial. *lear*, learning, cleverness (cf. S.E. *lore*). 'Flash'; showy of dress and manners: low.

leather-jacket   A small insect destructive of grass: coll. Ex its appearance.

leather-neck A Royal Marine: naval. By 1940, ob. in Britain.

left, be or **get** To be outdistanced metaphorically: orig. U.S.; anglicized ca. 1895. Abbr. *be* or *get left in the lurch*.

leg-pull A good-natured, innocuous hoax or deception: coll. Ex *pull* (someone's) *leg*.

leg-up, give someone a To assist him: coll.

lemon squash, n. and v. Wash: rhyming s.

lemon, the answer is a A derisive reply: c.p., orig. U.S. Ex the bitterness of a lemon as an eaten fruit. Also *lemon,* something undesirable.

lend A loan: coll.

let-down A disappointment: coll.

let 'em all come! A c.p. expressive of cheeky defiance: proletarian >, by ca. 1912, gen.

let her rip! Let it (etc.) go freely!; damn the consequences!: coll.

let in, v. To victimize; deceive, cheat: coll.

let on To admit; betray: dial. >, 'Don't let on that we're married'.—Hence, mostly in Australia and New Zealand, to pretend, make believe, give to understand: coll.

let down one's hair or **let one's hair down** To enjoy oneself thoroughly, let oneself go, be at one's ease.

let out To clear from all suspicion of guilt: coll. 'This new piece of evidence certainly lets him out.'

let's! Let us (sc. do something expressed or implied)!: coll. Often *yes, let's!*

let's hear from you! Hurry up!; look lively: military c.p. Ex the vocal numbering of a rank of soldiers.

letty A bed; a lodging; also v.i., to lodge: parlary; mainly theatrical. Ex It. *letto,* a bed.

level, on the Adj. and adv., honest(ly), fair(ly): coll., orig. U.S., anglicized by 1905.

level best One's best or utmost: coll.

liberate To gain illicitly or deviously; to steal: Army: 1944 (Italy) and 1945 (Germany). By humorous euphemism.

lick, v. To defeat, surpass; v.i., to ride at full speed: Australian.

lickety-split At full speed; in a tearing hurry: (mostly) juvenile: adopted ca. 1918 from U.S.A.

licks me, it It's beyond my comprehension: coll. Cf. *it beats me.*

lid A hat, a cap. By 1945, ob.

lid, dip one's To raise (lit., lower) one's hat: Australian.

lid on (it), that's put the That's finished it; c.p.

lifer One sentenced for life; penal servitude for life: orig. c.

lift To steal.

lift or **raise one's elbow** To drink, esp. to excess: coll.

light   Credit: workmen's; by 1960, ob.

light, adj.   Esp. *very light*. Rather short of money: coll. Also *light of*, short of (something); 'I'm light a haversack': (mostly Forces') coll.

light, put out one's   To kill.

light fantastic, the   The foot in dancing: coll. Ex Milton's 'Come and trip it as you go / On the light fantastic toe' (*L'Allegro*).

lighthouse   A pepper-castor: naval.

light out   To leave hastily: orig. U.S.; anglicized ca. 1900; now coll.

light up, v.i.   To light one's pipe or cigarette: coll.

lightning, like greased   Very swiftly: coll., orig. U.S. Tom Hood, 1842, 'I will come, as the Americans say, like greased lightning'.

lights   The eyes: S.E. till ca. 1810, then boxing s.

like, adv.   At end of phrase or sentence. Somewhat; as it were; in short, expressive of vagueness or after-thoughted modification: (dial. and) low coll. 'Of a sudden like.'

like it but it doesn't like me, I   Applied to food or drink: a semi-jocular c.p.: C. 19–20.

like it or lump it   To like or, disliking, put up with it: coll.

like that!, I   A derisive or indignant 'Certainly not', 'I certainly don't think so': coll.

Lilley & Skinner   Dinner: London rhyming s.

limes   Limelight: theatrical.

limey, Limey   An Englishman: U.S. > partly anglicized. Ex *lime-juicer*, a U.S. term for a British ship or sailor, lime-juice being served on British ships as an anti-scorbutic. Hence, esp. a Canadian name for a British seaman.

limit, the   Esp. in *that's the limit*. A person, act, or thing that is the extreme (or beyond) of what one can bear, esp. in jocular use: coll., orig. U.S., anglicized ca. 1908.

line on, get a   To get information about, or a clue to: coll., orig. U.S., anglicized ca. 1923. Ex marksmanship.

lines, hard   Bad luck: coll., prob. orig. nautical.

line-shoot   A tall story, a boasting; *line-shooter*, -shooting, he who indulges in, indulgence in, this practice. Ex *shoot a line*, q.v. Also cf.:

lines book   A book kept in the Mess for the recording of exaggerations by its members. Sometimes called a *shooting gallery*: R.A.F.

lino   A coll. abbr. of *linoleum*. Among printers and journalists, a coll. abbr. of *linotype*, itself contracting *line of type*.

lions in the army, they tame   A Regular Army c.p. (Frank Richards, *Old Soldiers Never Die*, 1933).

lip   Impudence; abuse: low.

listen, n. An act or period of listening: coll. Usually *have a good listen* (coll.) or *do a listen* (s.) but also as in ' "Out you'll go . . . and give a good listen" '.

lit (slightly), **well lit** (quite) Tipsy.

little Mary The stomach: coll. Ex Barrie's *Little Mary*.

little something A dash of spirits: coll. 'Would you like a little something in it?'

live with, can or **be able to** (Mostly in negative.) To be able to play (person) on level terms: sporting.

live wire An indefatigable but not necessarily reliable news-gatherer: journalistic coll.

livid Furiously angry; very much annoyed.

Lizzie A (cheap) motor-car, orig. and mainly a 'Ford'. By personification. Also *tin Lizzie*. Occ., from ca. 1924, *Liz*; but ob. by 1950.—(Also *lizzie*) Cheap *Lis*bon red wine: low.

lob To arrive; *lob back*, to return: Australian.

lob in To arrive.

local A public-house in one's own district: coll.

loco A coll. abbr. of *locomotive*, an engine.

loco, adj. Insane; crazy: Canadian orig. (U.S.). Ex the effects of the loco weed.

locum Abbr. *locum tenens*: medical, clerical coll.

locus(t); also locus, or **locuss** To drug a person and then rob him; to stupefy with drink: c. > low s.

log Abbr. *logarithm*: coll.

lollipop, lollypop A sweetmeat: coll.

lollop To lounge about; to bob up and down; to proceed clumsily by bounds: coll. Hence adj. and n. *lolloping*.

lolly A sweetmeat: dial. and, in Australia and New Zealand, coll. Ex *lollipop*.

lolly Short for *lollipop*, rhyming s. for 'shop'.—Money: Cockney. Cf. *sugar*.

London particular A thick London fog (cf. *pea-souper*): coll.

Londony Characteristic of London: coll.

long, the The summer vacation: university (*vac*) coll.

long drink of water Unhappy-looking man.

long firm A swindling group of phantom capitalists: commercial coll.

long-haired chum A female friend or sweetheart: tailors' >, in C. 20, also soldiers' and sailors'.

long shot A bet laid at large odds: turf s. >, in C. 20, gen. coll.

long sight, not by a Not by a long way: coll.

long time no see I haven't seen you for a long time: British and American c.p. In British usage, it derives ex Far East pidgin; in

American, either from the British phrase or from Amerindian pidgin. Perhaps the most widely used c.p. in the world.

long tot   A lengthy set of figures for addition, esp. in examinations: coll. Ex *tot,* itself abbr. *total.*

long 'uns   Long trousers: boys' coll.

longer & linger   Finger: rhyming s.

loo, the   The water closet. Ex Fr. *l'eau.*

look alive   To be alert; bestir oneself: coll.

look-in   A chance of success: sporting.

look in, v.i.   To watch television: coll.

look-see, occ. **looksee**   A look-round, an inspection. Ex pidgin, hence, nautical, *look-see,* to look and see. Hence, a periscope or a telescope: resp. military and naval.

look sharp   To be quick; to hasten: coll.

look up, v.i.   To improve: coll. 2. V.t., to visit, after an absence: coll.

loony, often **looney,** occ. **luny**   Crazy; hence, a lunatic: coll. Ex *lunatic.*

loony-bin   A lunatic asylum: orig. Cockneys'.

loop, up the   Mad: military.

loop the loop   Soup: rhyming s.

loopy   Slightly mad.

loose end, at a   Unoccupied; having nothing to do: coll.

loose off, v.i. and v.t.   To fire a machine-gun.

loot   A lieutenant: naval and military.

Lord Lovel   A shovel: rhyming s.

lord of the manor   A 'tanner', i.e. sixpence: rhyming s.

lot, a; lots   A considerable quantity or number; adv., a good deal: coll.

lot, the; the whole lot   The whole of a stated quantity or number: coll.

lots   Many; much: coll.

lounge-lizard   A sleek adventurer frequenting lounges in the expectation of women, their money and caresses: U.S., anglicized by 1925; by 1935, coll.; by 1960, slightly ob.

lousy   Contemptible; mean: S.E. till C. 20, when, esp. after 1918, coll. and used as a mere pejorative.

lousy with   Full of: orig. military, as in 'lousy with guns'; now esp. 'lousy with money'.

lovely (a)   A pretty girl.

lovely, adj.   Attractive, delightful; excellent: coll.

lovely grub!   Very nice indeed!: Forces' c.p.

low, lie   To bide one's time; keep quiet: s. > coll. Orig. U.S.; the popularity of Joe Chandler Harris's *Uncle Remus* (1880) popularized the phrase. Low coll., or rather sol., is *lay low* in this sense.

S.S.D.—H

lowbrow, n. and adj.   One who is not intellectual: orig. U.S.; anglicized ca. 1923; by 1932, coll. Cf. *high-brow.*

low-down   Information: U.S., anglicized ca. 1930.

lowest form of animal life, the   A reporter: journalistic. Hence, an A.C.2: R.A.F.

luck, down on one's   Unlucky; impoverished: s. till ca. 1920, then coll.

lucky man, the   The bridegroom: feminine coll.

lucky, touch   To experience good luck: coll.

lugger and the girl is mine!, once aboard the   A male, either joyous or derisively jocular, c.p.: by 1950 slightly ob. Ex that very popular song, David Slater's *Once aboard the Lugger,* 1917, and A. S. M. Hutchinson's novel, *Once Aboard the Lugger—the History of George and Mary,* 1908.

lumbered, ppl. adj.   Pawned: low; by 1940, ob. Arrested; in prison: c. > low s.

lumbered   Short of cash; financially embarrassed: London's East End.

lumping   Great; heavy; bulky; awkward, ungainly: coll. and dial.: often as intensive, as in 'lumping great fellow *or* load'.

lurk   'Is mostly applied to the several modes of plundering by representations of sham distress' (Mayhew) c. > low s.; ob. by 1930. Hence, in Australian low s., 'a plan of action; a regular occupation' (C. J. Dennis); by 1960, slightly ob.

lush   A drunkard: low.

lush, adj.   (Of a girl) extremely attractive: Services'. Ex *luscious.* (Of creature comforts) rich; appetizing; plentiful: Services'.

lushington   A drunkard: rather low: ob. by 1960 †. Of hotly disputed origin.

lyre-bird, be a (bit of a)   To be (a little) apt to tell lies: Australia: C. 20; ob. by 1940. Punning *liar* and (native to Australia) *lyre-bird.*

M

---

ma   Abbr. of *mamma*. A coll.

macaroni   An Italian: somewhat low. Ex the national dish. A 'pony' (£25): rhyming s.; by 1950, slightly ob.

mack, or **mac**   A coll. abbr. of *mac*(k)*intosh*.

Mackay, the real   The real thing, the genuine article: coll. Ex the *true* head of the Clan *Mackay*.

mad money   A girl's return fare, carried lest her friend dumps her, or she him: Dominions coll. Ex *mad*, angry.

madam   *A proper madam*, a girl with a bad temper; *a proper little madam*, a girl child with one: lower-middle and lower classes.

madam, it's (or **that's**) **all**   It's all nonsense or bunkum or 'eyewash': originally low, but by 1940, general.

made of money?, do you think I'm; you must think I'm . . .   A c.p. to a financial importunate.

madza   Half; *madza caroon*, half a crown; *madza saltee*, a halfpenny; *madza poona*, half a sovereign: Parlary. Ex It. *mezzo*.

mag, v.i.   To talk (noisily), chatter; to scold: coll. Ex the magpie.

mahogany, the   A dining-table: coll.; ob. by 1945.

main-brace, splice the   To give out a double ration of grog, to celebrate some special event: nautical.

Major Stevens   Evens (in betting): rhyming s.

major, the   The sergeant-major: military and marines' coll.

make   To steal: orig. c. To catch (a train, boat, etc.): coll. Ex the S.E. sense, orig. nautical, 'arrive at'.

make it   To succeed; to become prosperous; hence, to cope with anything: coll., adopted from U.S.A. ca. 1933.

make, on the   Intent on booty or profit.

make one's pile   To amass a fortune: coll.; orig. U.S.

105

maleesh or **malish,** or properly, **ma'alish** (pronounced *mahleesh*) Never mind: military. Arabic word.

mamsell A French girl: coll. Ex Fr. *ma'amselle.*

man, old A chief, a captain, an employer; father; husband: all coll.

man & wife A knife: rhyming s. Contrast *trouble and strife.*

man for my money, the The right person: coll.

manage To succeed against odds; contrive to make the inadequate serve: coll.

map A dirty proof: printers'.—Face, head, skull: military and proletarian.

marge Margarine: coll.

marines, tell that (tale) to the *I* don't believe it, whoever else does!: c.p., orig. nautical.

mark A fancy or preference.—A prospective victim: c. > low s.

mark, easy A person easily fooled or cheated: U.S., anglicized by ca. 1930.

marmalade Synonymous with *scrambled eggs*: R.A.F. Ex the *gold*-coloured braid.

marrying, vbl. n.; **marry,** v.t. Stockbrokers' s. A broker receiving simultaneous orders to buy and sell the same security can marry the deal, put one bargain against the other.

marvellous As used in Society since ca. 1920—and since 1943 elsewhere—is s. for 'pleasant' as 'nice'; a mere counter of a word! Maurice Lincoln, *Oh! Definitely*, 1933, 'If you forbade that girl to say "marvellous", then stopped her from saying "definitely", she couldn't speak at all.' Still very common as late as 1964.

mash Mashed potatoes: coll. verging on sol. Even *mashed*, in this sense, is coll.

Massey-Harris Cheese: Canadian. Ex the Massey-Harris self-binder + the costiveness of cheese.

mat A matter, esp. in *what's the mat?*: schoolboys'.—A matinée: theatrical coll.

mat(e)y Characteristic of a 'mate' or chum; friendly: coll.

maths A coll. abbr. of *mathematics.*

matlo(w) A sailor: mainly nautical and, in C. 20, also military. Ex Fr. *matelot*, a sailor.

matric A coll. abbr. of *matriculation.*

mauley, occ. **mawley** or **morley** A fist, the hand; hence, handwriting, a signature: low; slightly ob. Perhaps ex Shelta.

mazuma Money; esp. cash: Canadian, adopted from U.S. Ex Yiddish.

mean to say, I A coll. tautological form of *I mean*, itself verging on coll. when, as frequently, it connotes apologetic modification or mental woolliness.

measly Contemptible; of little value.

meat-ticket A variant of *cold-meat ticket*.

med, medical, medico A doctor, whether physician or surgeon or both combined; a student of medicine: coll.

Med, the The Mediterranean.

meet An assignation: Australian coll.

meg; megger A megaphone.

menace A person that is a bore or a general nuisance: coll.

mending, vbl.n. Something to be repaired.

mensh!, don't Don't mention it!: a lower-middle class c.p.

merchant A fellow, 'chap': S.E. in mid-C. 16–early 17, lapsed till ca. 1880, then revived as a coll. (esp. among actors) verging on s. Cf. *customer* and *client*.

Meredith, we're in A c.p. uttered when one succeeds in entering a place (e.g. a tea-shop) just before closing-time.

merry-go-round A pound (£1): rhyming s.

Mespot Mesopotamia: orig. military.

mess, lose the number of one's To be killed: naval.

mess about, v.i. and t. To play fast and loose; swindle, put off: coll.

messer A bungler, muddler: coll.

Met, the The Meteorological Office: Services'. Hence *Met man* or *Mets*, Meteorological Officer.

Metro, the The underground-train system of Paris: hence, occ. that of London.

mick, mickey or **micky**, occ. **mike** (Or with capital.) An Irishman: more gen. in Canada, Australia and New Zealand than in Britain. Ex *Michael*.

mid A midshipman: coll. Also *middy*. Both are ob.

middle A middle-weight: boxing coll.

middle-aged spread Paunchiness coming in middle age: coll.

miffy, adj. Easily offended: coll. and dial.

mike A wasting of time; idling, esp. in *do* or, occ., *have a mike*, to idle away one's time: proletarian. Prob. ex S.E. *mich(e)*, to skulk.—A microphone: from ca. 1927.—A microscope: medical students'.

mike, do a To decamp; to evade duty: military and low.

mike at, take a To have a look (at): low.

milky, n. A milkman: non-aristocratic coll.—Milk: nursery coll.

milky, adj. Cowardly, esp. *turn milky*: c. > low s.

mince-pies Eyes: rhyming s.

mind how you go! A c.p., common only since ca. 1942 and addressed to someone either caught in traffic or slipping on, e.g., a banana skin; hence, since ca. 1945, also metaphorically.

mind your back! Get out of the way!: Cockneys'.

mingy Miserly, mean; hence, disappointingly small: coll. Thinned ex *mangy* and prob. influenced by *stingy*.

minnie A German trench-mortar or the projectile: military: 1914–18.

Minnie The *Ministry* of Information.

minnow Usually in pl. A torpedo: naval.

minus (Predicatively) without; short of: coll., as in '*minus* one horse'. As an adj., lacking, non-existent: coll. 'His Latin is certainly minus.'

miss, give (e.g. it) a To avoid, or cease from, doing something: coll. Ex billiards *give a miss in balk*.

miss one's guess To be mistaken: Canadian coll. Ex U.S.

missis, gen. **missus** (Always occurring as either *the missus* or, less gen., *my, your, his*, etc. *missus*.) A wife: dial. > (low) coll.—(Among servants) a mistress of the house: coll.

mistake, and no Undoubtedly; for certain: coll. Also *and no error*.

mitt A glove; hence, hand: *mitten*.

mix it To fight vigorously: Australian.

mix-up Confusion; a mess, a muddle: coll. A general scrimmage.

mizzle or **mis(s)le** To decamp; depart slyly: c. > low s. Ex Shelta *misli*. Hence, *do a mizzle*.

mo A moment, esp. in *half a mo*: low coll.

moan, v. To complain, grumble; to do so habitually: naval. Also n.

moaning Minnie A variant of *Mona* (see Clara).

mob A gang of criminals, esp. of thieves: c. > low s. A military unit, esp. a battalion or a battery.

mobs of A large number, even a large quantity, of; e.g. *mobs of stones—birds—water*: Australian coll.

mods The first public examination for B.A.: Oxford University coll. Ex *Moderations*.

moggy A cat: Cockneys' (and dial.). Hence, *mog*.

moke An ass: s. and dial. Ex Welsh Gypsy *mokhio*.

Moll A woman, a girl: c. > low s. Ex *Moll*, a pet-form of *Mary*.

Mona See *Clara*.

monaker, monarcher, monnaker, mon(n)eker, monica, esp. **mon-(n)iker** A name; occ. a title: orig. tramps', c., it > ca. 1900, gen. though somewhat low s. Perhaps ex *monogram*, for an early and still current sense is 'signature'.

money, in the Receiving good wages or a large salary: coll.

money for jam or **old rope, it's** (It is) sure money; esp. money easily obtained or earned: coll. Hence, (it's) too easy!

money to burn, have To have plenty to spend; to be rich: coll.

mongey Food: military, esp. in W.W. I. Ex Fr. (*du*) *manger*.

monica, monicker, moniker   See *monaker*.

monk   *Monkey*, the animal: (low) coll.

monkery, occ. monkry; preceded by *the*   The country; tramps or other vagrants collectively; the practice of going on tramp: tramps' c. > low s.; by 1945, slightly ob. Hence, a district: grafters' s.

monkey   £500: sporting. (In U.S. $500.) Among stockbrokers, however, *monkey* = £50,000 of stock, i.e. 500 shares of £100. Cf. *pony*.—A mortgage; a writ on a ship: nautical.

monkey of, make a   To make someone look ridiculous: adopted from U.S.A. ca. 1930.

monkey out of, make a; be made a monkey of   To use, be used, as a dupe, esp. as a cat's paw: adopted ex U.S. servicemen.

monkey up, get one's   To make, but esp. to become, angry: s. and dial. Also *one's monkey is up*. 'Perhaps alludes to animal side brought uppermost by anger' (W).

monnaker, monneker, monnicker, monniker   See *monaker*.

mono   A monotype machine or process: printers' s. coll. Cf. *lino*.

month of sundays   A long time: coll.

mooch, v.   (Also *mouch;* cf. *mike*, q.v.) To idle, sneak, hang about (often with *about*); slouch (with *along*): low s. and dial. Perhaps ex *mike*, v., influenced by Fr. *mucher*, to hide, skulk. Hence, the corresponding n. *mooch* and the agent *moocher* and the vbl.n. *mooching*.

moon, v.   (Esp. with *about, along*, or *around*.) To idle, lounge, or wander as in a dream: coll.

moon, shoot the   To depart by night, with one's valuables, without paying the rent: coll.

moonlight flit, flitting   A removal of household goods by night without paying the rent.

mop up   To kill, slaughter; defeat utterly: mainly military and naval.

moral   Likeness; counterpart. Rare, except in *the very moral of*: (low) coll.—A 'moral certainty': orig. and still mainly racing.

more like   Preposition. Nearer: coll. Abbr. *more like it*, better, more acceptable or reasonable or sensible: coll.

more power to your elbow!   A c.p. of encouragement.

moreish (occ. more-ish); morish   That makes one desire more: coll.

morgue, the   Obituaries kept ready for notabilities likely to die shortly: journalistic.

morning after the night before, the   A c.p. applied to the effects of a drinking-bout.

moron   A half-wit: U.S.; anglicized, 1929, as coll. Ex the technical sense, 'one of the highest type of feeble-minded', itself ex Gr. μωρός, foolishly stupid.

mortal An intensive coll., as in 'every mortal thing'. Tediously long: coll., as in 'three mortal hours'.

mosey, occ. **mosey off** To decamp; depart quickly: U.S.; anglicized ca. 1890; slightly ob. *Mosey along,* to jog along.

moskeneer, occ. **moskeener, moshkeneer, moschkener, moskuiner** Often shortened to *mosk,* whence *mosker* and *mosking* (n.).

mother makes it, like Very well cooked; extremely tasty: coll. Ex many married men's stock complaint, 'Umph! not like (my) mother makes it'.

mother of pearl A girl: rhyming s.

mother's (or mothers') ruin Gin.

mouldy, adj. Worthless: coll., as in 'a mouldy offer'.

Mounties, the The Royal Canadian *Mounted* Police Force: Canadian coll.

mourning As n., two black eyes. Hence, *half-mourning,* one black eye. Esp., however, *in mourning,* bruised, black, either (of eyes) *to be in mourning* or (of persons) *have one's eyes in mourning*: mostly pugilistic. Also applied to dirty fingernails.

mouse A black eye: Cockneys'.

mouse trap Cheese: naval (lower-deck). Obviously because mouse-traps are baited with cheese.

mouthful A long word, esp. a name, that 'fills' the mouth: coll.

mouthful, say or **speak a** To say something important or arresting: U.S., anglicized ca. 1929.

mouthpiece A defending counsel: c. > low s.

movie Of the cinema: coll., in *a movie star.* Ex:—A moving picture: coll., orig. U.S.; anglicized ca. 1913. Esp. in pl. *movies,* moving pictures: the cinema.

mozzy A mosquito; *mozzy net,* mosquito net.

much! Short for the ironic *not much!*: Services' coll. ' "He never goes out with Waafs"—"Much!" ' (He very often does.)

much!, not Certainly not!: coll.

much of a muchness Of much the same size or value; very much alike: coll.

muck Anything vile or disgusting: coll. A failure: coll., as in 'make a muck of it.' Also v.

muck, as Exceedingly; as much as is possible: coll. Esp. *sick as muck,* thoroughly disgusted or disgruntled.

Muck, Lord A person, in the speaker's opinion unjustifiably, important or esteemed: (low) coll.

muck about To wander aimlessly; potter about: s. > coll.

muck in, v.i. To share rations, sleeping quarters and certain duties. Hence, v.t., *muck in with.*

muck-sweat Perspiration; orig. and properly if dust or dirt has accrued: proletarian coll. Hence, *be in a muck-sweat,* to be flurried or flustered; to be 'all hot and bothered'.

muck-up, n. A 'mess', confusion, spoiling.

muck up To litter: (low) coll.—To spoil, ruin, e.g. a plan. Hence, as n., a complete failure; confusion or muddle.

mucker A heavy fall; esp. in *come a mucker*; often fig., come to grief.

mud in one's eye A tie: rhyming s.

mud, one's name is One has been heavily defeated; one is in disgrace.

mud-hook An anchor: nautical.—In the game of crown and anchor: nautical and military.

muff Orig. in athletic sport, a clumsy or a stupid person: coll.— Hence, a failure: coll. To bungle, esp. at games; to fail in an examination: s. > coll.

muffin-worry A tea-party: coll.

mug The face.—Hence, the mouth: † by 1920.—A fool; an easy dupe; a 'duffer'. Something into which one can pour anything.

mug, v. To grimace: theatrical; by 1945, slightly ob.—To strike, esp. punch in the face: boxing; slightly ob.—To study hard: mostly schools' and universities'. As v.t., esp. *mug up.*

muggins A simpleton, 'juggins'; a fool: U.S., anglicized ca. 1880; by 1945, slightly ob.

mulga A lie; *mulga wire,* an unfounded report, usually incorrect; *it came over the mulga,* a c.p. applied to a tale of doubtful authenticity: Australian.

mull, v. To spoil, muddle, orig. and mainly athletics: coll.

mullock Rubbish; a worthless thing: Australian coll. Ex the mining j. senses, rock without gold, refuse of gold-workings, themselves ex Eng. dial.

mullock, poke (v.t. with **at**) To tease; to deride: Australian. Ex preceding. Cf. *poke borak.*

multy An intensive adj. and adv.: low and Parlary. Ex It. *molto,* much, very.

mum Mother, esp. as term of address: orig. dial., now coll. Also *mums.* Ex *mummy.*—A proletarian variant of *ma'am.*

mummy Mother, esp. as term of address: orig. dial.; now coll. Ex *mother* via *mammy,* q.v.

mum's the word! Silence: coll.

mumsie Mother: domestic and nursery coll.

mungaree or **munjari; mungarly** Food; scraps of bread; a meal: Parlary, and tramps' c. > low s. Ex It. *mangiare,* to eat, hence food, via Lingua Franca.

mungy   Food: naval and military. Either ex Fr. *manger* or a re-shaping of *mungaree*.

mur   Rum: back s.; very gen. in W.W. I among soldiers.

murder, cry blue   To make an excessive outcry.

murky   Containing secrets, 'shady'; discreditable: esp. (e.g. *his*) *murky past*: jocular coll.

Murph, ex Murphy   A potato. Ex the very common Irish surname.

muscle in   To intrude violently on another's 'racket': American c., anglicized ca. 1928 and, by 1935, > gen. s. = to poach, fig., on another's preserves. Ex *muscle one's way in*. To profit by another's advantage or good luck: Services'. Current among civilians since ca. 1935, in the nuance 'to force oneself upon others (*muscle in on* them) in a criminal racket'—the Amer. sense.

mush   (Pronounced *moosh*.) The mouth: boxing, then low. In New Zealand, the face.—The guard-room; cells: military. Perhaps ex dial. *mush*, to crush.—Porridge: nautical coll. A particularization of the S.E. sense.

musical   (Of horses) with defective respiration.

mutt   A 'stupid', a fool, a gawk: U.S., anglicized 1918. Ex synony-mous coll. *mutton-head*.

Mutt & Jeff   The British War Medal and Victory Medal: military. Cf. *Pip, Squeak and Wilfrid*.

mutter & stutter   Butter (n., v.): rhyming s.

muzzy   (Of places) dull, gloomy; (of weather) overcast: coll. and dial. Prob. ex dial. *mozey*, hazy, muggy.—Stupid, hazy of mind, spiritless: coll. Stupefied, more gen. stupid, with liquor: coll. and dial. Blurred, indistinct: coll.

my gentleman or **my lord; my lady**   He or she: derisive coll.; by 1960, slightly archaic.

my oath, Miss Weston!   On my word of honour!: naval. Ex the respect felt for Miss Agnes Weston, the naval philanthropist.

myxo   Myxomatosis.

N

nab   To catch; to arrest.—To seize; to steal: low s. Both senses, orig. c.

Nafy or **Naffy; properly NAAFI;** loosely **Narfy**   The canteen: naval and military coll. Ex the 'Navy, Army, and Air Force Institute'.

Naffy gong   The 1939–45 star: Services'. Also called the *spam medal.* Ex the resemblance of N.A.A.F.I. shoulder-strap colours to the ribbon colours.

nag   A riding horse (esp. if small) or pony: coll., except in Scotland and the North of England, where dial.

nail   A cigarette: military.

nail, v.   To catch or get hold of or secure; hence, to rob or steal. To catch or surprise (a person) in a fix, a difficulty, hence, to arrest (a person). To succeed in hitting.

nailer   An exceptionally good or notable event, thing or person (esp. . . . .); a gen. term of excellence: coll.; by 1945, rather ob.

name, get a   To get a (very) bad name: coll.

name, to one's   Belonging to one: coll.

name (or number) on, had one's   (Of a bullet) that hit a soldier: military coll. in W.W. I.

Nancy Lee   A flea: rhyming s.

nanny-goat   A she-goat: coll.

nanny-goat   Totalizator: racing s., rhyming on *tote.*

nantee or **nanti** (rare) or **nanty**   No; not any. Also absolutely: I have none; 'shut up!' (abbr. *nantee palaver,* q.v.); stop! (e.g. 'Nanty that whistling!'): Parlary and, by 1900, gen. theatrical. Ex It. *niente,* nothing.

nap & double   Trouble (n.): rhyming s.

napoo; rarely **napooh**   Finished (esp. empty), gone; non-existent; dead; 'it's no use arguing any longer', '(it's) no good': orig. and mainly military, esp. in W.W. I; ob. by 1939. Ex Fr. *il n'y en a plus*, there is none left.

napper The head: s. and dial., esp. in *go off one's napper*, go mad; by 1960, ob.

nappy A napkin: nursery coll.

nark A police spy; a common informer: c. >, by 1940, low s. Often *copper's nark*, i.e. 'nose'; ex Romany *nak*, the nose. Hence, a spiteful or nagging person; also, and esp., someone on inquiry from head-office: mostly clerks' and factory workers'.

nark, v. To watch: c. > low s.; ob. V.i., to act the informer; ob. To annoy, exasperate: low s. ex dial. In Australia, it also = to foil.

nark it! 'Shut up!'; be quiet!: military and low. Hence, Stop it!

nasty piece of work An objectionable person: coll.

natch! Of course!: Canadian: adopted ex U.S. Ex *naturally!*

natter To talk aimlessly, endlessly, irritatingly; to talk when speech is forbiden; Services'.

natural, for (or **in**) **all one's** (esp. **my**) For or in all one's life; ever: coll. Perhaps an allusion to *for the term of his natural life*.

naturally! Of course: coll.

nav A navigator: naval and R.A.F.

navvy A navigating officer: nautical.

navvy's (or **navvies'**) **piano** A pneumatic drill: roadmakers' and builders'.

navvy's prayer book, the A shovel: navvies': ca. 1870–1910. (D. W. Barrett, *Navvies*, 1880.) Ex the prayerful attitude involved in its use.

Navy!, thank God we've got a A military c.p. muttered when things are going wrong.

neaters Undiluted rum: naval officers'. (By process of 'the Oxford-er'.)

neck Impudence; very great assurance. Ex Northern dial. Esp. *have a neck*, to be impudent, to make an outrageous request: Australian.

neck, talk through (the back of) one's To talk nonsense.

necking, vbl.n. and ppl. adj. Love-making. Ex U.S.; adopted in England ca. 1928, esp. in *necking* (cf. *petting*) *parties*. Lit., hugging each other around the neck.

neddy An ass, C. 17–20: coll. Ex *Edward*; occ. abbr. *ned*. Hence, a fool: coll. and dial. ob. A life-preserver: c. > low s.

needful, the *Ad hoc* money: coll.

needle (With *the*) irritation; nervousness; hence (without *the*), ill feeling: 1899, Clarence Rook, *The Hooligan Nights*, 'It was a fight with the gloves. But there was a bit of needle in it. It was all over Alice.' Hence also as adj.

needle, v.   To irritate, annoy.

needle, cop, get, or **take the; needle, give the**   To become annoyed; to annoy.

Nellie Duff!, not on your   Not likely!: a c.p. *Nellie Duff* rhymes on *puff,* life.

nerve   Impudence; supreme 'cheek': (orig. low) coll.

nervy   Impudently confident: slightly ob. 'Jumpy', having bad nerves; excitable or hysterical: coll.

net   A let: lawn-tennis coll.

never a dull moment!   An ironic c.p. in times of danger or excitement: mostly naval.

never, on the   On credit; by wangling: military >, by 1919, gen. Often *on the never-never.*

never never; or with capitals   Abbr. *never never country* or *land,* the very sparsely populated country of Western Queensland and Central Australia: Australian coll.

New South   New South Wales: Australian coll.

New York nipper   A kipper: rhyming s.

newt, drunk as a   Very drunk indeed.

newsie (or **-sy**), n.   A newspaper seller.

Niagara Falls   Stalls (of a theatre): theatrical rhyming s.

nibble   To consider, eagerly but carefully, e.g. a bargain, an offer; v.t. with *at.* Coll.

nibs   Self; *my nibs,* myself; *your nibs,* you or, as term of address, 'friend'; *his nibs,* the person mentioned: c. > lcw s. > gen. s.; by 1960, ob.

nice and   Nicely, in sense of 'very': coll.; 1846, D. Jerrold, 'You'll be nice and ill'.

nice as pie   (Of persons) very polite, very sweet and agreeable: coll.

nice work!   A c.p. in approval of a favourable arrangement or of a good piece of work.   Since ca. 1944, often extended to *nice work—if you can get it!*

nick   Good physical condition or health: usually *in the nick.*—(Always *the.*) A prison; a police-station: c. >, by 1945, low s.

nick   To catch, esp. unawares; to get hold of.—Hence, to arrest: low s. To steal; purloin: low.

nicker   A £1 currency note: c. > low, esp. racing and grafters' s. Pl.: *nicker.*

nicknames   Inseparable or inevitable, are of two classes: general; particular. The general denote nationality (*Fritz, Frog, Ikey, Jock, Mick, Taffy*) or a physical trait (*Bluey, Bunty, Snowy, Tich, Tiny*).

The particular, which are the inseparable nicknames *par excellence,* attach themselves to certain surnames; like the general, they are rarely bestowed on women. The following are the most frequently heard:—*Betsy* Gay; *Blanco* White (cf. *Chalky*); *Bodger* Lees (cf. *Jigger*); *Bogey* Harris; *Brigham* Young; *Buck* Taylor; *Busky* Smith (cf. *Dusty* and *Shoey*); *Chalky* White; *Charley* Peace; *Chats* Harris; *Chatty* Mather; *Chippy* Carpenter; *Dan* Coles; *Darky* Smith; *Dinghy* Read; *Dodger* Green (cf. *Shiner*); *Dolly* Gray; *Doughy* Baker (cf. *Snowy*); *Dusty* Miller and, occ., Jordan, Rhodes, Smith; *Edna* May; *Fanny* Fields; *Flapper* Hughes; *Ginger* Jones; *Granny* Henderson; *Gunboat* Smith; *Happy* Day; *Hooky* Walker; *Jack* Sheppard (-erd, -herd); *Jesso* Read; *Jigger* Lees; *Jimmy* Green (cf. *Dodger*); *Johnny* Walker (cf. *Hooky*); *Jumper* Collins or Cross; *Kitty* Wells; *Knocker* Walker or White; *Lackery* Wood; *Lottie* Collins; *Mouchy* Reeves; *Nobby* Clark(e) and, occ., Ewart, Hewart, Hewett, Hewitt; *Nocky* Knight; *Nutty* Cox; *Pedlar* Palmer; *Piggy* May; *Pills* Holloway; *Pincher* Martin; *Pony* Moore; *Rattler* Morgan; *Shiner* Black, Bright, Bryant, Green, White, Wright; *Shoey* Smith; *Shorty* Wright; *Slinger* Woods; *Smoky* Holmes; *Smudger* Smith; *Snip* Parsons, Taylor; *Snowy* Baker; *Spiky* Sullivan; *Spokey* Wheeler, Wheelwright; *Spud* Murphy; *Taffy* Jones, Owen and, as above, any Welshman; *Timber* Wood (cf. *Lackery*); *Tod* Hunter, Sloan; *Tom* King; *Topper* (occ. corrupted to *Tupper*) Brown; *Tottie* Bell; *Tug* Wilson; *Wheeler* Johnson; *Wiggy* Bennett. (A small Army group consists of Arabic words: e.g. *Eska, Jebbel, Ketir Mug*, and *Mush*.)

These 'inseparable' names app. arose first in the Navy (e.g. *Pincher, Nobby, Tug*) and soon—by 1890 or so—reached the Army; W.W. I effectually distributed them among the lower classes, a few (e.g. *Dolly* and *Tug*) among the upper classes. They derive from the commonness of some phrase, as in '*Happy* Day' and '*Hooky* Walker'; from an historical or a vocational association, as in '*Pedlar* Palmer', '*Dusty* Miller', and '*Shoey* Smith'; from a merely semantic suggestion, as in '*Lackery* (or *Timber*) Wood' and '*Shiner* White'; rarely from a neat phrasal connexion as in '*Jumper* Cross' (*jump across*); occ. from a well-known trade article or advertisement, as in '*Blanco* White', '*Pills* Holloway' and '*Johnny* Walker'; from a famous personage, as in '*Pincher* Martin', '*Nobby* Ewart', '*Spiky* Sullivan'—the largest of the ascertained-origin groups; and from some anecdotal cause or incidental (or local) notoriety, as in '*Rattler* Morgan' and '*Wiggy* Bennett'.

niff A sniff; C. 19–20; an unpleasant odour: Cockneys'. Hence, the adj. *niffy*.

nifty Smart, (somewhat blatantly) skilful: orig. U.S.; anglicized ca. 1890.

night & day A play: rhyming s.

nightie, nighty   A night-dress: coll.

nines, to or **up to the**   To perfection; admirably: coll.; esp. *dressed up* or *got-up, to the nines.* Perhaps ex *nine* as a mystic number connoting perfection.

nineteenth hole, the   The bar-room of a golf club-house: golfers'. A golf-course has 18 holes.

nip   To catch, snatch, seize, neatly, take up smartly (also with *away out, up*): chiefly dial. To move, to go, quickly or promptly: dial. > s. Often with *out* or *up*; *nip in* = to slip in, *nip along* = to depart hurriedly, or to move fast.

nipper   A boy, a lad (esp. if under say 12): orig. proletarian. He 'nips about'.

nippers, the   Ex preceding. The lowest form: many Public Schools'.

nippy   Lively; nimble, active; sharp or prompt. Ex *nip*.

Nips   Japanese: adapted ex U.S. *Nipponese.*

nips in(to), put the   To ask a loan (from a person): Australian and New Zealand. Cf. *sting.*

nit, n.   A simpleton, a moron, a fool: Australian. Short for the synonymous and general *nit-wit,* a coll. adopted from U.S.A.; *nit* = Ger. *nichts.*

nix, nicks   Nothing. Prob. ex. coll. Ger. *nix* (= nichts).

no can do   Cannot do; impossible: pidgin and 'passe-partout' English.

no dice; no soap   The deal's off: Canadian. The latter, fairly common elsewhere in the British Commonwealth, prob. rhymes on *no hope.*

no, don't tell me—I'll (or **let me**) **guess!**   A c.p. Sometimes *no* is omitted: occ., *now* for *no.*

no go (it is, etc.)   No use!; it's impracticable or impossible.

no names, no pack-drill   A military c.p.: 'No names, no punishment.' Hence, fig.: 'No names, no slander (or libel).'

no odds!   It doesn't matter; never mind: coll.

Noah's ark   A lark (whether bird or, more gen., fun); (mostly n. and esp. among urban labourers): rhyming s.

nob   The head.—Hence, a person of rank, position or wealth.

nobba, occ. **nobber**   Nine, esp. as adj.: Parlary. E.g. *nobba saltee,* ninepence. Ex Sp. *nova* or It. *nove.*

nobble   To strike on the head; to stun. To tamper with a horse, e.g. by laming it, to prevent it from winning: the turf.—Hence, to obtain a person's help or interest by underhand methods; to appropriate dishonestly; to swindle out of; to seize, catch, get hold of.

nobby   Very smart, elegant or fashionable; ob.

noble   A chiefly school-girlish coll. of approbation, esp. in *that's* (*very*) *noble of you*: by 1955, slightly ob.

noise like a(n) . . . , make a   To pretend to be a (thing); (momentarily) to suppose oneself to be an (animal; occ. a person): a c.p. locution. Dorothy Sayers, *Unnatural Death*, 1927, 'And now we'll just make a noise like a hoop and roll away'.

non-com   A non-commissioned officer: coll.

nonsense   A fiasco; an absurdity.

north & south   The mouth: rhyming s.

nose on   To give information to the police about (a person): c. > low s.

noser   A blow on the nose: mostly boxing.—A strong head-wind: nautical coll.

nos(e)y   Inquisitive. *Nosey Parker*, a prying person; hence *nosey-parkering*, inquisitive(ness).

nosh   To eat furtively between meals: children's.

not half, adv.   Much, very; as in 'not half screwed, the gent was!': (mostly Cockney) ironic coll.—An exclamation, esp. of emphatic assent; as in ' "Did you like it?"—"Not half!" '

not her—him—me—you,—it (just) isn't or **wasn't**   It doesn't—or didn't—truly suit her (etc.); it isn't or wasn't in character: c.p. Apparently it originated in the smart fashion shops of Society.

not to worry!   Don't worry; there's nothing to worry about: Services': C. 20. Suddenly, in 1957–58, it began to be generally and widely used. 'You are *not to worry*.'

nothing to write home about   Unremarkable; unusual; mediocre: coll. During W.W. I, Australian soldiers preferred *nothing to cable home about*.

notice, not so as (occ. **so that**) **you'd**   Not so much—or to such an extent—as to be noticeable: coll.

nous   Intelligence; commonsense or good sense. Academic s. Adopted ex Gr.: cf. *hubris*.

nowhere, be   To be badly beaten, hopelessly out-distanced: coll.

nozzler   A punch on the nose.

number, have (someone's)   To have someone sized up or potentially mastered. Ex telephony.

number one   One's self or one's own interests, esp. in *look after*, or *take care of, number one*: coll.—The First Lieutenant: naval.

number is up, one's   One won't live (being destined for death) or, less often, is sure to be detected: the former a gen. coll.: the latter, military s.

nursey, nursie   A coll., mainly children's, form of *nurse*, n.

nut   The head.—Hence, brains, intelligence; esp. in *use one's nut*.

nut, off one's   Crazy.

nut, work one's   To think hard; to scheme: orig. dial.; >, ca. 1905, s., esp. in Australia.

nut out   To consider; work out: military. 'I've got to nut it out.'

nuthouse   A hospital, or a ward set aside for the (temporarily) insane; an asylum for the insane: adopted from U.S.A. 'They're *nuts!*'

nutty as a fruitcake   Insane. Cf. *nut, off one's.*

O

---

o.k., gen. **O.K.**   All right; correct; safe: suitable; what is required; comfortable, comfortably placed: orig. U.S. s.; >, ca. 1880, Eng. s. and, ca. 1895, Eng. coll.

o.k., O.K., v.i. and, more gen., v.t.   To pass as correct: orig. U.S.; anglicized as a coll. ca. 1900.

O.K. by me! it's   I agree, or approve: an Americanism anglicized by 1933.

oak   A joke: rhyming s.

oats, off one's   Indisposed: coll. Ex the stable.

object   A laughing-stock: coll.

observatory   The astrodome of an aircraft.

ocean pearl   A girl: rhyming s.

ocean rambler   A herring; a sardine.

ocean wave   A shave: rhyming s.

odds, above (Australian) or **over** (English) **the**   Outside the pale; exorbitant. Ex horse-racing.

odds, shout the   To talk too loudly or boastingly. Ex the race-course.

odds and sods   'Details' attached to Battalion Headquarters for miscellaneous offices; batmen, sanitary men, professional footballers and boxers on nominal duties, etc.: military.—Hence, hangers-on; miscellaneous persons.

off, adj.   Stale; in bad condition: coll. Hence, out of form: coll. Hence, in ill health: coll.

off, prep.   Having lost interest in: coll. 'I'm rather off dogs at present.'

off, be   To depart; run away: coll.

off it   To depart: coll. Hence also, to die.

office   A signal, a (private) hint; a word of advice; (in sporting s.)

120

valuable information. Esp. in *give the office*.—An aeroplane cockpit:
Air Force. Ex its speaking-tube and writing-pad.—An orderly-room:
military jocular coll.

offish Distant; reserved: coll. (Pronounced *off'-ish* and not, as in
sense 2, *off-fish'*.)—2. Official; authentic.

offsider An assistant: Australians' and New Zealanders'. Orig.,
a cook's offsider: coll. Hence, a 'pal': Australian.

oggin, the, occ. **hoggin** The sea: naval (lower-deck). The origin is
obscure.

oil, the Esp. *the dinkum* (occ. *good*) *oil*: the truth; hence, information. Australian and New Zealand.

oiled (Slightly) tipsy. Esp., *well oiled*.

okay (or **O.K.**) **by me, it's; O.K. by you?** Virtual c.pp.; certainly:
coll.; adopted ex U.S.

oke! 'O.K.' U.S. >, ca. 1930, anglicized, thanks mainly to 'the
talkies'.

okey-doke A variation of *O.K.*

old, adj. A vague intensive = great, abundant, excessive,
'splendid'; now only with *gay, good, grand, high*, and similar adjj., as
in 'a high old time', and with *any* as in 'any old time' or 'any old how':
coll.

old battle-axe An old, or an elderly, woman that is resentful and
vociferous, thoroughly unpleasant, usually arrogant, and no beauty.
Common to the U.S., Canada, Britain; not unknown in Australia,
New Zealand, South Africa.

old-fashioned look A glance of quizzical disapproval.

old girl Esp. in address. Wife; mother: coll.

Old Harry, play To play the devil: coll.

old lady One's wife or mother: coll.

old man The captain of a ship; hence, the officer in charge of a
battalion.—Husband: jocular coll. Father: coll. A coll. vocative. Cf.
old boy, chap, fellow.—A master, a 'boss'; governor of a prison;
headmaster: coll.

Old Newton (got him, took him, etc.) Often shortened to *Newton*,
refers to a pilot crashing, esp. if fatally: R.A.F. Gravity is an aircraft's implacable foe; Isaac Newton discovered the laws of gravity.

Old Nick The devil: coll.

old pot & pan 'Old man', i.e. husband, father; occ. 'old woman',
i.e. wife, woman: rhyming s. († by 1915 for a woman).

old soldier An experienced, esp. if crafty, man: coll. Esp. *come the
old soldier*.

old sport A coll. term of address; by 1945, ob.

old sweat An old soldier of the Regular Army: military. Ex his
strenuous efforts.

old thing A familiar term of address: coll.

old top A s. vocative: ca. 1919–40.

old woman Wife; mother: coll.—Jocular where not proletarian.

oldie An old trick or an old story; hence, an old film or play: coll.

oldster An elderly or an experienced person: coll. It complements S.E. *youngster*.

omee; omer; omey; homee, homey A man; esp. a master, e.g. a landlord: Parlary. Ex It. *uomo*.

omnium(-)gatherum A mixed assemblage of things or persons: coll. The L. *omnium*, of all + *gather* + mock L. ending *-um*.

on, adj. Ready and willing: coll., as in *Are you on?*, are you agreed, prepared, willing?—Possible; arranged. 'It's not on.'

on, prep. To be paid for: coll., as in 'The lunch is on me'.

on the floor Poor: rhyming s.

one, a A very odd or amusing person. 'He's a one!'

on at, be or **go** To nag (someone); reprove constantly: coll.

one-er, oner, wunner A person, a thing, of great parts, remarkable (e.g. a notable lie), most attractive, dashing; an expert. Perhaps *oner* is ex *one*, something unique, influenced by dial. *wunner*, a wonder.

one in the eye A misfortune, a set-back, a snub.

one of those things, often preceded by **it's just** A c.p. of resignation; used when the inexplicable and annoying or baffling occurs.

one-pip(per) A second lieutenant: military.

onion The head, esp. in *off his onion*, crazy.

oodles A large quantity, esp. of money: U.S.; anglicized ca. 1890.

oojah Sauce; custard: Services'.

ooja(-ka-piv or **ka-pivvy)** A gadget; anything unnamed. Origin doubtful.

op Operator; esp. *wireless op.*: nautical.—A surgical operation.

oppo 'My oppo' is my chum, pal, usual companion: Royal Navy and Royal Marines, hence also R.A.F. Hence, sweetheart or even one's wife.

ops Operations (in manœuvres): military. Also in R.A.F.: Operations Room; Operations Officer.

optic (Esp. in pl.) An eye: jocular coll.

oracle, work the To raise money; to succeed.

order of the . . . , the E.g. . . . *of the bath*, a bath; . . . *of the boot*, a kick, a violent dismissal; . . . *of the push*, a dismissal. All are coll. and essentially middle-class. Perhaps suggested by such *knight* mock-titles as *knight of the pigskin*, a jockey.

Orderly Buff; Orderly Dog An Orderly Sergeant; an Orderly Corporal: military.

organize To 'wangle' something; to get something deviously or illicitly; to obtain or arrange something (very) cleverly but not necessarily illicitly: R.A.F.; hence, general.

organized, get   So to arrange work, or a plan, as to achieve one's purpose; he who has done this *is*, or *has got, organized*: R.A.F.; hence, gen.

Oscar   Money, esp. coin: Australian rhyming s. on *cash*. Ex Oscar Asche, Australian actor (1871–1936).

Ouds, the   The Oxford University Dramatic Society: coll.

out, v.   To disable; knock out: boxing. Hence, to kill.

out, n.   An excuse; an alibi: adopted from U.S.A.

out-and-outer   A thorough bounder, an 'impossible' person.

out of commission   Out of order; not running: coll. 'We can't take the car; she's out of commission.'

out of this world   Incredible—incredibly good or beautiful or capable. 'Her singing is out of this world.' Orig. literary and cultured, verging on Society. Slightly affected.

out with   To bring out, to show: coll.: e.g. *out with a knife*. Hence, to utter, esp. unexpectedly or courageously: coll.

outside, adv.   In civilian life: naval coll.

outsider   A person unfit to mix with good society: coll.

over, be all   To make a great fuss of.

own, on its, or one's   On its or one's own account, responsibility, resources, merits: coll.—Hence, by oneself; alone; independently: coll.

own up   To confess; admit (v.t. with *to*): coll.

owner, the   The captain of a ship: naval. The captain of an aircraft: R.A.F.

owners, the   The British public: naval.

Oxford -er   At Oxford, it began late in 1875 and came from either Harrow or Rugby School. By this process, the original word is changed and usually abridged; then *-er* is added. Thus, *memorial > memugger*, the *Radcliffe* Camera > *the Radder* (for *the* is prefixed where the original has *the*). Occ. the word is pluralized, where the original ends in *s*: as in *Adders*, Addison's Walk, *Jaggers*, Jesus College. This *-er* has got itself into gen. upper-middle class s.

P

P.B.I., the   The infantry: infantrymen's coll.: since 1915. I.e. *poor bloody infantry*.

pa   A mainly childish form of *papa*, q.v.: coll.

paces, show one's   To display one's ability: coll. Ex horses.

pack it in; pack it up   To stop talking; to cease fooling or some foolish practice: Services'.

pack the game in   To desist; esp. abandon a way of life: proletarian. Hence, *pack it in.*

packet   A (large) sum of money lost or won in betting or speculating.

packet, cop or **stop a**   To be wounded, esp. if fatally; occ. *cop it*. Ex *cop* (q.v.), to catch; *packet* may be the missile.—Hence (only *cop a packet*), to have bad luck, meet with trouble.

pad the hoof   To go on foot: by 1960, slightly ob.

Paddy   A nickname (cf. *Pat*) for an Irishman: coll. Ex the very common Irish name, *Patrick*, of which *Paddy* is the Irish diminutive.

paddy   A rage, a temper: coll. Cf. *Irish*.

padre   A chaplain: naval, hence military and R.A.F., coll.; by 1945, S.E. Ex Portuguese (lit., father) as used, from ca. 1580, in India for any priest or parson.

pain in the neck, give one a   To bore intensely; to irritate.

pain in the neck   A tedious or boring or exceedingly irritating person.

pal   Chum, a friend, a friendly companion. Ex Romany, *pal*, brother, mate, ex Turkish Gypsy *pral*, *plal*, brother; ultimately related to Sanskrit *bhratr*, a brother.

pal, v.i.   To associate (*with*); become another's 'pal'.

pally   Friendly; 'thick'. Ex *pal*, n.

panic Preparations at full speed on a ship getting ready for sea: naval: 1914–18.

pannikin-boss or **overseer** An overseer in a small, 'unofficial' way on a station: Australian coll. Hence, 'a shift boss': coll.

paper Free passes to an entertainment; collectively, the recipients of such passes. Hence, v.

paper end, the The written and documentary aspect of some matter as distinct from the matter itself: Services', esp. R.A.F., coll.

par A *paragraph*, esp. of news: journalistic coll.

para A *paragraph*, esp. as part of a book: book-world coll.

paralysed, paralytic Tipsy.

pard A partner; a chum: orig. U.S.: anglicized ca. 1885, chiefly in the Dominions.

park, v. To place, esp. with implication of safety: coll. Ex military usage, to put in an artillery- or car-park, via *park a gun, lorry, car.*—2. V. reflexive (of persons): to place oneself; hence, to sit: coll.

parley voo, v.i. To speak French. Ex *parlez-vous*, do you speak (e.g. French)?

parnee, parn(e)y; esp. **pawnee** Water. Ex Hindustani *pani*, partly via Romany.

part, v.i. To pay, give, restore: coll.

part brass-rags To quarrel: naval. Bowen, 'From the bluejacket's habit of sharing brass cleaning rags with his particular friend'.

partial to Liking; fond of: coll.

partic Particular; esp. as adj. (fastidious): trivial coll.

party An aerial combat; a bombing raid; commando raid; a naval operation: Services'. By nonchalant meiosis.—A very busy day: Services'.

pash An infatuation; among school-children, one for a teacher. Ex *passion*. Cf. *rave*.

pass To fail to understand; have no concern in: coll. Ex euchre, although its post-1910 usage mainly derives ex bridge.

pass in one's checks To die: orig. U.S.; anglicized, esp. in Canada and Australia, ca. 1890. Ex setting one's accounts at poker.

pass the buck To pass on something one cannot trouble oneself with: Civil Service. An Americanism.

paste, v. To thrash. Perhaps ex bill-sticking.

Pat An Irishman; often in address: coll. Ex *Patrick*.

Pat Malone Alone: Australian and New Zealand rhyming s. Esp. *do a thing*, or *go, on one's Pat Malone* (hence *pat*).

pathetic Ludicrous. (Now coll.)

patter Mere talk, is now coll. It derives ex *patter*, to speak glibly, itself ultimately echoic.

Pav, the Any Pavilion theatre or music-hall.—(**pav.**) A sports pavilion: mostly schoolboys'.

paw A hand; coll.

pax Silence!; truce!: schoolboys'. Ex L. *pax*, peace.

pay A paymaster: naval coll.

pay-off Punishment; settlement for infringing the rules of the underworld: c. > low s.—Hence, retribution.

pay out To give (a person) his deserts: coll. 'He'll pay you out for that!'

pea in a colander, like a Flustered, agitated, jumpy. Running round in small circles.

pea soup A French-Canadian: Canadian. Ex the frequency of that dish on French-Canadian tables. Hence, *talk pea-soup*, to talk French-Canadian.

pea-souper A dense yellowish fog: coll.

peach, n. An attractive girl: orig. U.S. Esp. *a regular peach* or *a peach of a girl*. By 1950, ob.

peach, v. To blab: coll.

peachy Very pleasant. Ex U.S.

peaky, peeky Feeble, puny, sickly: coll. and dial.

pearl-diver An assistant-pantryman in charge of the washing of the saloon crockery; hence more generally.

pearlies Pearl buttons, esp. on a coster's clothes: coll. Hence, costermongers.—Teeth: non-cultured. By 1960, slightly archaic.

pecker The appetite. Ex † *peck*, to eat.—Resolution, courage. 'Keep up your pecker, old chap.'

peckish Hungry. Cf. preceding.

pecky Choppy (sea); (of a horse) inclined to stumble; (of kisses) like a bird's peck: coll.

peculiar Mentally deranged: coll.

peel To undress (v.i.).

peeler A policemen. (By 1945, rather ob.) Ex Mr (later Sir) Robert Peel.

peep-o' (h)! (To and by children.) Look at me!; here I am!, esp. as one emerges from hiding: coll.

peepers Spectacles.

peeved Annoyed; cross: coll. Ex *peevish*.

peg A drink (esp. of brandy and soda-water). Ex *peg* as one of the pins in a drinking-vessel.—A blow, esp. a straight or a thrusting one: s. and dial.—A wooden leg: coll. A tooth (esp. a child's): nursery coll.—A cricket stump: coll.—Abbr. *peg-top*: children's coll.

peg, v. To work persistently, 'hammer' away: coll.

peg, v.   To starve: Australian. Ex *peg out*, to die. To put someone on a charge: Army.

peg, on the (also **pegs, on the**)   Under arrest; having had one's pay stopped: military.

peg-leg   A person with a wooden leg: (low) coll. Ex S.E. sense, a wooden leg.

peg out   To die. Ex cribbage.

peg to hang things on!, it's nice to have a   A c.p., said by such an inferior in business as bears the brunt of a superior's mistakes.

pegged, be   To be due for trial for some 'crime': military.

peke   A coll. abbr. of *Pekin(g)ese*, sc. *dog* or *spaniel.*

pen   A penitentiary; a prison: low.

pen & ink   A stink; to stink: rhyming s.

penal   A sentence, or a term of penal servitude: coll.

penguin   A ground-staff, i.e. non-flying, member of the R.A.F.

penn'orth, pennorth, pen'orth; penn'worth   A year's imprisonment; mostly in combination: low s. Michael Harrison, *Weep for Lycidas*, 1934, 'Ronnie will get fourteen penn'orth. . . Fourteen years hard.'

penny-a-mile   A smile: rhyming s.

penny a pound; often merely **penny**   Ground: rhyming s.

penny-farthing   An old-fashioned, very high bicycle with a large and a small wheel: coll.; ob.

penny plain & tuppence coloured, originally **a penny plain and twopence coloured**   Since ca. 1890 has been a c.p. Meaning 'plain or fancy', the phrase seems to have, at first, referred to cheap fiction costing one penny with plain jacket and, with coloured-picture jacket, twopence.

penny's dropped!; or **the penny'll drop in a minute**   A c.p., belated appreciation of humour. Ex slot-payment in public lavatories.

people-in-law   One's husband's or wife's relatives, esp. parents, brothers, sisters: coll.

pep   Energy; spirited initiative: coll.

peppy   Energetic; spirited, e.g. work.

percentage   Profit; advantage. 'There's no percentage in it'— nothing to be gained by it.

perch, hop the   To die.

perfect day, the end of a   A W.W. I c.p. of indefinite meaning; occ. jocularly applied, by soldiers, to one who had evidently been 'celebrating'. Imm. ex Carrie Jacobs-Bond's song, *When you Come to the End of a Perfect Day.*

perfectly good. . ., a   An indubitably—or, merely, a quite—good, sound, satisfactory something or other: s. > coll.

perform, v.i.   To make a (considerable) fuss, to 'go on'.

period!   Finally; without extension or modification, palliation or repeal: originally journalists', authors', broadcasters'. 'Dead as a door-nail? Just dead. Period!'

perish, do a Nearly to die from lack of water: Australian.

perisher, do a To die from lack of water: Australian.

perishing, adj. A gen. pejorative, as in 'the perishing thing!' Also as an intensive.

perk up To recover health or good spirits: coll. and dial.

perks Perquisites.

perm A supposedly *perm*anent wave (of the hair): coll. Hence, to subject a person, or a person's hair, to a permanent wave: coll.

perm, n. A permutation: coll.

persuader A weapon, esp. a revolver.

persuasion Nationality, sex; sort, kind: jocular coll. Ex *persuasion*, religious belief, opinion.

petty A petticoat: coll.

pew A seat, esp. in *take a pew*.

pewy (Of country) so enclosed by fences as to form a succession cf small fields: sporting (esp. hunting). Ex the shape of the old-fashioned big, enclosed pews.

phenomenon A prodigy; a remarkable person, occ. animal, or thing: coll.

phiz (phizz), phyz; physog Face; expression of face: jocular coll. Ex *physiognomy*.

phoney, occ. **phony** Fraudulent; imitation, pretended, bogus, criminal: U.S.; fully anglicized ca. 1940. Ex the old English c. *fawney*, a worthless finger-ring, itself ex Irish *fainne*, a ring.

phos, phoss, even **foss** Phosphorus.

photo A photograph: coll.

photo finish; often reduced to **photo** (pron. **photer**) A Guinness: rhyming s.

phut, go To come to grief; fizzle out; be a failure: coll.

phyz See *phiz*.

pi, adj. *Pi*ous; sanctimonious: schools' and universities'.—*pi-jaw*. A serious admonition or talk; also v.: schools' and universities'.

piano (Often slovened to *piana*.) A cash register: Anglo-Irish. It plays a merry tune.

pic A picture: artists' and journalists'.

pick A toothpick: coll.—An anchor: nautical.

pick a bone with To eat a meal with: jocular coll.

pick-me-up A stimulating liquor: coll. Hence, anything (e.g. seaside air) with bracing effect.

pick on To nag at; annoy actively: coll. .

pick-up A chance acquaintance; also v. A pick-up match; hence, a team in such a match: coll.

pickle A predicament, an unpleasant difficulty: coll.—A troublesome child: coll. Also a merely mischievous child.

picnic A rough-and-tumble; noisy trouble: coll. 'An awkward adventure, an unpleasant experience, a troublesome job' (Morris): Australian; mostly *no picnic*, a difficult task; by 1918, coll.

picture A fine example; a beau-ideal: coll., as in 'a picture of health'; often ironical as in 'pretty picture', a strange figure. Hence, a very picturesque or beautiful object: coll., as in 'she's a picture'.

pictures, the The cinema: coll.

pidgin See *pigeon*.

pie A prize, treat, 'easy thing': U.S. s., anglicized ca. 1910.

pie in the sky Paradise; heaven. Ex the U.S. song, 'There'll be pie in the sky when you die'.

pie in the sky, when you die Good things or times that, promised, never come: adopted, ca. 1943, from U.S.A.

piece, say one's To say what one has intended to say, esp. in business or in moral duty: coll. Ex obligatory recitation at, e.g., a party.

pig-jump, -jumper, -jumping 'To jump . . . from all four legs, without bringing them together' (O.E.D.); a horse that does this; the doing thereof: Australian.

pig-sticker A long-bladed pocket-knife; a sword; a bayonet.

pig-sty The press-room: printers'.—An abode, a place of business: jocular coll.

pigeon; better **pidgin** Business, concern, duty, task. 'That's my pigeon.'

piggery A room in which one does just as one wishes and which is rarely cleaned: coll. Prob. suggested by S.E. *snuggery*.

piggy-wig; piggy-wiggy A pet pig: coll.

pigs aft The officers regarded as drinking in the Wardroom: lower-deckese.

pig's back, on the In luck's way: Anglo-Irish >, by 1914, gen.

pig's (ear) Beer: rhyming s.

pig's fry To try: rhyming s.

pig's whisper, in a Very quickly indeed; in a very short time: s. > low coll.

pigskin A saddle: sporting.

pile up To run (a ship) ashore: nautical coll. Hence, to smash (a motor-car) in such a way that it buckles up into a *pile* or heap: motorists' coll. In W.W. I, *pile up one's bus* was the airmen's phrase for 'to crash'; whence, a *pile up* or 'crash': R.A.F.; from ca. 1918.

pill A ball, esp. a black balloting-ball or a tennis ball.—(Of a person) a bore: slightly ob. by 1940.

pill, v.   To reject by ballot in a club election.

Pill-Box, the   Harley Street: London taxi-drivers'.

pimple   The head: low; ob. by 1940.—A hill: proletarian.

pimple & blotch   Whiskey (strictly Scotch): rhyming s.

pin, v.   To seize (a thing): by 1940, slightly ob. Hence, to steal, esp. if rapidly: low; ob. To catch, apprehend (a person): ob.

pin-up   An attractive girl, or her likeness: coll.: adopted ex U.S. servicemen. Extended, ca. 1955, to a handsome male, similarly 'honoured' by teen-age girls.

pinch, v.   To steal: c. until ca. 1880, then low s. Ex the pinching movement of predatory fingers.—To arrest: c. > s. Hence, *make a pinch*, to make an arrest: police s.

pine-apple   A Mills bomb: military; 1916–18. Ex the criss-cross of lines denoting segments.

pink, adj.   Mildly Socialistic. Prompted by *red*, Communistic.

pink, in the   In excellent health or spirits. Ex *in the pink of condition* (of racehorses).

pinkie, pinky   Anything small; orig. and esp. the little finger: (Scots) coll., mostly among children. Lit., the little pink one.

pinna, pinny   A pinafore: coll.

pins   (Rare in singular.) Legs: coll. and dial.

pins & needles   The tingling that accompanies the restoration of circulation in a benumbed limb: coll.

pip   A star on the tunic or jacket of a uniform: military. See also *pip, get* (or *have*) *the* and *give the*.

pip, v.   To blackball: clubs'. Prob. suggested by *pill*. To take a trick from an opponent: cards. To hit with a missile, esp. a bullet; to wound; to kill: military. To beat, defeat, e.g. in a race. To fail (a candidate).

pip, get or **have the**   To feel depressed: coll.

pip, give the   To depress; hence, to annoy or disgust: coll.

Pip, Squeak & Wilfred   The medals (or medal ribbons), 1914–15 Star, War Medal, Victory Medal: military. Ex three characters in a cartoon.

pipe, the   The Underground Railway: London taxi-drivers'.

pipe, v.   To talk; speak: coll. Esp. in *pipe-up*, speak up. To follow, to dog: detectives' s.; by 1940, ob. (Also *pipe off.*) Hence, to watch; spy on: low.

pipe an (or **one's**) **eye**   To weep: coll. 'An obscure variation on to *pipe away* . . ., with allusion to the boatswain's whistle' (W).

pipe down   To be quiet, cease talking: nautical coll.

pipe-opener   (An) exercise taken as a 'breather'.

pipes   A boatswain: nautical, esp, as nickname. Ex giving of orders by sounding a pipe.

pipped on the post   To fail or be circumvented after having been within reach of success or victory or one's goal: sporting > gen.

pirates   Gen. pl., 'Naval small craft on any irregular or detached duty': naval.

pitch, queer the   To spoil a sale, a performance: showmen's and cheapjacks'. Hence, to mar one's plans.

pitch a tale   To tell a story, esp. if romantic or pitiful: now coll.

pitch in   To set vigorously to work: coll. Hence, to take a hand; to begin eating: coll.

pitch into   To attack energetically, with blows or words (hence, to reprimand): coll.

pitch it (too) strong   To exaggerate: coll.

pittite   One sitting in the pit at a theatre: coll.

pitty   Pretty: nursery. Ex baby talk.

pity the poor sailor on a night like this!   A semi-jocular c.p. à propos of a stormy night.

pixilated or **pixolated**   Tipsy: Perhaps a blend of '*pixy-l*ed' and 'intox*icated*'.

plain   (Of drinks) undiluted, neat: coll.

plan, according to   Jocularly and often ironically among British soldiers, to mean 'willy-nilly': 1917–18. Ex Ger. *plangemäss*, a euphemistic misrepresentation in communiqués reporting loss of ground.

plank   To put down; pay readily: coll.

plant   Hidden plunder or valuables (*the plant*); a swindle or a cleverly planned robbery; a decoy: c. > low s. Hence, 'a plant set to detect motorists travelling at illegal speed (O.E.D.): 1909. To conceal, hide; to set in position; to post (a person); to select a person or a building for a swindle or a robbery; to plan or prepare by illegal methods; to dispose (cards) for cheating; (in mining) to salt; to deliver (a punch); to drive (the ball) into the goal or 'into' another player: boxing, football.

plaster   A mortgage: Canadian. Plaster on the house.

plaster, v.   To shatter (a bird) with shot: sporting.—Hence, to shell heavily: military.—Hence, to bomb heavily from the air: R.A.F.

plates (of meat)   Feet: rhyming s.

play, v.i.   To work in co-operation; to reciprocate; to agree: Services', also civilian. Short for the synonymous *play ball*.

play the game   To act honourably: coll. Lit., play to the rules; cf. *it's not cricket*.

play trains!, run away and   Don't bother me!: c.p.

play up to   To take one's cue from another: coll.

pleased as a dog with two tails   Delighted: coll.

plonk   Mud, esp. that of no-man's land: military: 1915–18. Ex the noise made when one draws one's feet from the clinging mire.—Cheap port, sold by the quart; hence any wine: Australian. Ex *plink-plonk*, Aus. soldiers' s. for Fr. *vin-blanc*.

plonk   To shell: military. Ex sound of impact and burst.

plough, v.   To reject in an examination: university s.

plug   A punch; a knock. To punch, esp. *plug in the eye*.—To shoot (v.t.). To try to popularize (a song) by dinning it into the public ear: coll. Hence, a piece of publicity.

plumber   An armourer: R.A.F. Facetious.—*The Plumber* is the R.A.F.'s s. name for an Engineering Officer. *Plumbers*, the engine room staff: naval.

plummy   Rich; desirable; very good.

plunger   A reckless better or speculator.—A Baptist: Church s.—A hypodermic syringe: orig. medical.

plute   A plutocrat.

podge   A short, fat person; such an animal: dial. and coll.

points to, give   To be superior to, have the advantage of: coll. Ex S.E. sense, to give odds to (an opponent).

poison   Liquor; a drink of liquor.

poisonous   A coll. intensive. (Cf. *putrid*.)

poke   To hit (someone): Australian. Also n.

pole on   To sponge on (somebody): Australian.

pole, up a or **the**   In difficulties; rather drunk, annoyed, irritated; in Australia, 'distraught through anger, fear, etc.; also, disappeared, vanished' (C. J. Dennis).

polio   *Polio*myelitis or infantile paralysis: coll., medical >, by 1958, general,

polish off   Summarily to defeat an adversary: boxing s. > gen. coll. = to finish out of hand, get rid of (esp. a meal) quickly.

poly, the   The Polytechnic Institute.

Pom   A *Pom*eranian dog.

pommy   A newcomer from Britain, esp. from England: Australian. Origin? Hotly disputed; prob. ex *pome*granate (ruddy cheeks).

Pompey   Portsmouth: naval, hence sporting. Perhaps ex its naval prison: cf. Yorkshire *Pompey*, a house of correction.

pong   A stink; to stink: low.

pongo   A monkey: showmen's.—Hence a nickname for a marine: naval.—Hence, a soldier: naval.

pony   Only a small sum, as a pony is a small horse: £25. Among brokers, a *pony* is £25,000 of stock, i.e. 25 £1000-shares.

pooch   A dog; an inferior dog: Canadian. Ex U.S.—Hence, a greyhound: Australian.

poodle-faker   A man, esp. a Service officer, that cultivates the society of women: Anglo-Indian, hence military, hence naval. Hence, *poodle-faking*. A reference to *lap*-dogs.

pooped   Exhausted; very tired: 'Must stop for a bit; I'm pooped.' Probably ex the nautical S.E. v. *poop.*

pop   A popular concert: coll.—A drink that fizzes from the bottle when the cork—'pop goes the cork'—is drawn: coll.—A pawning—to pawn. As = father, orig. U.S.; anglicized ca. 1930.

pop off   To die.

pop the question   To propose marriage: coll.; by 1945, slightly ob.

poppycock   Nonsense: U.S. s. anglicized ca. 1905; by 1930, coll.

pops   Popular concerts: music-lovers'.

porky, adj.   Of, concerning, resembling pork; obese: coll.

posh, adj.   Stylish, smart (of clothes), best; splendid. Of obscure and much discussed origin; but perhaps ex *polished.*

posh up   (Gen. in passive—esp. *all poshed-up.*) To make smart in appearance; to clean and polish: military > gen. Ex *posh,* adj.

poss, if   Possible: trivial coll.

possum, play   To pretend; to feign illness or death: orig. U.S.; partly anglicized ca. 1850. Ex the opossum's feigned death.

possy, possie   A position; esp, a dug-out, or other shelter: military, mainly Australian and New Zealand. Hence, mostly in the Dominions, a house, a lodging, etc.; a job.

post   Such mail as is cleared from one receiving-box or as is delivered at one house: coll.

postic; occ. **posty**   A postman: coll.

pot   A large stake or bet; hence, any large sum; a prize, orig. and esp. if a vessel (gen. of silver), given at a sports and games.—A person of importance, esp. *a big pot*: coll.—A person: in pejorative s. or coll. combinations, as *fuss-pot,* a fussy person, and *swank-pot,* a conceited one.—A china, or an enamel, mug: Services'.

pot   To shoot for the pot, i.e. for food; to kill by a pot-shot: coll.

pot, go to   To be ruined or destroyed; to get into a very bad condition: coll.

pot-walloper   A heavy drinker.

potatoes in the mould   Hence often *potatoes,* whence *taters.* Cold (adj.): rhyming s.

pots; runners; straws   Potatoes; scarlet runner beans; strawberries: greengrocers' coll.

potty   Trivial, insignificant. Ex *potter (about).*—Easy, simple; safe.—Silly; crazy: from ca. 1910.

poultice   A mortgage: Australian.

pounce   A severe, esp. if written, criticism: book-world coll.

pour   A 'continuous' rain; esp. a *steady pour* (all the morning): coll.

powwow A conference of senior officers before a battle, or during manoeuvres: military.

pozzy Jam: military, hence also naval. Prob. ex a South African language.

pram A perambulator (for infants): coll.

prang To crash-land an aircraft (usually v.t.): R.A.F. echoic. —Hence, to bomb (a town, a factory, etc.).—Hence, sometimes applied to non-flying accidents, as in 'He pranged his arm at rugger'.— Hence, n. in all three senses.

prawn, silly A pejorative applied to persons; esp. *you silly prawn* or *the silly prawn*.

preachy Given to preaching; as if, as in, a sermon: coll.

precious Egregious; (pejoratively) thorough; occ. an almost meaningless intensive: coll.

precious, adv. Exceedingly; very: coll, as in *precious few*.

pre-fab A pre-fabricated house.

prep *Prep*aration of lessons; the period of such preparation: school s.—A preparatory school (*prep. school*): orig., school s.

press on, regardless; press-on type 'I must press on, regardless' = I have urgent work to do, I must finish this job. Hence, *press-on type*, an energetic or very conscientious fellow: often derisive.

pretty, sit To be advantageously placed: orig. U.S. Ex fowls, esp. chickens, sitting prettily on the nest.

pretty as paint, as Very pretty: coll.

previous Premature; hasty: coll.

priceless (By itself, it =) ludicrous; extremely amusing. With n., egregious: e.g. 'priceless ass' (of a person): s. >, ca. 1935, coll.

pricey or **pricy** High-priced.

prink, v.t. To make spruce; in reflexive, to dress oneself up: coll.

prink, n. *The Prink* is the Principal, esp. of a women's College: girl undergraduates'.

prinking A fastidious adorning, mostly of oneself: coll.

prissy Effeminate: mostly women's: coll.: adopted, ca. 1943, ex U.S. servicemen. Perhaps a blend of *prim + sissy*, as Mitford M. Mathews has suggested.

private eye A private detective: adopted, ca. 1944, ex U.S. servicemen, with the late Raymond Chandler intervening.

prize idiot A (notable) fool: coll.

pro An actor: theatrical. One who belongs to *the* profession, i.e. acting.—Hence any professional as opp. to an amateur: coll.

prof A *prof*essor: U.S., anglicized ca. 1860.

prog Food; hence, food for a journey or picnic.

proggins A proctor: universities'.

prom A *prom*enade; a promenade concert: coll.

pronto Promptly; quickly: U.S., anglicized in 1918, esp. in the Navy and Army. Ex Sp. *pronto*, promptly.

prop Any stage requisite; a portable article used in acting a play: theatrical. Ex *property*.—A straight hit; a blow: pugilistic and low street. Ex *prop*, v.—A proposition, as in geometry: schools'.—A propeller: aviators' coll.

prop, v. To punch: pugilistic and low.

proper (Of things) excellent, admirable; (of persons) respectable, decorous; thorough; complete: coll. Hence as adv.: low coll.

proper do A very fine party or wedding-feast: working classes'.

props The property-man: theatrical.

pross, on the, adj. and adv. Looking for free drinks, etc.; on the cadge: theatrical > gen. s.

protected Uncannily or very lucky: Australian and New Zealand. Prob. ex *protected by the gods*.

proud, do one To treat very generously: coll.

proud, do oneself To treat oneself well, live comfortably: coll.

Pru, the The *Pru*dential insurance company.

prune; short for **Pilot Officer Prune** A pilot who takes unnecessary risks, has several 'prangs' on his record, and usually 'buys it': R.A.F. Created by S/Ldr Anthony Armstrong and L.A.C.W. Hooper ('Raff').

pub A *pub*lic house: s. >, ca. 1890, coll. and the minor pubs.'—Hence, *pub it*, to frequent 'pubs'.

pub-crawl; csp. do a P.-C. A liquorish peregrination from bar to bar. Hence *pub-crawler, pub-crawling*.

public A public-house: coll.

pud, n. Pudding: lower-class and lower-middle class, coll.

puddle, the The Atlantic Ocean.

puff Breath, 'wind': s. and dial.—Life; existence. As in *never in one's puff*, never. Rather ob.

pug A boxer: sporting.

pukka Certain, reliable; genuine; excellent: Anglo-Indian coll. In *pukka sahib* (in C. 20, often derisive), it connotes the acme of gentlemanliness. Ex Hindu *pakka*, substantial.

pull, v. To do; commit: U.S., adopted ca. 1925. Also *pull off*, to achieve. E.g., Georgette Heyer, *Behold, Here's Poison*, 1936, 'If Rendall pulled the murder, Hyde's out of it.'

pull down To earn (money).

pull in To arrest: c. >, ca. 1890, low s.

pull off To succeed with, or in effecting, something.

pull one's punches To exercise moderation, esp. in punishment or in blame: boxing coll. > general.

punish To handle severely, as in boxing—food and drink—the

S.S.D.—K

bowling, at cricket—a horse: coll. Hence *punisher, punishing* (adj.), *punishment*, in corresponding senses.

punk, adj. Worthless; decidedly inferior; displeasing, 'rotten': since ca. 1917, via American soldiers; low. Ex *punk*, touchwood.

pup, sell a To swindle, v.i.; esp. *sell one a pup.*

puppy(-)fat Fattiness that, acquired from eating starchy food, lacks substance: coll.

purge To dismiss from employment, esp. in passive.

purge A continual complaining, a notable complaint; also *purge-on* (by someone): Services'.

purler A headlong fall: coll.

push A thronging, a crowd, of people; hence, a gang or a group of convicts, of thieves, or, in Australia, of larrikins.—Hence, any company or party, group, association, or set of people; hence, military or a naval unit.

push, order of the A dismissal, esp. from employment; hence *give* or *get the push*: s. >, by 1910, coll.

push the boat out To be generous, act generously, with money; esp. to pay for a round of drinks: Navy and Army officers'.

push-bike A foot-propelling bicycle as opp. to a motor-cycle: coll.

push off To depart; hence, to begin, v.i., esp. of a game.

pusser is the inevitable n,autical shape of purser: coll.

pusser ship A very smart severely disciplined ship: naval.

put, stay Remain in position, firm, lit. and fig.; to continue to be safe or satisfactory: coll. Ex U.S.

put a bung or **sock in it** (Esp. imperative.) To 'shut up'; cease being noisy: military. Here, *it* is the mouth.—(In barracks or hut) to close the door (*bung* only).

put away To eat, drink, esp. in large quantities.—To put in gaol. To inform against.—To kill: coll.

put 'em up! Raise your arms!; Put up your fists!: coll. A variant is *stick 'em up!*, in both senses.

put (someone) in the picture To give (a newcomer) an idea of what is happening and enable to play one's part: Services' coll.

put it across (a person) To punish, get even with, revenge oneself on; to deceive, trick, impose on: coll., now verging on S.E.

put off To disconcert, disturb: coll.

put-on A deception, subterfuge, excuse: coll.

put the bite on To ask someone for a loan of money.

put up To show, achieve, e.g. *a good fight*; coll. to preconcert anything devious or underhand. To wear: military coll.; esp. medals.

put up job A pre-arranged crime or deception.

put (a person) up to To inform of or instruct in: coll.—To incite to (some act, to do something); to persuade (to do something): coll.

put years on me, you (or **he,** etc., **puts**)   A c.p. of disparagement.

putrid   A pejorative of the *awful* kind. Prob. suggested by *rotten*.

putty, up to   Of very poor quality; disappointingly inferior; (virtually) negligible: mostly Australian.

pyjams   Pyjamas.

Q

quack-quack   A duck: an echoic nursery coll.

quad   A prison: c. > low s.; usually *quod*, q.v. Prob. *ex quad-rangle*.—A *quad*rangle: coll.

quads; quins   Four, five, children at one birth: coll. For *quadruplets* and *quintuplets*.

quaint, adj.   As used from ca. 1920 (the practice was on the wane by 1949) to mean 'amusingly old-fashioned, entertainingly unusual, even funny in an odd way', was orig. upper-middle- and upper-class s.

quarter, the; in address, quarter   (The) quartermaster sergeant: military coll.

quarter bloke, the   The same; also, the quartermaster.

Queen Mary   A long, low-loading, articulated vehicle for transportation of aircraft by road: R.A.F.

queer, adj.   Drunk; in C. 20, esp. he *looks, looked, rather*, etc., *queer*; hence, unwell; giddy: s. >, in C. 20, coll. Of strange behaviour, (slightly) mad, orig. (*a bit*) *queer in the head*, as in Dickens.

queer, v.   To spoil, ruin.

queer bird, card, cove, fellow, fish; in pl., also queer cattle   A person odd in manner, strange in opinion.

queer stick   A very odd, or incomprehensible, fellow: coll.

queer street, in   In a serious difficulty; very short of money: c. >, ca. 1840, s. >, ca. 1890, coll. >, ca. 1930, S.E.

quick(e)y; occ. quickee   The act of backing a horse after the result of a race is known: sporting. Perhaps ex *quick return on one's money*. —A fast bowler: cricketers' coll.

quicky   A drink, esp. 'a quick one': Service officers'.

quid   A sovereign; hence, the sum of twenty shillings: low. Perhaps ex *quid pro quo*.

quidlet   A sovereign; £1: low. Diminutive of *quid*.

quids   Money, or rather cash, in gen. Ex *quid*.

quids in   Applied to a state of things when one is doing well: 'I'm quids in!' Short either for *quids in the till* or for *in, to the tune of quids* (pounds).

quiet, on the   Quietly, secretly: coll.

quins   See *quads*.

quit   To leave off in a very lazy or a cowardly manner, and *quitter*, a shirker, are C. 20 coll. ex U.S.

quite!; quite so!   Yes!; no doubt!; I agree: coll.: from the mid-Nineties. Cf. Fr. *parfaitement*.

quite a bit   Fairly often; a fair amount (n.), rather (adv.): coll. 'It hurts quite a bit.'

quizzy   In*quisi*tive.

quod   A prison: c. > low s. (Cf. *quad*.) Hence, v.

quote   A quotation; a quotation-mark: coll.

R

rabbit An inferior player of any game: s. >, by 1930, coll.

rabbit punch A cuff on the nape of the neck: pugilistic. Ex one method of killing rabbits.

racket A dodge, trick; plan; 'line'; occupation, esp. if these are criminal or 'shady': c. >, ca. 1860, low s. >, ca. 1930, gen. s. >, by 1945, coll. Ex *racket*, noise, disturbance.

racket, stand the To take the blame for one's gang: c. >, by 1850, s. >, by 1900, coll.—Hence, to pay the bill, stand the expense: s. >, by 1930, coll.

rag The curtain: theatrical and showmen's; hence, a dénouement, a 'curtain'.—The tongue; hence, talk; banter, abuse.—A jollification, esp. and orig. an undergraduates' display of noisy, disorderly conduct and high spirits: university >, ca. 1910, very common in Army and Navy, and by 1930, fairly gen. Hence, v.

rag-time, adj. Merry; carelessly happy-go-lucky; farcical: coll. Ex the Negro music and dancing so named.

raggie, raggy A particular friend (ex the sharing of brass-cleaning rags); mostly n. in pl., as *be raggies*, to be steady chums: naval.

rails, front or **head** The teeth: low, slightly ob.

rake it in To make money fast: coll. 'He's simply raking it in!'

rake-off A(n unlawful) profit; a commission: orig. U.S.; anglicized ca. 1920.

raker A very fast pace: coll.

ramp A swindle; hence, a swindle 'depending on an artificial boom in prices'.

rampage, on the Storming about: coll.

rancid Very objectionable or unpleasant: ca. 1910–40. Prob. after *putrid*.

rantan, on the On the spree; drunk: coll.

rap, take the   To be (punished or) imprisoned, esp. for another: orig. U.S.; anglicized ca. 1920.

rarze(r)   A 'raspberry': theatrical.

raspberry   A rude and disapproving noise; hence, a gesture or a sign made in disapproval: theatrical.—A reprimand: Services (esp. Army) officers'.

rat   Ex police spy: c. > low s.

rat   Short for *rat and mouse*, rhyming s. for a louse.

rat-shop   A shop or factory that employs non-union workers: proletarian.

rate of knots, at the   Very fast: naval coll.

rather!   (In replying to a question) I should think so; very decidedly: coll. Often emphasized as in Denis Mackail, *Greenery Street*, 1925, ' "Rather!" said Ian enthusiastically, "Oh, rather!" '

rats, the   Delirium tremens.

rattle   The commander's report of defaulters: naval.

rattler   A train; a bicycle.

ratty   Angry, irritated.

rave   A strong liking; a passion.

rave   An enthusiastic notice in the Press.

razzle-dazzle   A frolic, a spree; riotous jollity: U.S., anglicized ca. 1895, esp. *on the razzle dazzle*; after ca. 1920 often abbr. to *on the razzle* and applied to a drunken spree.

ready, or the ready   Money, esp. money in hand.

ready, v.   To pull a horse so that he shall not win: racing.—To contrive, manipulate, engineer; to bribe: low.

ready up   To prepare, or contrive, illicitly or not honourably: esp. Australian. Hence also n.

real, adv.   Extremely, very: coll.; esp. in *real nice*.

real thing, the   The genuine article (fig.): coll.

recap   Recapitulation: coll.: schools'.

red, in the   In debt; having failed to make one's expenses: commercial coll.

red, paint the town   To have a riotously good time: U.S., anglicized ca. 1890.

red, see   To be in, fly into, a rage: coll. Ex a bull's reaction to red.

red cap   (or with capitals)   A military policeman: military coll.

red 'un   A gold coin; an object made of gold, e.g. a watch: c. and low s.

reef (or two), **let out a**   To undo a button or so, esp. after a meal: nautical > gen.

ref   A referee: sporting.—A reference (as to ability, etc.): commercial.

ref, n.   A refectory: mostly religious Orders'.

ref, v.   To referee (a match): coll.

regimental   A downfall: military. Esp. *come a regimental*, 'to be court-martialled and reduced to the ranks'.—(*The Regimental*.) The Regimental as opp. the Company Sergeant-Major: military coll.

regs.   Regulations; as in *King's Regs*: Services'.

regular, adj.   Thorough, absolute: coll.

relieving officer, the   One's father, because he pays one's debts. By 1945, ob.

Rep   A repertory theatre; gen. *the Rep*, a specific theatre, or *the Reps*, the world of repertory: mainly theatrical.—A travelling salesman: one who represents a company.

repulsive   Unpleasant; extremely dull: orig., Society.

resting   Out of work: theatrical and music-hall coll.

rev   Form of address to a clergyman: non-educated.

reviver   A drink (rarely of non-intoxicants): orig., Society; now coll.

rhino   Money. By 1920, slightly—by 1960, very—ob. Origin problematic; perhaps an allusion to the size of a rhinoceros.— Rhinoceros: coll.

rib, v.   To make fun of; pull someone's leg: mostly Cockney s.

ribbons   Ropes forming the boundary: cricketers'.

ribby; on the ribs   Destitute; (of places) poverty-stricken, squalid: c. > low s.—Hence, (of things) inferior; (of conditions) unsatisfactory: mostly lower-class London.

rice-pudding, he couldn't knock the skin off a   A contemptuous c.p.

ricko   A ricochet: military.

ride   To keep girding at: Canadian.

ride, take (one) **for a**   To take a person in a motor-car and then, at a convenient spot, shoot him dead: U.S., anglicized ca. 1930, often loosely (i.e. in order to thrash).

rig   A trick or dodge; a swindling scheme or method: by 1940, ob. A prank: coll.: ob.—A (somewhat 'shady') manipulation of the money-market; a corner: s. >, ca. 1890, coll.—To manipulate illegally or illicitly: coll.; esp. *rig the market*.—To clothe; supply with clothes: coll. Hence the n. *rig-out*.

rigger   One who 'rigs' an auction or the market: now coll.

right, a bit of all   Excellent; mostly attractive, delightful: coll.

Right, Mr; Miss R.   The right person—the person one decides to marry: coll.

right in one's (or **the**) **head**   (Usually preceded by *not*.) Sound of mind: coll.

righteous, more holy than   Very holey or tattered.

rightio!, righty-o!, righty-ho!   All right!; certainly; gladly!

rights, catch (bang) to   To catch (a person) doing something he ought not to do: c. and low s.

ring, v. To change illicitly; simply to change or exchange; hence, to cheat (v.i.; also *ring it*).

ring, the dead Astonishingly or very similar: mostly Australian. Prob. suggested by the U.S. *be a ringer for*, to resemble closely.

ring a bell To recall something, as in 'Yes; that rings a bell' (evokes a vague memory). Ex the bell that rings when, in a shooting-gallery, one hits the bull's-eye. Adopted, ca. 1925, from U.S.A.

ringer, half, Pilot-Officer; **one-ringer,** Flying Officer; **three-ringer,** Wing-Commander; **two-ringer,** Flight-Lieutenant; **two-and-a-half ringer,** Squadron-Leader: Air Force coll.

ring in To insert, esp. to substitute, fraudulently.

rings round, run To beat hollow: Australian s. >, ca. 1910, fairly gen. coll. Ex sport.

riot act, (to) read the To reprove, administer a reproof: coll.

rip!, let her Let her go!: U.S., anglicized ca. 1875.

ripper A person or thing esp. good. Prob. ex *ripping*.

ripping Excellent; very entertaining; occ. it verges on the advl. as in 'A ripping fine story'.

rise To listen credulously; grow foolishly angry: coll. Ex a fish rising to the bait.

ritzy Rich; stylish, fashionable: adopted ca. 1935 from U.S.A. Ex the various Ritz hotels in the great capitals, esp. that in London.

road Way, manner; esp. in *any road*, occ. *anyroad*: non-cultured coll.—Direction; esp. *all roads*, in every direction: (mostly lower-class) coll.

road-hog An inconsiderate motorist. Ex U.S.

roar up (Of destroyers) to attack: naval coll. 'Roar in, roar up and roar out again.' To scrounge; to find by hustling: Army.—To reprimand: Australian.

rob the barber To wear one's hair long: coll.

Robin Hood, adj. Good: rhyming s.

Robinson Crusoe To do so: rhyming s.

rock A rock cake: coll.

rock, v. To startle (someone) with news or assertion: mostly R.A.F.

rock-creeper A coastal ship: nautical.

Rock, the Gibraltar: coll.

rocker, off one's (Temporarily) mad; extremely eccentric. Ex piece of wood enabling chair or cradle to rock.

rocket A severe reprimand: Services'.

rocks, on the (Of a strong drink) 'without water or soda, but simply poured over the rocks (lumps of ice)'. Ex U.S.

rocky, adj. A vague pejorative: e.g., unsatisfactory or unpleasant. Ex S.E. *rocky*, unsteady.—Penniless, or almost: coll.

rogue and villain A shilling: rhyming s.

roll, bowl, or pitch Despite all obstacles: coll.

roll up To appear on the scene: coll.

rolling Very rich: coll. Ex *rolling in money*.

Rolls A Rolls-Royce motor-car: coll.

romp home, or **in,** v.i. To win very easily: racing s. >, in C. 20, gen. coll.

roo, 'roo A kangaroo: Australian.

rook To cheat; defraud, and defraud of; charge extortionately.

rook(e)y; rookie A (raw) recruit: military. A perversion of *recruit*.

root To kick (a ball, a person). Hence, also n.

rooty; rooti Bread: military. Ex Hindustani. Hence:

rooty gong A long-service medal: Regular Army.

ropeable Angry; furious: Australian. Ex *ropeable* (i.e. *wild*) *cattle*.

ropey (Of a person) inefficient or dilatory or careless of appearance; (of an action, etc.) clumsy or inefficient; (of things, e.g. an aircraft, a meal) inferior: R.A.F.

rorty 'Noisily drunk and argumentive' (Granville): naval.

rorty; occ. **raughty** Of the best; excellent; dashing; lively; jolly; sprightly: costers'.—Hence, always in trouble: military.

Rory (O'More) A floor; a door: rhyming s.

rosebuds Potatoes: rhyming s. (on *spuds*).

rosy, always preceded by **the** Wine; orig. and properly, red wine; cf. the Fr. s. *le rosé*.

Rose (or Rosie) Loader or **Loder** Whisky and soda: rhyming s.

rot Nonsense, trash: s. >, ca. 1920, coll.

rot, v. To chaff severely: by 1960, slightly ob. Ex *rot*, n.

rots battleships, it; it rots your socks Water, as opposed to beer, is harmful: public-house c.pp.

rotten In a deplorable state or ill-health; ill; worthless; 'beastly'.

rotten An objectionable person. Ex *rot*, n. and *rotten*.

rough as a sand-bag (Of a story) much exaggerated; (of a person) uncouth or objectionable: military.

rough house Disorder; a noisy disturbance or struggle: coll. U.S., anglicized ca. 1910.

rough-house, v. To treat roughly: coll., orig. U.S.; anglicized ca. 1914.—Hence, to act noisily or violently: coll.

rough-neck, roughneck A rough, ignorant fellow: U.S., anglicized ca. 1910: coll.

rough on Hard for; bearing hardly on: coll.: U.S., anglicized ca. 1885.

rough up A violent quarrel, a 'free for all'.

round the bend   Crazy; mad. In 1957, the intensive *round the bend —and back again* was coined. Ex *Harpic*, a water-closet cleanser, advertised to '(clean) round the bend', whence the variant *clean round the bend*. The synonymous 'Harpic' lasted only a few years.

round the houses   Trousers: rhyming s.

rouse, v.i.   (Pronounced *rouss*.) To 'grouse', to scold (v.i.), esp. if coarsely: Australian. Perhaps ex *rouse a person*, to anger him. Constructed with *on* (a person).—(Also **roust**.) V.t., 'to upbraid with many words' (C. J. Dennis): Australian.

row   A disturbance; a noisy quarrel: now coll. Origin obscure. Hence, a noise.

row, v.   To make a disturbance; to quarrel.—To scold severely, to reprimand (v.t.); to criticize harshly or sharply: now coll.

royally   Splendidly; excellently: coll.: by 1945, rather ob.

rozzer; occ. **rosser**   A policeman: c. > low s.

rub-a-dub, n. & v.   A 'sub', to 'sub' (advance wages): workmen's rhyming s.—A 'pub'; a club: rhyming s.

rub-a-dub-dub   A public-house; night club: rhyming s.

rub down   To search (a prisoner) by running the hands over his body.

rub in   To emphasize annoyingly; insist vexatiously or unkindly upon; remind naggingly of, esp. as *rub it in*.

rubber(-)neck; (-)necking   A very inquisitive person; excessive curiosity: U.S.; anglicized ca. 1905. Ex stretching and swivelling one's neck.

rube; reub, reuben or **Reuben**   A country bumpkin: U.S., anglicized by 1931. Cf. *hick* (ex *Richard*).

ruck on   To 'split on a pal'; blab about (a person): c. > low s.

ruction   A disturbance, uproar, noisy quarrel, 'row': now coll. Ex *insurrection*.

rugged   Uncomfortable, characterized by hardship, 'tough'. 'The first night was a bit rugged—there being no bed, no conveniences in the hut.'

rugger   Rugby football: s. >, ca. 1910, coll. Ex *Rugby*, by Oxford-*er*.

rule over, run the (occ. **a**)   To search: c. >, ca. 1910, gen. s.

rum   Queer, odd, eccentric; strange; disreputable, questionable. A very old word, originally meaning 'excellent', of unknown origin.

rum cove   A very strange fellow; a 'queer fish'; orig. low.

rum go   A puzzling and not too respectable contretemps; a mysterious (not merely because wholly unexpected) occurrence or, esp., development of a plot, situation, etc.

rumble   To detect; fathom, understand. 'I soon rumbled he was in it when I heard . . .' Cf. *tumble to*, by which *tumble* may have been suggested.

rumbustious Boisterous: coll. Prob. a perversion of *robust*.

rummy Odd; singular. Ex *rum*, adj.

rumour!, it's a; often **'s a rumour** A military c.p. (1915–18) in retort on an opinion expressing a very well-known fact or on 'a statement emphatically (and, usually, disagreeably) true'.

rumpus An uproar; 'row', quarrel: coll. Prob. it is echoic.

run To charge with a 'crime': naval and military. Ex *run in*.—To arrest: military > gen. s.—To let the water run into (the bath): domestic coll.

run, get or **give the** To be discharged—to discharge—from employment.

run, on the Wanted by the police.

run out on To leave (someone) in the lurch: coll.

run (something) **fine** (Esp. *run it fine*.) To leave only a very small margin (esp. of time): coll.

run the show To 'manage' an enterprise, entertainment, etc.

run to seed; occ. hyphenated Shabby: coll.

run up the wall; make (someone) To become bewildered or scared or crazy; to cause someone to do so. Perhaps ex a famous exercise in Commando training.

rush, v.t. To cheat (gen. *rush out of*); esp. to charge extortionately: since ca. 1910, coll.

rush of brains to the head, (s)he's had a A c.p., depreciatory of a sudden bright idea.

rush one's fences To be impetuous: 'County' coll. Ex the j. of hunting.

rusty Ill-tempered; annoyed: coll.

rux Bad temper; (a gust of) anger, passion: Public Schools'. Either ex Lincolnshire *ruck*, a noise, a racket, or ex Kentish *have one's ruck up*, to be angry.

S

sack To dismiss one from employment or office; hence, *get* or *give the sack*. To expel; Public Schools'.—Bed; esp., *hit the sack*.

sack, the order of the Esp. as *get* or *give* (occ. *bestow, confer*) *the order* . . . A dismissal from employment, a discharge from office, a being discarded by sweetheart or mistress (rarely lover).

sahib A 'white man', a thoroughly honourable gentleman: mainly in the Services. Since ca. 1925, often derisive of 'Public School' morals and mentality. Ex Arabic and Urdu respectful address to Europeans.

sail into; v.i. sail in To attack, e.g. with one's fists; to begin vigorously on (e.g. a meal); to enter (a building, a room, etc.).

sailor's farewell A parting curse: nautical, military: C. 20. Also *sailor's blessing* and *soldier's farewell*.

salmon & trout Stout (the drink): rhyming s.

salt, n. A sailor; esp. one of long experience, when usually *old salt* (as in Hughes, 1861): coll. Occ., though by 1910, ob.: *saltwater*.

salt, v. To insert in the account books fictitious entries with a view to enhancing the value of a business to a prospective buyer: commercial. (Esp. *salt the books*.) Prob. suggested by:—In mining, to sprinkle or plant an exhausted or a bogus claim with precious dust, nuggets or gems: orig. s.; by 1910, coll. and now verging on S.E.—to introduce secretly into (a meeting) persons to oppose the speaker.

salt-cellar (Esp. in pl.) A very deep hollow, above the collar-bone, in the female neck: coll.

salt down or **away** To put by or store (money) away. Ex *salt*, to preserve with salt.

salt horse (or **beef**) **squire** A warrant as opp. a commissioned officer: naval; mid-C. 19–early 20.

salvage A military synonym of to *make* (steal), *scrounge, souvenir, win*. By meiosis.

Sam Hill Hell, e.g. 'What the Sam Hill?': Cockney euphemism.

samey Monotonous: coll.

san A sanatorium: coll.

sand Salt: nautical.—Sugar: Canadian.

sandman is coming, the Addressed to, or remarked of, children showing signs of sleepiness: a nursery coll. Ex rubbing eyes as if sand were in them.

sanfairyann! or **san fairy Ann!** It doesn't matter: military c.p.: from late 1914; † by 1939. A perversion of Fr. *ça ne fait rien* (that makes no odds). Variants: san fairy, san fairy Anna, and (Aunt) Mary Ann.

Santy Santa Claus: coll., mostly Canadian.

sardine tin A submarine: naval (lower deck).

sarga; sarge Sergeant: military coll.; *sarga* only, *sarge* mostly, in address.

sarky *Sarca*stic: (low) coll.

sauce Impudence, impertinence: coll. and dial. Hence, also v.

saucepan lid A pound sterling: rhyming s. (on *quid*).—A Jew: rhyming s. (on *Yid*).—A child: rhyming s. (on *kid*).—A mild deception, a 'leg-pulling'; hence also v., as in 'Now you're saucepan-lidding me': rhyming s. (on *kid*).

saucy Impudent or rude; impertinent: coll.—Hence, smart, stylish: coll.

sausage, v. To cash; esp. *sausage a goose's*, to cash a cheque. For *sausage and mash*, rhyming s., to cash; moreover, *goose's = goose's neck*, rhyming s. for a cheque. Cf.:

sausage, not have a To be penniless, esp. temporarily.

savage, adj. Furiously angry; unsparing in speech: mostly coll.

saved by the bell Saved by a lucky intervention: coll.; often as a c.p. Ex the bell signifying the end of a round in a boxing match.

saver A prudent covering bet: the turf.

savvy; also **sabby, sabe, savey, savie, savvey, scavey** Common sense or gumption; hence, acuteness, cleverness. Sp. *sabe usted*, do you know; imm. ex the v. *savvy*.

sawbones A surgeon.

sawn off (Of a person) short; small: Services' (esp. R.A.F.) coll.

sax A saxophone.

say!; I say! An introductory interjection; a mere exclamation: coll.

scab A workman refusing to strike, esp. one working while his companions are on strike: orig. U.S., anglicized ca. 1880. Hence as v.

scalawag; usually **scallawag, scallyway** A ne'er-do-well or disreputable fellow; a scoundrel. (Frequently playful like *rascal*.) U.S. s. anglicized ca. 1860 and >, ca. 1910, coll. Origin doubtful.

scale (also **scale off**) To run away; depart hurriedly or furtively; to disappear of one's own motion: mostly Colonial (esp. Australian).

Scapa Flow Folk-etymological elaboration of **scarper**, as if rhyming s. on 'to *go*': since ca. 1918.

scarce, make oneself To absent oneself, disappear: coll.

scare up To find, discover (e.g. *scare up money*): coll. Ex shooting game-birds.

scarper To run away: Parlary and Cockney s. Ex It. *scappare*. On the stage, it = to leave a play without giving notice.

scarper the letty To leave one's lodgings without paying: Parlary >, by 1900, theatrical.

scat! Go away: coll. Ex *scatter*.

scatty (Not very) mad; crazy: proletarian. Ex *scatter-brained*.

schizo A schizophrenic: psychologists', esp. psychiatrists', coll.

schlenter Dubious, untrustworthy; make-believe: South African: c. >, by 1900, low s. as n.: imitation gold; only in pl., imitation diamonds. Ex Dutch *slenter*, a trick.

schol A scholarship.

school A number or a group of persons met together in order to gamble.

schoolie or **-y** An instructor: naval coll.—An Education Officer: Services' coll.

schooner on the rocks 'A cooked joint surrounded by potatoes': naval.

scoff Food: South African coll. Ex Cape Dutch. Hence, a meal: now fairly gen. Also as v.: to eat voraciously; to eat; hence, to seize greedily, to plunder.

scoop News obtained and printed in advance of a rival newspaper: journalistic: U.S., anglicized ca. 1890: s. >, ca. 1920, coll.— A lucky stroke in business. Both senses have a corresponding v.

scoot To go (away) hurriedly or with sudden speed: orig. U.S.; now coll. Loosely, to go, to depart.

scorcher An exceedingly hot day: coll. Often a *regular scorcher*.

score, n. The gaining of points in games: coll. Hence, a notable or successful 'hit' in debate, argument, or keen business: likewise coll. Also as v.

scot A very irritable or quickly angered person. (Rather ob.) Hence, *scot*, a temper, or passion of irritation.

Scotch mist A sarcastic c.p. of the Services (esp. the R.A.F.), implying that one is either 'seeing things' or failing to see things he ought to see. ' "Can't you see my tapes? What do you think they are

—Scotch mist?" Hence, of noise, as in "That?"—"Well, it wasn't
Scotch mist." '

Scotch peg A leg: rhyming s.

scotty Angry; apt to grow easily annoyed. (Cf. *paddy*.)

scout, good A good, a trustworthy or helpful person: U.S.,
anglicized ca. 1920.

Scowegian (Pron. *Scow-wegian*.) A Scandinavian: Canadian
and nautical. Ex *Scandinavian + Norwegian*.

scrag To manhandle; properly (as in Rugby football), to twist the
neck of a man whose head is conveniently held under one's arm.
Hence, also n. Ex dial.

scram! Clear out!: U.S.; anglicized among devotees of the
cinema, ca. 1930. Prob. ex *scramble*.

scrambled eggs The gold oak-leaves on peak of the cap of any
officer from Group-Captain upwards: R.A.F.

scran Food, esp. broken victuals; a meal; bread-and-butter:
military.

scrap A scrimmage; fisticuffs. Hence as v.

scrape A shave: jocular coll.

scrape, bread and Bread with but a smear of butter: orig. schools'
coll.

scream An extremely ridiculous or funny person or thing, often
a perfect s.

screeve Any piece of writing; a begging letter. A drawing in
chalk on the pavement: orig., c.: from ca. 1855. Ex the v. V.t., to
write (esp. a begging letter).—Ex It. *scrivere*. Whence, v.i., draw on
the pavement with chalk; orig. c. Hence, *screeving*, n.

screever One who, for a living, writes begging letters; a 'pavement artist': orig., c. Ex *screeve*, v.

screw A skeleton key: c.: (Slightly ob.)—Hence, a turnkey or
prison warder: c., then low s.—Wages, salary.

screw, v. To break into (a building) by using a skeleton key;
hence, v.i. to burgle; also, to keep watch for one's burglar-con-
federate: c. and police s.—Hence, to look at: grafters'.

screwball, adj. and n. (An) eccentric: Canadian; adopted ex U.S.
Perhaps from billiards or snooker.

screwed Tipsy.

screwed on right or **the right way, have one's head** To be shrewd
and businesslike; be able to look after oneself: coll.

screwy Crazy, mad; (very) eccentric: proletarian.

scrimshank; occ. **skrim-,** v.i. To shirk work: military. Prob. a
back-formation ex:

scrimshanker; occ. **skrimshanker** A shirker: military. Origin unknown. Hence, *scrimshanking*, n.

scrounge, v.t.   To hunt for; cadge, to get by wheedling; to acquire illicitly; hence, to steal; also v.i.: military, then from ca. 1920, fairly gen. Ex dial, *scrunge*, to steal (esp. apples). Hence: *scrounge*, n., as in *do a scrounge*; *scrounger*; *scrounging*, adj. and n.

scrub   Esp. in *scrub it!*, cancel it!; forget it!: Services'. To wash it out (as, e.g., with a scrubbing brush).

scrub round   To agree to forget; to omit, to cancel, ignore: Services'. Also *scrub all round*.

scrumptious   First rate, excellent, 'glorious'.

scug   An untidy or ill-mannered or morally undeveloped boy; a shirker at games; one 'undistinguished in person, in games, or social qualities': Eton and Harrow.

scuppered   Killed, dead in battle: naval, hence military.

scutter   To go hastily and fussily, or excitedly, or timorously: coll. and dial.

scuttle   An undignified withdrawal: political.

sea-lawyer   A captious and argumentative, or a scheming, fo'c's'le hand: nautical coll.

sea miles than you've had (or **eaten**) **Pusser's peas, I've done** (or **had**) **more**   A boast of comparatively long service at sea: naval. (*Pusser*, purser.) Cf. the Army's and R.A.F.'s *get your knees brown!* (hot-country service) and *get some in!* (general).

search me!, or **you can** (or **may**) **search me!**   I don't know: c.p.: C. 20 (U.S., anglicized by 1910); slightly ob. by 1939. (*But you won't find it.*)

sec   A second: coll.—A secretary: coll.

sedulous ape   A writer that, aiming at a certain periodical, imitates the style, arrangement, etc., of its articles: authors' coll.

see off   To 'tell off', reprimand, scold severely.

see off   To dcfeat (in, e.g., a boat race): naval, hence also gen.

see off   To attend to (a task, an emergency) effectually.

sell   A successful deception or hoax; hence, a planned hoax; also, (great) disappointment.

sell-out   A contest for which all the seats are sold: sporting coll.

sell the pass   To give away an advantage to one's opponent(s); to betray one's own side: coll. Ex mountain warfare.

see (a newspaper) **to bed**   To set the presses in motion for printing of an edition: journalistic.

send-off   A God-speed; hence, a start in life, in business, etc.; occ. as adj.: coll.

send up   To commit to prison.

sentiments!, them's my   That's what I think about it: jocular c.p.

sergeant!, kiss me   A military c.p., intended to annoy and gen. uttered during the sergeant's final rounds of barracks, tents, etc.

S.S.D.—L

Either derisive of nursemaids' invitations or, less prob., reminiscent of Nelson's *kiss me, Hardy*.

sergeant-major A zebra: South African. Ex its very distinct stripes.—In the game of crown and anchor, the crown: military.

sergeant-major's Tea; orig., strong tea esp. if good, then tea drunk between meals: military. (The S.M. can get tea almost whenever he desires it.)

serve out, v. To take revenge on, to punish; retaliate on (a person) *for* .... boxing s. > gen. coll.

set, adj.; esp. **all set** Ready and willing; thoroughly prepared: coll.

set about To attack, set upon: coll.

set back To cost (a person) so much: U.S., anglicized by 1932.

set-out A set or display of china, plate, etc.; (of food) a 'spread'; a 'turn-out', i.e. a carriage 'and all': mainly sporting coll.—A person's costume or manner of dressing; an outfit, equipment; a public show or performance; a party; hence, a company or a set of people: coll.— A to-do or fuss: (low) coll.

settler A crushing remark; a knock-down blow; hence, any 'finisher' whatsoever: coll.

seven years are the worst, the first; often prefaced with **cheer up!** A military c.p. of 1915–18; then civilian.

Sexton (Blake) Cake: rhyming s.

sez you!; occ. **says you!** A derisive c.p.: orig. U.S., anglicized ca. 1928; by 1950, ob.

shackles Remnants and scrapings of meat in a butcher's shop: proletarian. Prob. ex *shackle*, abbr. *shackle-bone*, a knuckle-bone. Hence, stew; meat-soup: military.

shady Disreputable; not quite honest, not at all honourable: coll.

shagged (out) Weary, exhausted.

shake, n. Generic for instantaneous or very rapid action: coll. Esp. *in a shake, in a brace* or *a couple* (1840) *of shakes, in two shakes, in the shake of a lamb's tail* or jocularly *of a dead lamb's tail.*—Hence, a moment. 'Wait a shake.'

shake, v. To rob (a person); to steal (something): low.

shake, v. To stir up (the sluggards): Services', esp. naval, coll.

shake a leg (Esp. in imperative.) To hurry: coll., mainly military and nautical.

shakes, the Any illness or disease marked by trembling limbs and muscles: coll.—Hence, delirium tremens: coll.—Hence, extreme nervousness: coll.

shaky do A mismanaged affair, e.g. a bungled raid, work badly done, something that has—or very nearly has—serious consequences; also, a risky, haphazard raid necessitated by general policy; a (very) dangerous raid: Services', esp. R.A.F. Hence, an arrangement or agreement or contract that, apparently fair, is, in the fact, one-sided.

shambles Uproar; confusion; 'mess': Services' (mostly officers'). By 1945, also civilian. Ex the definition of S.E. *shambles* as, e.g., 'bloody confusion'.

shame to take the money, (it's) a That's money very easily come by: c.p.

shant A quart or a pot; a pot of liquor (esp. *shant of gatter*, a pot of beer): low s.

shark (Also *black shark*.) Lawyer: nautical coll.—A sardine: jocular nautical.—A professional punter: bookmakers'.

sharp end, the; the blunt end The bows—the stern—of the ship: naval jocular, in derision of landlubberly ignorance.

shattered; shattering Nervy, nervous; tiresome, upsetting, boring, unpleasant: Society > gen. middle-class. E. Waugh, *Decline and Fall*, 1928, 'My dear, how too shattering for you'.

shaver A fellow, chap: coll. Now mostly of young boy, or of a youth.

shawly An Irish fish wife, esp. of Dublin: Anglo-Irish. Ex the great shawl they wear.

shay sho!, you don't A jocular form of 'really!' Ex tipsy distortion of *say* and *so*. Also *I should shay sho!*

Sheba An attractive girl or woman; esp. as the counterpart of *sheikh* (as below): ca. 1926–39. Ex the Queen of Sheba, reputedly alluring.

shed To give; give away (something of little value): coll.

Sheeny, or s. A Jew; also as adj. Perhaps ex Yiddish (ex Ger.) *schön*, used in praising wares.—Hence, a pawnbroker.

sheikh; often incorrectly sheik A 'he-man'; hence a girl's young man': ca. 1926–39.

sheila A girl: Australian, hence New Zealand.

shekels Coin; money in gen.: coll. Ex the most important Hebrew silver coin.

shell-back A mature sailor, esp. if tough and knowledgeable: nautical coll.

shell out To disburse; pay (out); as v.i., to hand over what is due or expected, pay up: coll.

shemozzle; occ. shimozzel, s(c)hlemozzle, chimozzle A difficulty or misfortune; a 'row': East End, orig. and mainly. Ex Yiddish. Hence, loosely, 'an affair of any sort': proletarian and military.

shemozzle (etc.), v. To make off, decamp; generally pronounced 'mozzle'.

shenan(n)igan or -in; occ. shenan(n)iken, shi- (with either ending), and **shenanecking** Trickery, 'funny' games: orig. U.S.; anglicized ca. 1890. Origin obscure.

shevoo; often written **chevoo** A party, esp. in the evening: now mostly Australian. Prob. ex Fr. *chez vous.*

shew a leg (Esp. in imperative.) To rise from bed: nautical > also military. Lit., show a leg from under the bedclothes.

shicer A worthless person: low, ex Yiddish.—Hence, a welsher or defaulter: Australian racing.

shift To travel speedily: (mostly Australian) coll. 'He can shift!'

shicker, v.i.; occ. **shikker** To drink liquor; get drunk. Ex Hebrew *shikkur,* tipsy.

shickered; shick Tipsy.

shimmy A chemise: coll. The game of *chemin de fer:* Society.

shindig or **shindy** A spree or noisy merrymaking.

shine A fuss, commotion, row: coll. Esp. *make* (or *kick up) a shine.* Perhaps ex *shine,* brilliance, influenced by *shindy.*

shiners Money; coins, esp. guineas or sovereigns.—Jewels.—A cleaning-up parade: military.

shingle short, have a To have a 'tile loose', to be mentally deficient: Australian s. >, ca. 1910, gen. coll.

Shinner(s) A Sinn Feiner. Sinn Fein leaders and adherents: Anglo-Irish coll.

ship An aircraft: R.A.F.

ship, old A jocular address to a sailor: orig. and mostly nautical to a former *ship*-mate.

ship's Naval cocoa or tobacco: naval coll.

shiralee; shirralee A swag, or bundle of blankets, etc.: Australian. Ex an Aboriginal word.

shirt, lose one's; get one's shirt out To become very angry.

shirt on, put one's To bet all one's money on (a horse).

shirty Angry (temporarily); ill-tempered (by nature); apt to become quickly angered.

shocker An (extremely) objectionable person. Also 'complete shocker': a hopeless, a terrible, individual or object: Services' > gen.

shocking, adv. Shockingly: coll.

shoe A tyre, esp. of a motor-car: garages'.

shofel, shopel Counterfeit money; hence adj.: Cockney. Ex Yiddish *schofel,* worthless stuff.

shoot Amount, number; esp. the whole shoot.—Dismissal, esp. in *get* or *give* (a person) *the shoot.*

shoot! Go ahead; speak! In making a film, *shoot!* = use your camera now: orig. U.S.

shoot a—rarely **the**—**line** To talk too much, esp. to boast: R.A.F. since ca. 1928, Army officers' since 1940. Perhaps ex theatrical *shoot one's lines* (declaim them vigorously).

shoot down—shoot down in flames—shoot down from a great height

To defeat in an argument; to be right on a question of procedure, dress, drill, etc.: R.A.F. Obviously ex aerial warfare.—Hence, *shoot down*, as in '*Shot down*. Pulled up for not saluting or for being improperly dressed'; in gen., 'to reprimand a subordinate': R.A.F.

shoot (off) one's mouth   To talk boastfully or indiscreetly; to tell all one knows: orig. U.S.; anglicized, thanks to the 'talkies', in 1930–31.

shoot the amber   (Of a motorist) to increase speed when the amber light is showing, in order to pass before the red ('stop') light comes on: motorists' s. > coll.

shop   An engagement, 'berth': theatrical.

shop, v.   To lay information on which a person is arrested: c. > low s.

shoppy   A shop-girl or, less often, -man: coll.

short, n.   Same as *something short.*—A short film: coll.—A short circuit: electricians' coll.

short, something   (A drink of) undiluted spirits: coll.

short & sweet, like a donkey's gallop   Very short.

shot   A dram (of spirits): coll. (Ex U.S.) Dose of a drug; an injection.

shot, like a   Very quickly; immediately; hence, very willingly: coll.

shot down, ppl. adj.   Beaten in an argument: aircraft engineers': since 1917.

shot first, I'll see (him, her, gen.**) you; shot if—, I'll (or may I) be**   Mildly imprecatory or strongly dissenting.

shout, n.   'A call to a waiter to replenish the glasses of a company: hence, a turn in paying for a round of drinks. Also, a free drink given to all present by one of the company' (Morris); hence, one's turn to entertain another. 'It's my shout this time.' To stand drinks to even one person.

shout, n.   A summons (to duty): nautical, esp. stewards', coll.—An alarm: fire brigades'.

shove, the   A dismissal; esp., *get the shove* and *give the shove*, to be dismissed, to dismiss.

shove off   To depart: coll.: C. 20. Ware. Ex nautical sense, prob. on *push off.*

shover, also **shuvver**   A chauffeur: jocular coll.

show   Any public display; hence, a matter, affair, 'concern'; a group or association of persons, esp. in *boss the show*: coll.—A fight, an attack: military.

show, bad; good show   Phrase expressive of disapprobation and approval or praise: Services' (mostly officers') > gen.

show, do a To go to a public entertainment.

show, put up a To give a good account of oneself.

show, steal the To gain most of the applause: music-hall and variety.

show off, v.i. To act, talk, ostentatiously: coll.

shower!, what a What a poor, scruffy lot of men!: Services' c.p.

shrewdy A shrewd, esp. a cunning, person: coll.

shriek An exclamation-mark: coll.

shunt To shift the responsibility of (a thing) on to another person: coll.

shut-eye Sleep.

shut up (Esp. in imperative.) To cease talking; stop making a noise: now coll.

shy, v. V.i., to throw a missile jerkily or carelessly: coll.—V.t., to throw, toss, jerk: coll. Hence also n.

shy of Short of money; hence, of provisions: mostly Australian.

sick Disgusted; exceedingly annoyed or chagrined. Ex *sick* (*of*), thoroughly weary (of).—(Of a ship) 'in quarantine on suspicion of infectious disease' (Bowen): nautical coll.

sickening Unpleasant; inconvenient; (of persons) rude: Society coll.

sicks (occ. **sick**), **the** A feeling of nausea; esp. in *give one the sick(s)*, to get on a person's nerves.

side Conceit, swagger, esp. *put on side*, to give oneself airs.

side-kick A close companion; a mate, occ. an assistant, on a job: Canadian and Australian.

side-lever, gen. in pl. Hair growing down the cheek at the side of the ear.

side, on the In 1939–45 common in the British Army as a whole in sense 'additionally but very discreetly'.

sidy Conceited.

sig A signaller: military.

sight As adv., as in 'a sight too clever'. An oddity, often pejoratively ('You've made yourself a perfect sight'): coll.

sight, put out of To consume; esp., to eat: coll.

silence To knock down, to stun; hence, to kill.

silly; silly Billy (usually affectionate). A silly person: coll.

Simon Pure, the or **the real** The real or authentic person or thing: coll. Ex Simon Pure, that Quaker who, in Mrs Centlivre's *A Bold Stroke for a Wife*, 1717, is, for part of the play, impersonated by another character.

simp A *simp*leton: coll.: U.S., anglicized by 1931; by 1945, slightly ob.

sin bosun, the The ship's chaplain: naval.

since Pontius was a pilot, as in 'He's been in that mob since . . .': R.A.F. c.p., testifying to long service. A pun on *Pontius Pilate*. Of the same semi-erudite order are: *since the Air Ministry was a tent* and, referring to Air Ministry Orders, *since A.M.O.s were carved on stone.*

Sinbad the sailor   A tailor: rhyming s.

sin, like   Very vigorously; furiously. Here, *sin* = the devil.

sing small   To make less extravagant or conceited claims or statements: coll.

sink, v.   To 'lower' or drink.

sinker   A small, stodgy cake of the doughnut kind.

Sir Garnet; often **all Sir Garnet**   All right, whether as predicate or as answer to a question: from ca. 1880.

sis   Sister: coll.: mostly in address: orig. U.S.; anglicized before 1887.

sissie, sissy; occ. **cissy**   A namby-pamby boy. Ex *sissy*, sister.

sit-me-down   One's posterior: semi-nursery, semi-jocular.

sit on   To check, to snub.

sit, or **be sitting, pretty**   To be in a very advantageous position. Ex sitting hens?

sit up & take notice   To take (a sudden) interest: coll.; orig. U.S., anglicized by 1900.

sitter   In cricket a very easy catch; an easy mark or task; a certainty.—Hence *for a sitter*, certainly, assuredly.

sixer   Six months' hard labour: low.—Anything counting as six, esp. in cricket: coll.

size up   To gauge, estimate; to regard carefully (in order to form an opinion of): coll.

skates, put on (one's); get one's skates on   To hurry; evade duty; desert: military >, by 1919, gen.

skating rink   A bald head: jocular.

skedaddle   To run away, decamp, hastily depart: coll. Perhaps echoic.

sketch   A person whose appearance offers a very odd sight: coll. 'Lor', what a sketch she was!'

sketchy   Unsubstantial (meal); flimsy (building, furniture); imperfect: coll.

skew-gee   Crooked; squinting: low coll. Ex *on a* or *the*.

skew-whiff, adj. and adv.   Crooked(ly); askew.—Hence, tipsy.

skin, v.t.   At cards, to win from a person all his money; to fleece. —Also *skin alive*. To thrash; orig. U.S., anglicized ca. 1895.

skin-game   A swindling game.

skint   Very short of or wholly without money: jocular and military. For *skinned.*

skip A dance: Anglo-Irish coll.—A portmanteau; a bag, a valise: grafters'.—Short for:—

skip it! Don't trouble! Forget it!: coll.: adopted ca. 1939 from U.S.A.

skipper A master, a boss: coll.—Ex *skipper*, a sea captain. A military captain: naval, hence military, hence R.A.F. coll. Always *the skipper* and not *Skipper So-and-So.*

skirt, a bit of A woman, a girl.

skite A boaster; boasting: Australian. Ex *blather-skite.* Hence, *skiter.*

skive, v.i. and v.t. To evade a duty: military.

skivvy; occ. **skivey** A maid servant, esp. a rough 'general'. Ex *slavey,* q.v.

skrimshank, -er See *scrimshank, -er.*

skunk A mean, paltry, or contemptible wretch: coll.: orig. U.S.; anglicized ca. 1870. Ex the stink-emitting N. American beast.

sky-pilot A clergyman, esp. if working among seamen: nautical s. >, by 1895, gen. s. >, by 1910, gen. coll.He pilots men to a haven in the skies. Hence, loosely, an evangelist.

sky the towel To give in, yield: boxers' >, by 1910, soldiers' coll.

slab A slice of bread and butter: streets'.

slack Impertinence, decided 'cheek': dial.> s. > coll. Ex the † *slack-jaw.* A period of inactivity or laziness: coll. Hence, *slacker.* Ex *slack period* or *spell.*

slam To strike or punch (someone).

slang To abuse, scold, violently: coll.

slap-happy Boisterously happy; esp., recklessly happy: coll.: adopted in 1942 from U.S.A. Back-slappingly happy.

slap-up, adj. Excellent; superior, first-rate.

slash, v.i. To cut a person across the face with a razor: c. > low s.

slasher Any person or thing exceptional, esp. if exceptionally severe: coll; slightly ob.

slats The ribs: U.S., whence Australian and Canadian. Ex shape.

slaughter A wholesale dismissal of employees: workmen's.

slavey, A hard-worked 'general' servant.

slick, adj. Not-quite-honestly smart: coll., adopted—via Canada —ex U.S.—Neat or smooth; attractive, desirable: Canadian: adopted, ca. 1946, ex U.S. 'Boy, look at Jane! There's a slick chick.'

slide (Esp. in the imperative.) To decamp: coll.: U.S., anglicized ca. 1890. Occ. *slide out.*

slimy Deceitful; treacherous: coll.

sling To utter: coll.—To use (e.g. slang); relate (a story): s. >, ca. 1910, coll.

sling a yarn To relate a story: now coll.

sling language or **words**   To talk: now coll.

sling off, v.i.   To utter abuse or cheek or impertinence; v.t. with *at.*

sling one's hook   To make off; decamp.

sling the bat or **the language**   To speak the vernacular (esp. of the foreign country—orig. India—where one happens to be): military.

slinky   (Of gait) slyly smooth; glidingly and unobtrusively sensuous or voluptuous. Ex *slink,* to move stealthily.

slip, v.i., esp. **be slipping**   To weaken, physically; go downhill, fig.; lose grip, ground, status, etc.: coll.

slip into   To begin punching a (person) vigorously.

slip it across or **over** (a person)   To hoodwink.

slip up, v.i.   To make a mistake, to fail: U.S., anglicized ca. 1910 as a coll.

slippy   Quick, spry, nimble; esp. *look slippy.*

slob   A 'softy', a fool, a (stupid) lout: in New Zealand, Australia, England.

slog   (A period of) hard, steady work: coll.—A hard punch or blow; (at cricket) a hard hit: coll. Ex the corresponding vv., whence, in turn, *slogger* and *slogging.*

slope, v.   To make off; run away, decamp: coll.—Hence, to leave (lodgings) without paying.

sloppy   Very sentimental: coll. Cf. *slushy.*

sloppy   Slack, careless, negligent.

slosh   To hit, esp. resoundingly. Echoic.

sloshy   Emotional, sentimental; corresponding n.—*slosh.*

slow   Old-fashioned; hence, (of things) tedious, dull, boring; (of persons) humdrum; dull: coll.

slug   To strike heavily: dial. > coll. Cf. *slog.*

slummy   One who lives in a slum: coll.

slush   Food: nautical.—Counterfeit paper money: c., orig. U.S., anglicized ca. 1924; by 1945, also low. s.

slushy   A ship's cook: nautical coll. Ex *slush,* refuse fat.

slushy, adj.   Extremely sentimental: coll. Ex *slushy,* washy, rubbishy. Cf. *sloppy,* q.v.

sly-boots   A sly or crafty person: coll.

smack   A 'go'; an attempt (*at*): coll.

smack in the eye   A rebuff, refusal; severe disappointment; setback: coll., esp. in Australia.

smack it about!   Get a move on!: naval.

smacker   £1, note or coin.

small beer of, think no   To have a high opinion of (persons, mostly oneself): coll.

small-parter   A player of small parts: theatrical.

smarm; occ. smalm, v.i.   To behave with fulsome flattery or insincere politeness: coll. Ex *smalm, smarm,* to smooth down, as hair with pomade. The word prob. represents a blend:? '*smarten* with *cream*'.

smarmy   Apt to flatter fulsomely, speak toadyingly or with courteous insincerity: coll.—Ex *smarmy,* (of hair) sleek, plastered down: coll.

smart Alec   A know-all, an offensively smart person: coll; orig. U.S., anglicized by 1930. Also *smart Alick.*

smarty   A would-be clever, cunning, or witty person: U.S., anglicized—as a coll.—ca 1905.

smasher   Anything unusually excellent; an extremely pretty girl.

smashing   Excellent; very attractive: the adj. corresponding to *smasher.*

smell   To make smelly, fill with offensive odour: coll. 'That cigar smells the place out.'—(Esp. with negative.) To approach at all, be even compared with in ability. 'Smith can't smell Grimmett as a batsman.'

smelly   'Shady', dishonourable, illicit. Perhaps after *fishy.*

smithereens   Small pieces or fragments: coll. and dial., orig. Anglo-Irish.

smoke, like   Rapidly.

smoke, the (big)   London.

smoke-ho; -oh; smoko   A cessation from work in order nominally to smoke, certainly to rest: coll. Hence, a cup of tea: Australian coll.

smoodge, v.i.   To flatter, wheedle, speak with deliberate amiability: Australian. Perhaps ex Yiddish, but prob. ex 'to *smoothe*'. Hence, to make love, pay court: Australian. Hence, *smoodger,* the agent, and *smoodging,* the action.

smooth as a baby's bottom; like a b.b.   Smooth-shaven; (second only) expressionless: coll.

snaffle   To 'appropriate', to seize a thing for oneself: mostly military. Adopted from underworld.

snake-juice   Whiskey: Australian.

snakes, see   To have delirium tremens: U.S.; anglicized ca. 1900.

snak(e)y   Bad tempered: Australian.

snap out of it!   Wake up!; realize the truth!; 'be your age!': adopted, ca. 1933, from U.S.A.

snap, soft   An easy matter, business, project; an easy job: coll.

snappy!, make it   Look lively!: coll. (orig. U.S.).

snare   'To acquire; to seize; to win' (C. J. Dennis): Australian.

snazzy   Fashionable, smart: Australian: adopted, ca. 1943, ex U.S. servicemen. Also, by 1954, English s.—Perhaps a blend of *sn*appy + j*azzy.*

sneak   To filch; steal furtively: coll.—To tell tales (v.i.): schools':
by 1930, coll.

sneezed at, not to be   Not to be underrated, disregarded, despised:
coll.

snide (occ. **snyde**)   Anything spurious, esp. base coin or sham
jewellery: c. > low s.—Hence, a contemptible person: c. > low s.
Ex Yiddish.

sniffy   Scornful, disdainful: coll. and dial.

snifter   A dram. Prob. ex U.S. *snifter*, a small drink of spirits.—
Any thing or person excellent, or very big or strong. Ex dial. *snifter*,
a strong breeze.

snip   A bargain; a certainty; an easy win or acquisition; hence,
an easy job.

snitch   The nose: dial. and low s.—Hence (cf. *nose*, n.), an
informer, esp. by Queen's evidence: only in *turn snitch*.—To purloin.

snogging, be or go   To be—to go—courting a girl; to be or go
love-making: R.A.F.

snooker, v.   To delude, trick, 'be too much for'. Ex the game:
cf. S.E. *euchre*.

snoop; snoop around   To pry; go about slyly: orig. U.S.; anglicized, as a coll., ca. 1905; by 1935, virtually S.E. Ex the Dutch
snoepen. Hence *snooper, snooping*, one who does this, and the action;
also *snoopy*, adj.: all anglicized ca. 1920.

snooty   (Of persons) unpleasant; supercilious: Society and near-
Society, then gen. Adopted ex U.S.

snooze, v., hence also n.   To sleep, a sleep: c. > s. > coll. Origin
obscure.

snort   A 'pull'—a drink—of spirits: Society

snorter   Anything exceptional, esp. in size, severity, or strength:
coll.

snotty   A midshipman: nautical.

snotty, adj.   Apt to take offence; proudly conceited.

snow   Cocaine: U.S.; anglicized ca. 1920; c. >, ca. 1930, s.

snuff, up to   Alert; not easily tricked; shrewd: coll. Lit., of one
who knows to what dangerous uses snuff can be put.

snuff it, snuff out   To die: s. >, ca. 1900, coll. >, by 1920,
S.E.

snug   A bar-parlour at inn or 'public'.

snug as a bug in a rug   Very snug, cosy, comfortable: coll.

so-and-so   Objectionable person, as in 'that old so-and-so': coll.
Euphemistic.

so long!   Au revoir!: coll. (Origin obscure.)

soak   To charge (a person) an extortionate price; to tax heavily:
orig. U.S.; anglicized by 1914.—To borrow money from.

soap & water   Daughter: rhyming s.

soapy   Unctuous; ingratiating; given to 'soft soap'.

sob sister   A female writer of articles for the sensational news-papers, esp. a woman journalist replying to women readers' in-quiries: journalistic, adopted ca. 1930 from U.S.A.

sock   To hit; strike hard; drub, thrash.

sock in it!, put a   Be quiet!; stop talking, *it* being the offender's mouth: military >, by 1920, gen.

socks, pull up one's   To brace oneself, to make an effort. Ex that significant preparation for action.

soft, adj.   Half-witted: coll. and dial.—Foolishly benevolent or kind; constantly helping others without thinking of oneself: coll.

soft number   An easy task: military. Perhaps ex music.

soft soap   Flattery; 'blarney': U.S.; anglicized ca. 1860. Hence as v.

softie or **softy**   A silly, very simple, or weak-minded person: coll. and dial.

soldier bold   A cold: rhyming s.

solid   Severe; difficult: Australian and gen. coll.

solitary   Solitary confinement: prison s. >, by 1900, coll.

some, & then   And many, or much, in addition: U.S., anglicized by 1919. Prob. a mere elaboration of the Scots *and some*, and much more so, as in the 'She's as bonny as you and some' of lexicographer Jamieson.

some hopes!   It is *most* unlikely: a c.p.

something good   A good racing tip; hence, a profitable affair, a safe but not generally known investment: coll.

soogey   To scrub, to scour: naval, echoic—unless ex *squeegee*.

sooner   A shirker: naval. Ex *sooner dog*, one that would sooner feed than fight.

soppy   Foolishly sentimental: coll. Hence, *be soppy on*, to be foolishly fond of (a person).

sort, a bad or **a good**   A bad, a good, fellow or girl, woman: coll.

sort out; also, **take on**   To tease; leg-pull (v.t.): Cockneys'. To pick a quarrel with and use force upon someone: Services'. To choose (someone) for a job, esp. if unpleasant or arduous: Services'. In Australia, to reprove or reprimand (someone).

sound egg   A very 'decent' fellow. Denis Mackail, 1934, 'Another and infinitely superior sex still remained, full of stout fellows, sound eggs, and great guys.'

soup & gravy, the   The Navy: rhyming s.

soup, in the   In a difficulty; in trouble: coll.: orig. U.S. anglicized ca. 1895.

sourdough   An experienced old-timer in the north-west: Canadian;

by 1910, coll. It arose during the Yukon gold-rush and refers to the
sour dough carried for use in emergency.

sour(-)puss A morose person. Ex Am. *sourpuss*, a sour face.

souse A getting drunk; to get drunk.

south, put down Lit., to put into one's pocket; hence, to bank,
not to spend.

south-paw or **southpaw** A left-handed boxer: pugilistic: U.S.,
anglicized ca. 1934. Ex U.S. baseball s.

sov A sovereign (coin): coll. Hence, *half-sov*. By 1945 ob.

sozzled Tipsy. Prob. ex dial. *sozzle*, to mix in a sloppy manner.

spade A Negro. Ex the colour of the card-suit.

spades Coloured people, esp. Negroes and West Indians: low,
e.g. Teddy boys'. In cards, a 'dark' suit.

spank, v. To smack, slap, with the open hand; hence n.: coll.
and dial. Echoic.—To move quickly and briskly; to ride, drive,
smartly or stylishly at a smart trot or a graceful canter: dial. > coll.
Whence the adj. *spanking*.

spare, adj. Idle; loafing.

spark To send a wireless message to (ship or person): nautical
and wireless operators'.

sparks (Nickname.) A wireless operator. Ex electrical sparks.
The X-ray department: medical students'.

sparring partner, one's One's companion or friend: coll. Ex
pugilism.

spasm The verse of a song, stanza of a poem: jocular coll.

spats Those stream-lined covers over landing-wheels which are
in aircraft designed to reduce air-resistance.

speak the same language To have the same sort of upbringing,
hence the same general ideas: coll.

spec, on On chance; as, or at, a risk; esp. on the chance of making
a profit.

specimen A person: esp. with *bright, poor*, etc.

specs Spectacles for the sight.

speed-merchant One who motors at high speed: U.S.; anglicized ca. 1920.—Whence, a very fast bowler: cricketers'.

speedo A speedometer: motorists'.

spiel A hard-luck story: tramps' c. and low s. A grafter's patter.
Ex the corresponding v.

spieler; occ. **speeler** or **speiler** A gambler, esp. a card-sharper;
a professional swindler: Australia and New Zealand. Ex Ger. *spieler*,
player, esp. at cards, a gamester.—Hence, a glib and crafty fellow;
a 'weaver of hard luck stories'.

spiffing First-rate, excellent; (of dress) fine, smart, spruce: dial.
and s. > coll. By 1945, archaic.

spiflicate, or **spifflicate** 'To confound, silence, or dumbfound' (Grose); hence, to handle roughly, treat severely, to thrash; hence, to destroy, kill; hence, to do something mysterious (and unpleasant) to, often as a vague threat to children. Of unknown origin.

spiky Extreme in Anglo-Catholic dogma and practice: ecclesiastical. Ex the stiffness and sharpness of opinions and attitude.

spill, v. To cause to fall from vehicle or horse; hence, from a boat, a box, etc: coll. To confess, divulge: c. > low s.

spill the beans To blab; to divulge important facts; to confess; to lay information: U.S., anglicized by ca. 1927.

spin, go for a To go for a drive in a motor-car; occ. on a motor-cycle: coll.

Spit A Spitfire fighter 'plane.

spit & a drag, a A smoke on the sly: naval. Ex *spit and drag*, a cigarette: rhyming s. (on *fag*).

spit & polish Furbishing; meticulous cleaning: naval and esp. military: coll. >, ca. 1920, S.E.

spit out To confess: esp. *spit it out!*: coll.

spiv One who lives by his wits—within the law, for preference; orig. by 'the racing game': c. >, by 1935, low s.>, by 1950, coll. Ultimately akin to *spiffing*.

splash Ostentation; a dash; a sensation: coll.: esp. in *cut* or *make a splash*. Ex noisy diving. A small quantity of soda-water (added to whiskey, etc.): coll.

splendacious; splendiferous Very splendid, remarkably fine, magnificent; excellent: jocular coll.

splice, v. To join in matrimony: esp. in passive. Ex lit. nautical sense.

splice, sit on or **(upon) the** To play a strictly defensive bat: cricketers'.

split A split soda: coll.—Hence, a half-size bottle of mineral water; a half-glass of spirits: coll.—A division of profit, orig. of loot: c. > low s.

split, v.i. To turn informer, give evidence to the police: hence, to give evidence injurious to others. To divide, or share in, profits: low.

split, (at) full At full speed: coll.

split with To break off acquaintance with; to quarrel with: s. >, ca. 1910, coll. In C. 20, occ. absolutely, as in 'For good reasons, we don't wish to split.'

spondoolic(k)s, -ix; spondulicks (the most gen.), **-ics, -ix** Money; cash: U.S., anglicized ca. 1885.

sponge, chuck or **throw up the** To give in; submit: coll. Ex boxing.

spoof   A nonsensically hoaxing game. The name and the game were invented by Arthur Roberts the comedian (1852–1933).—Hence, humbug; hoaxing, or an instance of this.

spoof, v.t.   To hoax; humbug. Ex the n.

spoof, adj.   Hoaxing; humbugging. Ex the n. All three are, by 1960, slightly ob., except among those born before 1900.

spoon, v.i.   To make love, esp. if very sentimentally; hence, to flirt: coll.

sport   A 'good sport', one who subordinates his or her own personality or abilities to the gen. enjoyment: coll. Hence, *be a sport!* = don't be a spoil-sport!

sport, v.   To display in company or in public, showily or ostentatiously: s. > coll.—To shut (a door) esp. to signify 'Engaged': orig. and mainly university.

sporty   Sportsmanlike; sporting; generous: s. >, ca. 1920, coll.

spot   A drop of liquor: coll.—Hence, a small amount of; esp. *a spot of . . .*, e.g. lunch, hence of rest, work, pleasure, music, etc.: s. >, ca. 1930, coll.

spot, v.   To note (a person) as criminal or suspect: orig., underworld.—Hence, to guess (a horse) beforehand as the winner in a race: turf > gen. coll.—Hence, to espy; mark, note; recognize, discover, detect: coll.

spot, be in a   To be in a very difficult or dangerous position or condition: c. > gen. s.

spot, put on the   To determine and arrange the murder of: U.S., anglicized by 1930.

spout, up the   In pawn. Hence, in a bad way, bankrupt. (Of a bullet) in the rifle-barrel and ready to be fired: military.

sprat   A sixpence: by 1945, slightly ob. Prob. ex the smallness of the fish.

spread   A banquet; an excellent or a copious meal; hence, among sporting men, a dinner.

spree   A boisterous frolic; a period of riotous enjoyment. Origin problematic.

spring to   To be able to pay or give: hence, to be able to accomplish.

sprog, n.   A recruit: R.A.F. Prob. ex a recruit's confusion of 'sprocket' and 'cog', a sprocket being, like the recruit, a cog in a wheel. Hence also adj.

spruce, v.i.   To tell lies or 'tall stories'; v.t. to deceive thus: military. Hence, *sprucer*, one who does these things.

spruce up   To clean and dress oneself to go out or to go on parade: Regular Army coll.

spruik   'To deliver a speech, as a showman' (Dennis): Australian.

Perhaps ex Dutch *spreken*, to speak.—Whence *spruiker*, a plausible 'spouter'.

spud A potato. Origin hotly disputed.

spud-bashing Kitchen fatigue: Services'.

spun Exhausted, tired out. Checkmated; at a loss.

squalid A pejorative, synonymous with and prob. suggested by *filthy*: upper classes'.

square, v. To settle (a matter) satisfactorily: coll. Ex *square*, to balance (accounts).—Hence, to satisfy or win over, esp. by bribery or compensation; to get rid of thus: s. >, ca. 1910, coll.

square, n. An old-fashioned person, esp. about dancing and music: jazz-lovers': adopted, ca. 1938, ex U.S.—An honest citizen; anyone of healthily conventional morals and habits: Canadian: adopted, ca. 1955, ex U.S.—by 1958, also English.

square-bashing Drill, esp. by recruits on the parade ground: Army and R.A.F. The recruits 'bash' their rifles down.

square bit or **piece** A sweetheart: military. Ex:—2. **square bit, piece, pusher,** a respectable girl or young woman: low and military. Here, *bit* and *piece* = a girl or a woman. For *pusher* see *square-pusher*.

square one's yardarm To protect oneself in a manner inspectable by one's seniors: naval officers'.

square-pusher A decent girl: lower classes' >, by 1915, almost exclusively military; by 1939, ob.

square-pushing An instance, or the habit, of 'walking out' with a girl or young woman: military; by 1939, ob. Ex the military practice of strolling with nursemaids and other maids round the square.

squash To silence or snub (a person) crushingly: coll.

squeaker A foxhound: sporting.—A pig, esp. if young: coll.

squeeze A crowded assembly or (social) gathering: coll.—An escape, esp. if a narrow one: coll.—An illegal exaction: Anglo-Chinese coll.—An impression: police coll. Richard Keverne, *Menace*, 1933, 'Parry's "squeeze" of the key to the Bruges warehouse.'

squeeze-box A concertina; a piano-accordion.

squiffy Slightly drunk; hence, drunk in any degree. Ex *skew-whiff*.

squire A jocular term of address among men: coll.

squirt A paltry or contemptible person, esp. if mean or treacherous: coll.: U.S., anglicized ca. 1875. Hence, at Public Schools, an obnoxious boy.—A water-pistol: mostly boys'.

squish Marmalade: universities' and Public Schools'. Ex *squishy*, soft and wet.

squiz A brief glance (low Australian). Ex *squint* + *quiz*.

stab at, have or **make a** To attempt, endeavour, have a shot at: coll., orig. U.S., anglicized ca. 1929.

stacks Plenty (of).

stag Any such applicant for shares as intends to sell immediately at a profit or, if no profit quickly accrues, is ready to forfeit the deposit money: commercial.—Sentry-go: military.

stag-party A party of men: U.S., anglicized ca. 1870.

stake, v. To give, or to lend for a long while, something to (someone): coll. Apparently Canadian before it became English. 'Will you stake me to a dinner?'

stall Any pretext or excuse; a playing for time.

stall, v. To make excuses, allege pretexts, play for time.

stall off To avoid or get rid of evasively or plausibly; hence, to keep the mastery, maintain superiority, over (a competitor, be it horse, as orig., or man): sporting. Frequently *stall off the challenge of* (another horse in the race).

stand To pay for the drinks of: coll.

stand for To endure, tolerate : U.S., anglicized as a coll. in early 1920's.

stand-in A deputy; one who takes your turn of duty: Services' coll. Ex:

stand in for To take (someone's turn of duty; to stand by fo r him: Services' coll. Ex the theatre.)

stand up To keep (someone) waiting, esp. at an assignation: c. >, by 1940, s.

star turn The central or most important person: coll. Ex the music-halls.

start, v. To start (i.e. begin) to complain or reprimand or abuse or boast or reminisce: coll. Thus ' "When I was your age I was up and about at six in the morning." "Now don't you start," said Paula' (Gerald Kersh).

start A surprising incident or procedure; often *rum start*. Ex the start of surprise.

start in, v.i.; v.t. with on To begin work, one's job (on or at): coll.: U.S. anglicized ca. 1900. 'I start in, Monday.'

start on To tease, jest at, bully: coll.

start something E.g., 'Now you've started something!' To set afoot something that will have important or exciting consequences: coll. Ex U.S.

state A dreadful state, esp. of untidiness, confusion, dirtiness: coll. Agitation, anxiety, state of excitement: coll.

stay, come to To become permanent, established, recognized: coll.; orig. U.S., anglicized in 1890's. Hence, (of merchandise, etc.) to secure a position in public favour as fulfilling a general need: coll.

steady, the Buffs! A c.p. of adjuration or of self-admonition: military, hence also naval. Of anecdotal origin.

S.S.D.—M

steam ahead, away   To put on speed; hence, to progress rapidly, to work vigorously: coll.

steam tug   A 'mug', a simpleton: rhyming s.

steamed-up   Heated; angry.

steep   Excessive, resp. of price, fine, taxes; hard to believe, esp. of stories: U.S., anglicized ca. 1880.

step   A stepfather or stepmother; a step-brother or -sister: coll.

step on it   To hurry.

stew, v.i.   To study hard: mainly schools'.

stewed   Tipsy.

stewed prune   A tune: rhyming s.

stick   A dull, stupid, awkward, or (in the theatre) incompetent person: S.E. until mid-C. 19, then coll.—Esp. in *give* (a child) *the stick*, and *get the stick*. A beating with a stick: coll.—A mast: nautical coll.

stick   To put up with (things), tolerate (persons). 'He could not "stick" her.' Also *stick it*, to continue, without flinching, to do something. To cheat (a person) out of money or in dealing; impose illicitly upon; hence, to persuade (someone) to incur an expense; 'let in' for: coll.

stick one's neck out   To ask for trouble. By exposing one's head.

stick (someone) **for** (a thing, a price)   To charge someone too much; make someone pay (so much).

stick it in or **on**, v.i.   To charge extortionately; v.t., *stick it into* or occ. *onto*.

stick it out   To go on enduring: coll.

stick out   To persist in demanding (e.g. money), v.t., *for*; (v.t. with *that*) to persist in thinking: coll.

stick-up, n., ex **stick up**, v.   A hold-up robbery; to hold up and rob: Canadian and Australian.

stick up for   To champion (a person): coll.; U.S. >, almost imm., British.

sticker   A commodity hard to sell; hence, a servant that a registry office has difficulty in placing; a lingering guest: coll.—A slow-scoring batsman hard to dislodge.—A pointed question, a startling comment, an embarrassing situation: coll.

sticker   A small, sticky-backed poster: coll.—Usually pl., *stickers*, such goods 'in short supply' as are slow in coming from manufacturers or wholesalers: tradesmen's.

sticks   Household furniture: coll.—Hurdles: sporting.

sticky   (Of stock) not easy to sell: Stock Exchange: s. >, by 1920, coll.—(Of persons) unpleasant or obstinate.—Of situation, incident, work, duty: unpleasant; very difficult: 'We had a sticky time'.

sticky, n.   A 'sticky', i.e. damp and difficult, pitch: cricketers' coll., esp. Australian. (Cf. the preceding entry.)

sticky-beak   An inquisitive person: Australian. Ex a bird that, searching for food, gets its beak sticky.

sticky dog   A sticky wicket: cricketers'.

stiff   A corpse: U.S., anglicized ca. 1880. Medical students *carve a stiff* (dissection).—Because cramped by lack of money.—Esp. in Australia (ex U.S.), a term of contempt (often jocular), as *you stiff!*, *the big stiff.*

stiff, adv.   Greatly. Only in *bore* (one) *stiff* and *scare stiff*: coll. Lit., to death.

stiff upper lip, keep a   To be firm, resolute; to show no, or only slight, signs of the distress one must be feeling: coll.

still & all   Nevertheless: coll.

sting   To demand or beg something, esp. money, from (a person); to get it thus.—To swindle, often in a very mild way and esp. in the passive voice.

stinger   Anything that stings or smarts: coll.

stink   A disagreeable exposure; considerable scandal.

stink, like   Desperately hard or fast or much, as in 'working like stink'.

stinker   A contemptible person. A very sharp or an offensive letter, a stinging criticism, a pungent comment or a crushing argument; anything (very) difficult to do.

stinking   Contemptible; (of a blow, criticism, repartee, etc.) sharp; extremely drunk.

stinko   Exceedingly drunk: orig. clerks'.

stinks   Chemistry: universities' and Public Schools'.

stir   A prison: c. >, ca. 1905, low s. Ex Romany *stariben, steripen*; cf. also Welsh Gypsy *stardo*, imprisoned.

stiver   Esp. in *not a stiver*, not a penny: coll. Ex *stiver*, a small Dutch coin.

stodge   Heavy eating; gorging; hence, a heavy meal: mostly schools'.

stoke up, v.i.   To eat; nourish oneself: coll. Ex stoking an engine.

stone-ginger, a   A certainty.

stones, on the   On the street, i.e. destitute: coll.

stony; short for **stony-broke**   Penniless. For semantics, cf. *hard-up*.

stooge, n.   A learner (as in 'Q learner') at a divisional or a corps H.Q. in the Army. Either ex *student* or perhaps ex U.S. *stooge*, a comedian's butt or a conjurer's assistant (a 'feed'), itself either ex *stool pigeon* via *studious* (mispronounced *stew-djus*) or ex *student*. Hence, a deputy; a stand-in. Hence a second-rater, one without importance.

stooge, v.   To fly over the same old ground as before: R.A.F. Hence, to be an assistant.

stooge around   To 'hang about', waiting to land; hence (also *about*), 'to idle about, on the ground, or in the air' (Jackson): R.A.F.

stool pigeon   An informer: c. > low s.; orig. U.S.; anglicized by 1916.

stop, v.   To receive (a wound); esp. in *stop* (a *nasty one,* a *Blighty*).

stop me if you have (or **you've**) **heard this one**   A c.p. by an imminent 'story-teller.

stop-out, n.   A person given to stopping out late at night: coll.

stop up   To sit up instead of going to bed: coll.

story-teller   A liar: euphemistic coll.

stoush, n.   A fight; v.t., to fight, esp. to beat in a fight (anything from fisticuffs to a great battle): Australian.

stout fellow   A reliable, courageous, and likable fellow: coll. Ex S.E. *stout-hearted fellow.*

Strad   A *Strad*ivarius violin: coll.

strafe; occ. **straff**   A fierce assault; hence, a severe bombardment; hence, a severe reprimand: military >, by 1919, gen.—To attack fiercely; to bombard: military. Ex the Ger. toast *Gott strafe England,* 'may God punish England!'—Hence, to punish, to damage; hence, to swear at, to reprimand severely: military >, by 1918, gen.; by 1940, ob.

straight   (Of an utterance) outspoken; (of a statement) unreserved: coll. Hence, *straight talk,* (a piece of) plain speaking.—Of persons or their conduct: honest, honourable; frank: coll.—(Of accounts) settled: coll.

straight!   Honestly!; it's a fact!: coll.

straight & narrow, the   The straight and narrow path of virtue or honour: coll.

straight as a dog's hind leg   Crooked: jocular.

straight from the horse's mouth   (Of information, news, etc.) genuine, authentic, correct: sporting s. > coll.

straight-up, adj.   Correct; the truth: low.

straight up!   Honestly!

straight wire, the   The genuine thing; esp., authentic news: Australian.

strap(-)hanger   A passenger holding on to a strap in omnibus, train, etc.: s. >, ca. 1930, coll. Hence, 'to *strap-hang*' (v.i.).

strapped   Penniless: English and Canadian.

streak   to go very fast; esp. *streak off* (*like greased lightning*): coll.

stream-lined   (Of women) tall, slim, graceful; (of clothes) neatly and closely tailored. Ex aircraft stream-lined to reduce air-resistance.

street, not up my (his, etc.)   That's not my concern; not my strong point; not my method: now coll.

streets ahead (of) or **better (than), be**   To be far ahead (of) in a race; hence, to be much superior (to): coll.

strength of it, or **this** or **that** or **the other, the**   The 'real' meaning or significance, as in 'What's the strength of him (or his) coming here?': coll.

strides   Trousers: theatrical.

string on   To befool, to 'lead up the garden path'.

stripes; old stripes   A tiger: jocular coll.—(Also *stripey*.) A sergeant of Marines: naval, esp. as a nickname. Ex his badge of office.

strong on   Laying great stress on: coll.

struck on   (Low) coll. form of *struck with*, charmed by a person —of the opposite sex.

stuck into it!, get   Work hard!; don't dally!: military. Ex digging (a clayey trench).

stuck on   Enamoured of: rare among upper classes.

stuck-up   Unjustifiably 'superior'; offensively conceited or pretentious: coll.

stuff   Copy; one's MS.: coll., journalistic and authorial.—Shell-fire; esp. with adj., as *heavy stuff*.—Often employed as a coll., to connote vagueness in the speaker's mind or intention, or to imply ignorance of the precise term or name, as in Christopher Bush, *The Case of the April Fools*, 1933, 'Made his escape down the creeper stuff'.

stuff to give the troops!, that's the   That's the idea; that's what we want: coll.; orig. (1916) military >, by 1919, gen. coll. Since 1917, often *that's the stuff to give 'em!*; since ca. 1920, often *that's the stuff!*, which may have been the original.

stuffed shirt   A pompous fool: upper and middle classes'. Adopted ex U.S.

stuffy   Irritable; sulky; obstinate, difficult': U.S. anglicized c. 1895 as a coll.; hence, easily shocked, strait-laced.—Stand-offish: Services'.

stumer; occ. stumor   A forged cheque or a worthless one (an 'R.D.'). Hence, a counterfeit banknote or a base coin. Hence (often as adj.), a sham; anything bogus or worthless.

stump up, v.t. and v.i.   To pay, disburse.

stunner   An exceedingly attractive woman or thing; a person excellent *at* doing something, or a thing excellent in quality or remarkable in size: coll. Cf.:

stunning   Excellent; delightful; extremely attractive or handsome: coll.

stunt An item in an entertainment: coll.; ob. Ex U.S. *stunt*, an athletic performance, any (daring) feat, itself perhaps ex German *stunde*, an hour (O.E.D.), or, more prob., ex Dutch *stond*, a lesson (W).—Hence, an enterprise undertaken to gain an advantage or a reputation.—Hence, any enterprise, effort, or performance. Hence, a dodge, a (political, commercial or advertising) trick or novel idea. —An attack, a raid; a bombing-sortie: military. Hence, also v.i.

style, cramp one's To prevent one from doing, or being at, one's best; to handicap or check one: orig., upper-class coll. Ex athletics or racing.

sub A substitute: cricketers' coll.—A subscription: coll.—An advance of money, esp. on wages: coll.—A submarine: naval and Air Force coll.

sub-fusc The 1913–16 variation of *dim* (insignificant, lacking character), q.v.: Oxford University. Hence, (of dress) modest, of quiet colour.

suck-in, n. and v. To deceive; deception; cheat.

suck up to To toady to: schoolboys'.

sucker A greenhorn; a simpleton: coll.: U.S., anglicized by 1920.

sudden death A decision by one throw (not, e.g., by two out of three). Hence, a decision by one game, as in lawn tennis when the set-score is 5-all: s. >, by 1930, coll.

sugar Money: low > respectable. Ex *sugar and honey*.—A term of address to a girl. Ex U.S.

sugar and honey Money: rhyming s.

sugar daddy An oldish man spending lavishly on a young woman: U.S., anglicized ca. 1931.

Sunday-go-to-meeting clothes and **togs** Sunday clothes: resp. coll. and s.

sundowner A drink taken at or about sundown: India, Ceylon, Singapore, the East Indies, Australia.

sunny side up 'An egg fried so that it is done on one side only, the yolk not broken, and not turned over': Canadian restaurants' >, by 1942, also English restaurants'.

sup A supplement: coll.

super Extremely strong, capable, intelligent; hence, excellent, 'swell'. Prob. ex *superfine*.

super A supernumerary: coll.—A superintendent of a station: Australian.—A police superintendent, esp. in address.

sure! Certainly!; with pleasure!; agreed!: coll.: early C. 18, in England, whence it fled to the U.S.; re-anglicized ca. 1910.

sure!, to be Of course!: coll.—Often concessively: admitted!; indeed!: coll.

sure-fire Certain; infallible: coll.; U.S. anglicized ca. 1918.

sure thing! The same as *sure!*: coll., orig. U.S.

swab A naval officer's epaulette: nautical jocose or pejorative. Ex the shape of a *swab*, anything for mopping up.

swaddy; swaddie; swoddy A soldier: naval and military s. Among soldiers, in late C. 19–20, usually a private and esp. as a term of address.

swag Any quantity of goods, esp. a pedlar's wares or a thief's booty, esp. as recently or prospectively obtained: c. >, ca. 1850, low s. >, by 1890, gen. s. in the wider sense, any unlawful gains or acquisition. Perhaps ex dial. *swag*, a large quantity.

swagger, adj.—Smart, fashionable; 'swell'; rather showy or ostentatious: (orig. Society) s. >, ca. 1930, coll. Ex S.E. *swagger*, superior or insolent behaviour.

swaggie, swaggy A man carrying a 'swag': Australian coll.

swallow (or swaller) and sigh Collar and tie: theatrical rhyming s.

swallow the dictionary Esp. in *must have swallowed the dictionary*, applied to one who uses very long words: coll.

swan around (Of tanks) to circle about; (of persons) to wander either in search of a map-reference or aimlessly: Army. Ex the manoeuvres of swans queening it on pond or stream.

swan around To 'tour' unauthorized: Army.

swank To behave showily or conceitedly; to swagger; to pretend (esp. to be better than, or superior to, what one is): dial. >, ca. 1870, s., though not gen. till ca. 1901.

swank(e)y, adj. Showy; conceited; pretentious; pretentiously grand: dial. >, ca. 1910, s.

swap, swop An exchanging; an exchange. Also v. Ex S.E. *swap*, an act of striking (esp. the hand as a sign of a bargain made); or more imm. ex the S.E. v. Hence *s wapper*, and *swapping*.

swarry; occ. **swarree, swarrey** A soirée or social evening: coll.; by 1945, somewhat ob.

swear & cuss A bus: Cockney rhyming s.

swear off To renounce: lower classes' s. >, ca. 1900, gen. s. >, ca. 1920, coll.

sweat Hard work; a difficult task: C. 14–20: S.E. until C. 20, then s., esp. in *an awful sweat.*—A long run taken in training: Public Schools'.

sweat on the top line; be sweating . . ., the more gen. form. To be eagerly expecting or on the eve of obtaining something much wanted: military. Ex the game of House.

swede-bashing Field training, as opposed to *square-bashing* (parade work, drill): Army and R.A.F.

sweet In the speaker's opinion, attractive, very pleasant: coll.

Sweeney Todd, the The Flying Squad: London rhyming s.

sweeten To bribe.—To contribute to (the pool), increase the stakes in (the pot, at poker): card players'.—V.i., to bid at an auction merely to run up the price: mainly auctioneers'.—V.t., to increase (the collateral of a loan) by furnishing additional securities: financial.

sweetie A sweetheart: coll. ex U.S.

sweetie (or **-y) pie** In address: dear; 'sweet'.

swell, n. A fashionably or smartly dressed person; hence, a (very) distinguished person, a lady or gentleman of the upper classes: s. >, in late C. 19, coll.—Hence, one who has done something notable or who is expert *at* something: s. >, in late C. 19, coll.

swell, adj. Excellent, whether of things (e.g. *a swell time*) or of persons considered as to their ability (e.g. *a swell cricketer*): by 1950, except in U.S.A., slightly ob.

swig To drink deeply, eagerly, or much (esp., strong liquor).—V.t., with the liquor as object, as in 'he just sat there swigging beer'.

swindle A lottery, a speculation; a toss for drinks.—Something other than it appears to be, a 'fraud': coll.

swing it To get something by trickery; to shirk or malinger, esp. if successfully.

swipe To appropriate illicitly; steal; loot: U.S., anglicized ca. 1900.

swipes Small beer; hence, any beer.

swish, adj. Smart; fashionable: by 1950, ob. Ex dial. *swish*, cognate with dial. *swash*, gaudy.

swiz, occ. **swizz** A 'fraud'; great disappointment: late C. 19–20 schoolboys'. Ex synonymous *swizzle*, itself perverted *swindle*.

swot, swat (Hard) study: Public Schools' and universities'.—One who studies hard. Hence, *swot* (*swat*) up, to work hard at, esp. for an examination: to 'mug up'.

synthetic (Of news) suspect; (a person) pretending to be something more than he really is: Services'. In the R.A.F. it is often applied to the theory as opposed to the practice of flying.

T

ta! Thanks!: coll., orig. and mainly nursery. Ex a young child's difficulty with *th* and *nks*.

tabs Curtains: theatrical.

ta-ta's (or -tas), go; go for a ta-ta (Of a child) to go for a walk: (proletarian) nursery coll. Ex *ta-ta*, good-bye!

tack (Cooked) food: coll. Ex nautical *soft*, or *hard, tack*, bread or ship's biscuit.

tackle, v.   To lay hold of; encounter, attack: coll.: orig. U.S.— Hence, to enter into a discussion, etc., with (a person), approach (on some subject): coll.—Hence, to attempt to handle (a task, situation), or to understand or master (a subject). Hence, to begin to eat, try to eat: coll.

Taffy   A Welshman: coll. Ex a (supposed) Welsh pronunciation of *Davy*.

tag along   To go along; to go. Perhaps ex *tag (oneself) on to a person and go along with him*.

tail of, get on the   To attack an opponent in the rear: Air Force coll. and since 1915.

tailor-made, adj. and n.   (A) machine-made (cigarette): naval > gen.

tails   A tail-coat, as opp. a jacket; a dress-suit, esp. and properly the coat only: coll.

take, v.i.   To be a good (*well*) or bad (*badly*) subject for photographing: coll. 1889, B. Howard, 'The photographers . . . say a woman "takes" better standing' (O.E.D.).

take a dim view of   To disapprove; think silly, inefficient, objectionable: Services'.

take a (or the) mike out of   To insult or annoy (a person) with a verbal attack: Cockneys'.

175

take a toss To 'fall for' a person: coll.

take-down, v.t. To deceive grossly; to swindle: coll. (orig. Australian). Hence, also n.

take evasive action To avoid a difficulty or a danger; to depart tactfully, or prudently escape; to evade a debt or an unpleasant task.

take in To deceive, impose on, swindle: coll. Hence, also n.

take it To accept, endure, punishment courageously or cheerfully: boxing.—Hence, to endure trial and adversity without whining or cowardice.

take (something) lying down To submit tamely: coll. Either ex boxing or ex cowed dogs.

take off To mimic, parody; mock: coll. Hence, n.

take on To grieve, to distress oneself greatly: coll and dial.— To become popular, 'catch on'. V.t., to engage (a person, or army) in a fight, a battle: coll.

take (one) down a peg To lower (a person's) pride: coll.

take the can back To be held responsible for a mishap; hence, to be imposed on. (Cf. *carry the can.*)

tale, tell the To tell a begging-story; to make love; to tell an incredible or a woeful story; hence, to explain away (esp. one's own) military offences: Services'.

talk big To talk braggingly or turgidly: coll.

talk to To rebuke, scold: coll.

talk turkey To talk business; to talk sense: Canadian (ex U.S.A.) coll; adopted in England ca. 1930. The substantial and succulent part of a (Christmas) dinner.

talkie, talky A moving picture with words: 1928 (S.O.D): coll. >, by 1935, S.E. On *movie.*

tall (Of talk) grandiloquent, high-flown: coll. Hence, extravagant; exaggerated: U.S., anglicized, esp. *tall talk* or *tall story,* ca. 1880; by 1920, coll.

tan (one's hide) To beat severely; to thrash: coll.

tanner A sixpence. Ex the obsolete c. *simon,* sixpence, via 'He (Peter) lodgeth with one Simon a tanner' (Acts. x. 6—cf. 32).

tantrum (Esp. in pl.) A display of petulance; a fit of anger: coll: origin unknown.

tap (a person) for To ask (him) for (money).

taped, have or **have got** (one) Here, *taped* = sized-up; so seen-through as to be rendered incapable of harm; orig. (1916), military >, ca. 1920, gen. Ex *tape,* to measure (something) with a tape, with esp. reference to the Engineer-laid tapes along which the Infantry lay waiting for the signal to attack when there was no trench or sunken road convenient as a jumping-off place.—Hence, since 1920, *taped* often = arranged, or settled, as in 'We have the whole thing taped'.

tapes   Rank-stripes: Army and R.A.F. coll.

tar(r)adiddle   A lie, esp. a petty one: coll.; origin unknown; by 1930, slightly ob.

tarp   A tarpaulin.

tart   A girl, a woman (but if old, always *old tart*). Orig. endearingly; cf. *jam-tart*.

tash   Moustache: Services'.

Tassy, Tassie   (Pronounced Tazzy.) Tasmania.

tasty   Pleasant, attractive; excellent.

tater; 'tatur; tatie, tato; tattie   A potato: dial. and low coll.

tatty   Fussy, esp. clothes or decoration. Inferior; cheap: Australian.

tea fight   A tea-party: coll.

tea-leaf   A thief: c. (from ca. 1905) >, by 1930, low s. Rhyming.

tea-pot lid   A Jew: Cockney rhyming s. on *Yid*; often shortened to *tea-pot.*—A child: rhyming on *kid.*

teacher!, please   (With upraised hand.) A c.p., indicating that the speaker wishes to make a remark; *thank you, teacher,* a c.p. connoting irony or derision towards someone permitting condescendingly or explaining pompously.

tear, v.i.   To move violently; rush (*about*): coll.

tear a strip off (someone); as v.i., usually *tear off a strip*   To reprimand: R.A.F., hence also naval.

tear, on the   Having a wildly enjoyable time: Anglo-Irish.

tearing   Violent; passionate; roistering; rollicking: coll.

teaser   A 'poser'; a difficult ball in cricket.—A preliminary advertisement (specifying neither article nor advertiser), prior to an advertising campaign: advertising coll.

tec; 'tec   A detective.—(**tec** or **tech,** esp. preceded by **the.**) A *tech*nical college or institution: coll.

tee up   Mostly as in 'It's (all) teed up' or fully arranged and virtually assured: Army officers'. Ex golf.

teen-ager   A person aged from thirteen to nineteen, esp. 15–17: coll., adopted in 1945 from U.S.A.; by 1960, familiar S.E.

teeny; teeny-weeny   Tiny: coll. Ex child's pronunciation; the second, a reduplication suggested by *wee.*

tell me the old, old story!   A c.p. (often, too, a chant sung in unison), in retort either on rumours of good times or on specious promises: military; by 1950, ob. The first line of a Nonconformist hymn.

tell off   To scold, blame, rebuke severely: coll. Hence, the n. *telling-off.*

tell the world!, I'll I say so openly or emphatically: U.S., anglicized in 1931.

tell you what, I'll; I tell you what; tell you what I'll tell you something; I suggest: c.p.

telling you!, I'm There's no argument necessary: coll. Ex 'I'm not arguing; I'm *telling* you'.

telly, the Television: non-cultured coll. Properly but rarely *tele*.

temperament, throw To lose one's temper: theatrical.

tenner A £10 note; (a sentence of) ten years' imprisonment.

tenpence to the shilling, only Weak in the head.

terrible As a mere intensive, is coll.; esp. 'very large or great; excessive'.

terribly A frequent intensive ('excessively, extremely, very greatly'), coll.

terrier A member of the Territorial Army.

terrific; terrifically Excessive, or very severe or great; extremely, excessively.—Hence, 'great'; very: orig. Society.

thank you for those few kind words! A semi-ironic c.p.

thanks for saving my life, or **thanks! you've saved my life** A jocular c.p. addressed to one who has just 'stood a drink'.

that, at (Estimated) at that rate or standard; even so; in that respect; unexpectedly; in addition; what's more; yet, however; in any case, anyway: U.S., anglicized ca. 1885. Charles Williams, *The Greater Trumps*, 1932, has ' "Try me and let me go if I fail. At that," she added with a sudden smile, "I think I won't fail" '; and 'The nearest village to his grandfather's, Henry told them, and at that a couple of miles away'.

that shook him (or **me** or . . .) That astonished, surprised, perturbed, perplexed, baffled, him: Services', esp. the R.A.F. Intensively: 'I was shaken rigid (or rotten)'.

that's all I wanted to know! A c.p. of confirmation of, and resentment against, disagreeable facts.

that's fighting talk! A jocular c.p., retorting upon a pretended affront.

that's just too bad! A c.p., implying that an appeal to consideration, or restraint, has failed.

theatrical An actor or actress: stage coll.; by 1960, slightly ob.

then (or **and then) you woke up?** A c.p., implying disbelief in a tall story.

there, all Shrewd, alert, smart; *not all there*, mentally deficient: coll.

there's a war on A c.p. of 1939–45: cf. the *c'est la guerre* of 1914–18.

thick Familiar, intimate: coll. Excessive in some unpleasant way;

intolerable, unjust. Hence, indelicate; esp., *a bit thick*, rather indecent.

thick ear   (Esp. *give one a t.e.*) An ear swollen as the result of a blow: (low) coll.

thin   Disappointing; unpleasant; distressing; esp. (*have*) *a thin time*, to go through hardship or a thoroughly disagreeable or distasteful experience.

thing   A fad; a moral, or an intellectual, kink; an obsession. 'She hated bits on the carpet. She had a "thing" about them and always picked them up.'

thing, the   (Always in predicate.) That which is suitable, fitting, fashionable, correct: coll.—Hence, the requisite or notable point: coll. By 1950, slightly archaic.

things   Personal effects carried with one at a given time; impedimenta: coll.—Clothes; hence, esp. such garments, etc., as, in addition to her indoor dress, a woman dons for going out in: coll. 'Take off your things—and we will order . . . tea' (O.E.D.).

things are looking up!   A c.p. directed at someone wearing a new suit or a new car.

things (will) happen (even) in the best-regulated families, these (occasionally **such**)   An apologetic or an explanatory domestic c.p., applied to a family quarrel or misfortune.

thingummy; often **thingam(m)y**   A thing or, occ., a person one does not wish to, or cannot, specify, or the name of which one has forgotten: coll.

think   An act or period of thinking; an opinion: coll.

think!, I don't   This c.p. reverses the ironical statement it follows: 1837, Dickens, ' "Amiably-disposed . . ., I don't think," resumed Mr. Weller, in a tone of moral reproof' (O.E.D.). It often elicits the dovetail, *I didn't suppose you did.*

think up   To invent, by taking thought; esp. by racking one's brains, to hit upon, to devise: U.S. coll., anglicized ca. 1905.

this child   I; myself; I myself: orig. U.S., at first esp. among Negroes; partly anglicized, mostly in the Dominions, in late C. 19; by 1950, ob.

this is it!   Uttered when an approaching shell or bomb seems to indicate one's imminent death: Forces' c.p. Ex U.S.A.

this is the life   A c.p. dating from several years before, but popularized by soldiers in 1914–1918. Also, *it's a great life!*

this is where you want it accompanied by a tap on one's own forehead.   You need brains: c.p. The same gesture accompanies the c.p. *he's got it up there*, he's intelligent.

thought did!, you know what   A c.p. comment upon '*I think . . .*'.

three   A Rugby three-quarter: sporting coll.

three sixty-five; usually written '365'. Eggs-and-bacon: commercial travellers'. Because eaten for breakfast every day of the year.

thrilled   Pleased; content: Society coll.

thriller merchant   A writer of 'thrillers': publishers' and authors'.

thrilling   Pleasant; apt: Society coll.

throat, have a   To have a sore throat: coll.

throb   Such a person as, usually of the opposite sex, mightily appeals to someone: schoolgirls'. Short for *heart-throb*.

throw   To fail to extract the full meaning or emotional content out of one's lines as one might: theatrical coll. Ex 'to *throw* away'.

throw a party   To give a party: U.S.; anglicized ca. 1924.

throw it up against, at, or **to one**   To reproach or upbraid one with: coll. (*to*: low coll.).

thruster   One who, in the field, thrusts himself forward or rides very close to the hounds: hunting coll. Hence, among motorists, one who thrusts his car ahead of others: coll.

thump, v.   To defeat; to thrash (severely): coll.

thumping   Unusually large, heavy, or, of a lie, outrageous: coll.

thundering   Very large or great; excessive. Hence also as adv.

tick   An objectionable or meanly contemptible person. Ex the insect parasite.—Credit, trust; reputed solvency.—Hence, a score or reckoning, a debit account.—A second moment; properly, the time elapsing between two ticks of the clock: coll. Esp. *in a tick* or *two ticks*.

tick off, v.   To reproach or blame; esp. to reprimand. 'I ticked him off good and proper.'

ticker   A watch. By 1960, slightly ob.—The heart.

ticket, work one's (occ. **the**)   To obtain one's discharge from the Army by having oneself adjudged unfit: s. >, ca. 1910, coll.

ticky, tickey, or **tickie;** occ. **tiki, tikki, tikkie**   A threepenny piece: South African coll.

tiddler   A stickleback: nursery coll.

tiddly, n.   See **titley.**—Adj., drunk: low. Ex *titley*, n.—Little: dial. and nursery coll. Hence (?), particularly smart: naval.

tiddly (or **tiddy**) **oggy**   A Cornish pasty: Navy. Ex *tidbit*.

tidy   In amount, degree, considerable: coll. Hence, *a tidy penny*, very fair earnings, etc.

tiff   A slight quarrel, a briefly peevish disagreement: coll. Hence, also v.

tiffy   An engine-room *artificer*: nautical. Hence, any artificer or fitter: mechanics'.

tiger   A formidable opponent: sporting coll.

tight   (Of a contest) close; (of a bargain) hard.—(Of a person) close-fisted: coll., U.S.—(Of money) hard to come by; (of the money market) with little money circulating.—Tipsy: orig. U.S. Cf. *screwed*, lit. screwed tight, hence, drunk.—Cramped; over-worked; meticulous: artists'.—(Of balls) in contact, (pockets) with small openings: billiards.

tight, sit   To stay under cover; not to budge: coll.

tight-wad   A person mean with money: adopted, ca. 1934, from U.S.A. He keeps his hand closed tight upon his wad of notes.

tile   A hat. By 1940, archaic.

tile loose, (have) a   (To be) slightly crazy.

timber   A wooden leg; hence, any leg. A wicket, the wickets: cricket coll.

time, do   To serve a term in prison.

times go, as   As things are at present: coll.

tin   Money, cash; orig. of small silver coins, which tend to wear thinly smooth and thus look tinny.

tin ears, have   To be unmusical.

tin fish   A torpedo: naval.

tin hat   A soldier's steel helmet.

tin lizzie   A Ford motor-car; *Lizzie*.—Hence, any (cheap) motor-car.

tin tack   A racing track: rhyming s.

tin tack, get the   To lose one's job. Rhyming on *sack*.

tinge   A commission allowed to assistants on the sale of outmoded stock: drapers'.

tinkle   A telephone-call; mostly *give* (someone) *a tinkle*, to telephone to them: trivial coll.

tiny   Is an inevitable nickname of very big men: lower classes'; late C. 19–20. Contrast *Tich*, q v.

tip, v.   To give a 'tip' or present of money. Hence, v.i., as in 'Did he tip handsomely?': both now coll. To give private information, a friendly hint, about: coll. Esp. to indicate a horse as a probable winner, a stock as a profitable investment.—Hence to supply (a person) with 'inside' information: likewise now coll.

tip off   To give inside information to.

tip the wink   To warn with a wink.

tip-top   At the very top; excellent; 'splendid': coll. Hence, also adv.

tipple   Liquor.

tired, be (born)   To dislike work; to be lazy.

titfer, short for **tit-for-tat**   A hat: rhyming s.

titivate, tittivate; occ. **tiddivate, tidi-, tiddyvate**   To put finishing or additional touches to (one's toilet, oneself): coll. Prob. ex *tidy*, with a quasi-Latin ending on *cultivate*: O.E.D.

titley In C. 20, usually *tiddly*, occ. *tiddley*. Intoxicating liquor. Hence, a little drunk. Hence: Tipsy.

tizzy A sixpence. Prob. a corruption of obsolete *tester*.

tizzy A 'state'; esp. *get into a tizzy*. Perhaps ex S.E. *hysteria*.

toast, (had) on Swindled. By 1960, slightly ob.

toasting-fork, -iron A sword: jocular coll.

toasty Warmly tinted: artists'.

to coin a phrase An ironic c.p., mildly apologetic for the immediately preceding or ensuing triteness (often a cliché): since ca. 1935, but general only since ca. 1949.

toe-ragger A term of contempt: Australian and South Pacific. Ex Maori *tua rika rika*, a slave.

toe the line To appear in an identification parade: c. and police s.

toes up, turn one's To die.

toff A 'swell'; a 'nob' (well-to-do person): proletarian: by 1950, slightly ob. Ultimately ex † *tuft*, a 'swell'.

toffee, not for Not at all. 'That fellow X. can't bat for toffee.'

toffee-nosed Supercilious; conceited: proletarian.

togged-up, all Dressed up; 'dressed to the nines'. Cf.:

togs Clothes: c. > low s. > ca. 1860, gen. s.; in C. 20, usually jocular. Ultimately ex L. *toga*.

tolly A candle: Public Schools'. Ex *tallow*.

tom A girl. Ex *tomboy*?

tomfoolery Jewellery: rhyming s.

Tom Thacker Tobacco: rhyming s. (on *bacca*).

Tom Thumb Rum: rhyming s.

tommyrot Nonsense.

Tommy Tucker Supper: rhyming s.

ton, a 100 of anything: pounds, runs, m.p.h., etc.

tonk To strike: Public Schools'. Ex dialect.

tons (of) Plenty of: coll.

tony Stylish; high-toned: coll.

too much of a good thing Excessive; intolerable: coll.

too right! Certainly!; 'rather!': Australian.

tool, v.t. and v.i. To drive: sporting.

toot, at or on the Immediately; at high speed: military: 1914–18. Ex Fr. *tout de suite* (pron. toot sweet), whence also the military c.p., *the tooter the sweeter*, the sooner the better.

toot, v. To drink heavily (at one session): naval. '*Exercise toot* is the Wardroom description of a mild "pub-crawl"; on the other hand, *Operation toot* is a monumental drinking party' (Granville).

tooth brush A tooth-brush moutache: coll.

toothpick A very narrow fishing-boat with pointed prow: mainly nautical.—A bayonet: military.

tooting!, too damn   Certainly! Perhaps ex *Tooting Common*, with a pun on *common*, usual, general.

tootle, v.   To go; esp, *tootle off*, to depart. Ex dial.

tottle-oo!; loosely, **toodle-oo!**   Goodbye! By 1945, ob.

tootsie, tootsy; tootsie (or -y) **-wootsie**   A child's, a woman's, small foot: playful or affectionate coll.

top, go over the   To leave one's own trench and join in the attack on the enemy: military coll: 1914–1918.

top-hole   Excellent; 'splendid', 'topping'. By 1960, rather old-fashioned. On S.E. *top-notch*.

top of the world, (sit) on   (To be) prospering; esp. to be it and show it: U.S., anglicized ca. 1930.

top off or **up**   To finish; to conclude; to put the finishing touch to: coll. Both senses derive ex *top* (or *top up*), to put the top on, to crown.

topper   A thing or person excellent or exceptionally good: coll.; by 1930, ob.—A top-hat: coll.

topping   Excellent in number, quantity, or quality; 'tip-top'. Ex archaic S.E. *topping*, eminent.

tops, the   as in 'He's the tops'—admirable, the best possible; most likable: coll.: adopted, ca. 1943, from U.S.A.

torn it!, that's   That has spoiled it, ruined everything: c.p. (orig. low).

tosh   Nonsense. Perhaps *bosh* perverted.—Hence, very easy bowling: cricketers'.

tot   The sum-total of an addition, an addition sum: coll. Ex *total*. A very young or small child: dial. and coll. Esp. *tiny tot*. A very small quantity, esp. of spirits.

tot-up   An adding-up; to add up: coll.

tote, v.   To carry: U.S. coll., partly anglicized ca. 1910. Ex Negro *tota*, to pick up, to pick up and carry, to carry.

tote   A totalizator: Australian coll. >, ca. 1901, gen. British coll.

tottie; occ. **totty**   A Hotten*tot*: S. African coll.

touch, n.   The obtaining of money from a person, e.g. by a loan; hence, the sum of money obtained at one time, esp. by cadging or theft. To receive (money), to approach (a person) *for* money, to get from (a person) the money one asks (*for*).

tough   Morally callous or commercially unscrupulous; also n.: coll. Ex two U.S. senses: *tough*, criminal, vicious, and *tough*, a rough, esp. a street bully.—Unfortunate; severe. Ex U.S. *tough luck*.

tough, make it   To raise difficulties: coll.

towny, adj. and n.   A town-bred person; characteristic of a town or a city: coll.

toys   The mechanical parts of a 'plane: armourers' and flight

S.S.D.—N

mechanics' (R.A.F.).—Equipment, vehicles, etc.; to a Gunner, his guns: Army.

trad Traditional; also elliptically as n, esp for 'traditional music' (notably, popular.)

trade, the The submarine service: naval: W.W. I and II.

traffic Wireless messages sent or received: wireless operators' coll.

train(-)driver Leader of a large formation of aircraft: R.A.F.

train(-)smash Fried tomatoes: Navy (lower-deck). Ex the colour of flowing gore, the aspect of mangled limbs.

trains!, go and play; also *run away and play trains!* A derisive c.p. of dismissal.

tram (it) To travel by mining-district tramroad; hence, by tram-car: coll.

tramp, n. and v. (To go on) a walking excursion: coll.

transmogrify To change, alter; esp. to metamorphose utterly or strangely: humorous coll.

trap A policeman, esp. *the traps*, the police. By 1950, ob.—The mouth; esp. *shut your trap!*: low. Ex the earlier *potato-trap*.

trapes; traipse To walk aimlessly, untidily, listlessly; to gad about: coll. Hence also n.

traps Personal effects; belongings; baggage: coll. Ex S.E. *trappings*.

travel To admit of, to bear, transportation: coll. To go, move, fast: coll.

tray, trey Three, whether as number or as set: c. >, ca. 1910, low s. Ex *tray, trey*, the 3 at dice or cards.—Hence (also *tray-trey-bit*), a threepenny piece.

treasure (Of a person) a 'gem' or 'jewel': coll.

treat Something very enjoyable or gratifying; the pleasure there-from or the delight therein: coll. Adv. (*a treat*): most gratifyingly; very well indeed: low coll. All senses: ultimately ex *treat*, entertainment offered by another person.

tree, up a Cornered; done for; in a serious difficulty; penniless: coll. Ex U.S.

trek To depart: coll., orig. and mainly South African. Ex *trek*, to journey by ox-wagon, hence to migrate—itself ex Dutch.

tremendous As a mere intensive (= astounding; immense): coll. Hence, tremendously.

trey See *tray.*

trick A person, esp. a child, alert and amusing: Australian and New Zealand coll.

trick A tour of duty; a turn at the wheel: naval; Canadian railroadmen's.

trick cyclist A psychiatrist: orig., Army. By 'Hobson-Jobson'.

tricks?, how's   How are you; how are things going? Ex cards.

trig   Trigonometry: coll., esp. schools' and universities'.

trike   A tricycle; to ride a tricycle: (low) coll.

trim   To cheat; to fleece. Prob. ex S.E. *trim*, to thrash.

trim one's jacket   To thrash a person: coll.

trimmer   A person or thing that *trims* or thrashes, lit. or fig.: e.g. a stiff letter, article, review; a redoubtable competitor, fighter, runner (human or animal); a severe fight, blow, run, etc.; an especially well-delivered ball at cricket: coll.

tripe-hound   A reporter: orig. and mainly newspapermen's.

tripper   An excursionist: coll.

Trojan   Ex the Trojans, who manfully defended Troy against the Ancient Greeks. A brave, plucky, or energetic person (rarely of a woman); esp. in *like a Trojan*, very energetically: coll.

trot, on the   Gadding about: Society coll.—In succession: Services', then general.

trot out   To bring out (a person, hence an opinion, etc.) for inspection; hence, to exhibit: coll. Ex the leading out of a horse to show his paces.—Hence, *trot it out!*, speak up, or confess!

trouble & strife   A wife: rhyming s.

trump   A very good fellow, a 'brick': coll. Ex playing-cards. Cf.:

trumps, turn up   To turn out well, prove a success: coll. Ex games of cards.

trunk   A trunk call: coll., among telephonists and constant telephone-users.

trust (him) as far as I could throw (him), I would not   A c.p. applied to an unreliable person.

try it on the dog   To experiment at the risk or expense of another, esp. a subordinate or a wife or husband: theatrical s. >, ca. 1905, gen. coll. Ultimately ex experimenting with meat on a dog or with poisons on animals.

try-on   An attempt to 'best' someone; an extortionate charge, a begging letter.

try-out   A selective trial: coll. Ex U.S.

try this for size!   A c.p. used in horseplay and accompanying a playful punch: variant, *how's that for centre?* (perhaps originally Army, ex marksmanship). The former probably derives ex drapery salesmen's jargon.—Hence, (*try this for size only*) also in contexts far removed from horseplay.

tub, v.t.   To wash, bathe, in a tub; hence, v.i., to bath in a tub, esp. on rising: coll.

tube   The tunnel in which runs an underground electric train: coll. Hence *the Tube*, such a railway.

tuck A hearty meal, esp. of delicacies; usually *tuck-in*, also as v. Hence, food; esp. delicacies: orig. and mainly schools'.

tuck-shop A (school) pastry-cook's shop.

tucker Rations, orig. of gold-diggers; hence, food: Australian > also New Zealand.—Hence, *earn* or *make one's tucker*, to pay for one's board and lodging. Cf. *tuck*.

tug An uncouth person; esp. if dirty and none too scrupulous.

tum; tum-tum Variants of *tummy*.

tumble To understand, perceive, something not obvious, something hidden; v.t. with *to*: low. Perhaps ex *tumble on*, chance on (a thing).—(Of values, prices, stocks.) To fall rapidly in value: commercial s. >, ca. 1920, coll.

tummy Stomach: coll. Perhaps, orig., a children's corruption of *stomach*.

tunk To dip—e.g., bread—in a liquid (esp. gravy or tea or coffee): coll.: adopted from U.S. servicemen. Ultimately ex Ger. *tunken*.

tuppeny-ha'penny Inferior; insignificant: urban coll.

turf out To kick out; to expel. Perhaps ex *put out on the turf*, i.e. outside.

turkey, talk See *talk turkey*.

turn A momentary nervous shock of fear or other emotion: coll. Ex S.E. *turn*, an attack of illness or faintness.

turn down To reject (an application); curtly say *no* to (a request, suggestion, invitation); refuse to accept (a suitor for one's hand): U.S., anglicized, esp. in the Dominions, ca. 1900.

turn in To go to bed: coll., orig. nautical. Ex turning into one's hammock.—V.t., to abandon, to desist from doing.—Hence, *turn it in*, to die.

turn it up! Stop doing that! esp. stop talking.

turnip An old-fashioned, thick, silver watch; in Anglo-Irish, a cheap Ingersoll. Also called a *frying-pan*.

turps Turpentine: coll. By abbr.; -s, collective.

turtle doves Gloves: rhyming s. Also *Turtles*.

tweaker or tweeker A slow leg-break spinner: cricketers'. Whether the bowler or the ball.

twee Dainty; chic; pleasing: coll.: ca. 1904–39.

tween(e)y, tweenie A *between*-maid: coll.

twenty-firster A coming-of-age: universities', orig. Oxford.

twerp An unpleasant or objectionable or foolish or 'soft' person (rarely female): since ca. 1910.

twicer One who goes to church twice on Sunday.—One who asks for two helpings; hence, one who persistently tries to get more than his due: Australian. Hence (?), a cheat, a liar: mostly commercial.

twig To see, recognize, perceive; hence, to understand, v.t. and v.i.

twiggez-vous?   Do you understand?: ca. 1898–1940.

twist   To swindle, to cheat.

twister   A 'shady' fellow, swindler, a crook; a shuffler, a prevaricator.

twit   A contemptible or very insignificant person.

two-and-eight   A fluster, a confusion, emotional state, attack of nerves: rhyming s.

two cents' worth, my, his, etc.   My opinion for what it's worth: Canadian c.p.; adopted ex U.S.

two-ten   A shopkeepers' code c.p. 'Keep your *two* eyes upon his, or her, *ten* fingers.'

two feet one backyard   A jocular c.p. applied to very large feet. Punning 'Three feet (make) one yard'.

two-time   To double-cross (someone); **two-timer,** a double-crosser, or merely one who doesn't 'play the game': adopted, ca. 1939, from U.S.A.

two twos, in   In a moment; immediately: coll. Lit., in the time taken to say *two* twice.

two-year-old, like a   In a very lively manner; vigorous(ly): coll. Ex race-horses.

tymp, occ. **timp**   A tympanist, whether a drummer or a player of the tympan: musical.

type   'Classification of person. Thus, "He's a poor type, a ropey type, a dim type, a brown type". In the R.A.F. the word is universal in this sense, and derives from its common use in connection with aircraft. Used since the Great War' (1914–18): C. H. Ward Jackson. This 'etymology' is correct; I think, however, that there has been influence by the French-slang *type*, a chap, a fellow.

typewriter   A fighter, boxer: rhyming s.

U

---

uckers The game of ludo: Navy (lower-deck).

ugly as sin Extremely ugly: coll.

ugly customer A vigorous boxer, not too scrupulous, but very difficult to knock out: pugilistic coll.

uke Ukulele: musicians' >, ca. 1930, gen.

umbrella A parachute: Services'.

ump An umpire: sporting, esp. cricketers'.

um(p)teen, um(p)teenth An undefined number; of an undefined number: military, to disguise the number of a brigade, division, etc.; orig. signallers' s. *Umpteen(th)* is still common, though rather in the sense '(of) a considerable number', as in *for the umpteenth* time. Ex *um*, a non-committal sound + *-teen*.

uncle; gen. **my, his,** etc., **uncle** A pawnbroker; hence, *uncle's*, a pawnbroker's shop. Prob. ex the legend of rich or present-giving uncles.

Uncle Fred Bread: rhyming s.

Uncle Ned Bed: rhyming s.

under the influence Tipsy: coll. Abbr.*under the influence of liquor.*

under the weather Tipsy: nautical.—Unwell: coll.

undercart Undercarriage of an aircraft.

undercome(-con- or -cum-)stumble To understand: illiterate or jocular coll.

undergrad An undergraduate: coll.

undergraduette A girl 'undergrad': s. >, by 1930, coll.

undies Women's, hence occ. children's, underclothes: (orig. euphemistic) coll.

unearthly hour, time A preposterously early hour or time: coll.

ungodly; unholy Outrageous; (of noise) dreadful: coll.

188

unload, v.i. and t.   To drop (bombs) on the enemy: Air Force jocular coll.: since 1915.

unstuck, come   To go amiss; to fail.

up, v.   To rise abruptly, approach, begin suddenly or boldly (to do something): coll. and dial.

up, adj.   Occurring; amiss: as in 'what's up?', What's the matter?, or, when *up* is emphasized, What's wrong?: coll.

up against   Confronted with (a difficulty): coll.: U.S. >, by 1914, anglicized. Esp. in the phrase *up against it,* in serious difficulties.

up-and-downer   A violent quarrel: lower classes'. Ex changing positions of participants.

up the wall, adv.   Hence, occasionall y, an adj. (in the predicate). Awry; (of supposed facts, calculations, premisses) fallacious; crazy. 'It's enough to send you up the wall.'

up to   Obligatory (up)on; (one's) duty; the thing one should, in decency, do: coll.: U.S., anglicized ca. 1910. Ex poker.

up to a thing or two, be   To 'know a thing or two': coll.

up to much, not   (Rather) incapable; (of things) inferior: coll.

up to mud   Worthless: mostly Australian.

upper storey, the   The head; the brain.

uppers, (down) on one's   In (very) reduced, in poor, circumstances: U.S. coll., anglicized ca. 1900.

uppity   Above oneself; conceitedly recalcitrant or arrogant. Either an arbitrary elaboration of *uppish* or a blend of *uppi*sh + haugh*ty*.

ups-a-daisy!; upsi- or **ups(e)y-daisy!; up-a-daisa, -daisy, -daisey, -dazy**   A cry of encouragement to a child to rise, or as it is being raised, from a fall, or to overcome an obstacle, or when it is being 'baby-jumped': coll. An elaboration on *up.*

upstairs, come or **go**   To gain height: R.A.F.

use for, have no   To consider superfluous or tedious or objectionable: coll. Ex U.S.

use one's loaf   To think (esp. hard or clearly); to be ingenious, exercise ingenuity. In rhyming s., *loaf = loaf of bread,* head.

useful   Very good or capable; (extremely) effective or effectual. 'He's a pretty useful boxer.'

useful, n.   An odd-job man, a handyman: Australian.

usual, (as) per   As usual: coll.

utter   To speak; to make any vocal sound (e.g., of pain or pleasure): mostly Society. Ngaio Marsh, 1938, '. . . If you stare like a fish and never utter'. Short for *utter a word* or *a sound.*

V

---

vac   A vacation: mostly universities' coll.

vackie, better **vacky**   A person, esp. a child, evacuated overseas or from city to country. Ex *evacuee.*

vain, take one's name in   To mention a person's name: coll.

vamos, vamoos, vamoose; illiterately, **vamoosh**   To depart, decamp, disappear: U.S. coll., anglicized as s. Ex Sp. *vamos,* let us go.

varsity, the   One's university; hence—without *the*—adj.: coll. (Unpopular at Oxford and Cambridge.)

veg(es)   Vegetable(s): eating-houses' coll. 'Meat and two veg.'

velvet, on   In an easy or advantageous position: sporting coll.

Vera Lynn   A (drink of) gin: rhyming s.

vert or **'vert**   A convert to another religion (esp. to Catholicism): coll.

vet   A veterinary surgeon: coll.—Hence, *the vet,* the medical officer: military: 1914–18.—To cause (an animal) to be examined by a 'vet': coll.—Hence, to examine, occ. to treat, (a person) medically: coll. Hence, to revise (a manuscript): a book-world coll.—Also, to sound, or ask questions of (a person), in order to discover his abilities or opinions: coll.

vice, the   The Vice-Chancellor, -President, etc.: coll.

view   'R.A.F. types do not "have an opinion", but instead "take a view". Thus, "He took a poor view when Bert snaffled his popsie" ': R.A.F. coll. Ex the aerial view they get of things.

viewy   Designed, or likely, to catch the eye.

violet   An onion: Navy (lower-deck).

viva   A viva-voce examination: university coll. Hence also v.

vocab   A vocabulary; a glossary or dictionary: Public School coll.

vote   To propose, suggest: coll. Only with *that* . . .

W

wacko! A variant of—and inferior to—*whacko!*

wacky, or **whacky** Unusual, out of the way, little known; esp. *wacky news*: adopted from U.S.A. by journalists ca. 1942. Cf. *whack, out of.* Also, in gen. use since 1944, for 'incorrect, unreliable' (news) and 'eccentric' (persons).

wad A fortune. Ex *wad of bank-notes.*

wadge, wodge A lumpy mass or bulgy bundle: coll. Ex S.E. *wad* on *wedge.* Hence, the adj. *wodgy.*

wads (Rare in singular.) Buns; occ., small cakes sold at a canteen: military.

waffle Nonsense; gossip(ing); incessant or copious talk: printers' > gen. Also v. Ex dial. *waffle*, a small dog's yelp or yap.

waffle (Of an aircraft) to be out of control (esp. *waffling,* losing height); to fly in a damaged condition or uncertainly: R.A.F.—Hence, to dither: Services' (mostly officers').

wag, hop the; play the wag To play truant.

wait To postpone (a meal) for an expected person: coll. To wait at; only in *wait table,* to wait at table: servants' coll.

wait for it! Don't be in too much of a hurry: (orig., military) coll. Ex the order given in fixing bayonets.

wait till (or until) you get it?, will you have it now or A c.p., addressed to someone either impatient or in a hurry.

wakey, wakey! Wake up: R.A.F. non-coms'. Ex nursery.

walkabout A journey: Western Pacific pidgin.—A walking tour; a riding (and walking) tour: Australian coll.

walk into To attack vigorously; hence, to scold or reprove strongly; to eat, drink, much or heartily of: coll. All three senses: by 1960, rather old-fashioned.

walk it To win easily: sporting.

walkie-talkie A wireless set, carried by one man, with both receiving and transmitting equipment: s. > coll.

walking-orders, -papers, -ticket A (notice of) dismissal: U.S., anglicized, esp. in the Dominions, ca. 1910.

wallaby, on the On tramp: Australian s. >, ca. 1910, coll. For *on the wallaby track*.

wallflower A girl keeping her seat by the wall because of her inability to attract partners: coll.

wallop A resounding, esp. if severe, blow: coll.—Hence, the strength to deliver such a blow: boxing. '(He) has a prodigious "wallop", but no great amount of skill.'—Liquor; esp. beer, ex its potency.

wallop To belabour, thrash: coll.'—Hence, fig., to get the better of: coll.

wallop, go (down) To fall noisily and heavily: coll. and dial.

waltz into To attack, 'walk into (a person).

waltz Matilda Esp. as vbl n., *waltzing Matilda*, carrying one's swag: Australian. Ex the song *Watzing Matilda*.

wangle A 'wangling'; some favour illicitly obtained: orig. military. Ex the v.—Hence, a swindle.

wangle, v.t. To arrange to suit oneself; contrive or obtain with sly cunning, insidiously or illicitly; to manipulate, to 'fake': printers' s. > fairly gen.; in 1914–18, a very common soldiers' word; since 1918, very gen. indeed. Esp. *wangle a job, wangling leave* (of absence). Perhaps ex dial. *wangle*, to shake.

wanky, wonky Spurious, inferior, wrong, damaged or injured: printers' >, by 1914, gen. In East Anglian dial., *wanky* is 'feeble'.

want down, in, off, out, up, etc. 'There is an extraordinary locution used here which omits "to get". "I want down" means "I want to get down". Cf. also "I want out, I want in, I want out of here, I want on (a tram), I want off"—and countless others.' Thus Dr Douglas Leechman, concerning a Canadian usage adopted, ca. 1954, ex the U.S.

want in; want out To wish to enter; to wish to go out: coll. of Scotland, Northern Ireland, and Canada. For *want to go in* or *out*.

want it!, it's up there (with a tap on one's forehead) **you;** or **that's where you want it** You should use your brains!: a lower-class and military c.p.

want to make something of it? A threatening retort to criticism or insult: c.p., implying readiness for fisticuffs.

war on!, there's a A military c.p. = 'hurry up!' or palliating a refusal. Occ. preceded by *remember*.

war paint One's best or official clothes, with jewels, decorations, etc.: coll.—Hence, make-up: theatrical.

warm, v.   To thrash: coll. Also *warm one's jacket*: cf. *dust one's jacket.*

warm, adj. Rich: coll.—Close to a sought object.

wars, have been in the   To show signs of injury, marks of ill or hard usage: coll. Ex a veteran soldier's scars.

wart   A youthful subaltern; a naval cadet.—An objectionable fellow: upper classes'.

wash   Nonsense; drivelling sentiment: ca. 1905–50. Ex *hog-wash*; cf. *bilge* and *slush.*

wash, v.   To bear testing or investigation; prove to be genuine: coll. Usually in negative.

wash, it'll all come out in the   It will be discovered eventually; hence, never mind—it doesn't matter!

wash-out   A failure (thing or person); a disappointment or 'sell'; a cancellation. Ex target-shooting.

watch my smoke!   You won't see me for dust!: nautical coll., virtually a c.p. Ex the smoke of a departing steamer.

water, make a hole in the   To drown oneself suicidally.

water bewitched   Weak tea.

water-waggon, on the   Teetotal for the time being: U.S., anglicized by 1908. Now often *on the waggon.*

waterworks, turn on the   To weep: coll.

Wavy Navy, the   The Royal Naval Volunteer Reserve.

wax   A rage; esp. *be in a wax*: by 1950, ob. Hence, adj.: *waxy.*

way?, are you in my   A reminder of egotistical obliviousness: c.p.

way, in a kind or **sort of**   A modifying tag: coll.

way, a little, or **rather that**   'Approximati.1g to that condition': coll. Dickens, 1837, ' "I'm afraid you're wet." "Yes, I am a little that way." ' (O.E.D.)

way out, on the   (Of a person) due for retirement or, esp., for dismissal: coll. Hence, (of things) wearing out, coming to end of useful 'life'.

weaken!, it's a great life if you don't   A military c.p. of 1915–18; by 1960, rather ob.

wear   To tolerate, put up with.

wear it!, I won't   I won't tolerate it!: Cockneys'. Hence, in the Services, wear it = to agree to, to accept it. Ex wearing—or refusing to wear—shoddy clothes.

weaving, get   (Esp., in imperative.) (See *get cracking.*) ' "Weaving" is a flying expression meaning a formation or flight in which the aircraft weave in and out of each other's paths' (Jackson).

webs   (A sailor's) feet: naval.

weed   A cigar, a cheroot: coll. Ex *the weed*, tobacco. A leggy, ill-compacted, and otherwise inferior horse: 1845 (O.E.D.); Lever,

1859. Perhaps ex *weedy.*—Hence, a thin, delicate, weak and soon-tiring person.

weedy (Of horses, dogs) lank, leggy, loose-limbed, weak and spiritless: coll.—Hence (of persons), lanky and anaemic; weakly: coll.

week, knock into the middle of next To knock out (lit. or fig.) completely: pugilistic s. > gen. coll.

week than a fortnight, rather keep you (for) a A c.p. formula directed at a hearty eater.

weenie, weeny Tiny: dial. > coll. Ex *wee* on *teeny.*

weepie, weepy A sentimental moving-picture.

weeping willow A pillow: rhyming s.

weigh in with To produce (something additional), introduce (something extra or unexpected): coll. Ex a jockey *weighing in*, being weighed before a race.

weigh up To appraise: coll.

weighed off, get To be received into prison: prison c.: since ca. 1925.

weight about, throw one's To swagger, unduly stress one's authority. Prob. ex boxing or circus.

weird Odd; unusual; wonderful.

well away, be To be rather drunk: coll. To be doing splendidly: coll. Orig. sporting: ex a horse that has, from the start, got well away.

well, what do you know! A c.p. expressive of incredulous surprise.

were you born in a barn? A c.p. addressed to one who leaves a door open: mostly in Britain and in Canada, yet hardly rare in Australia and New Zealand. Of the same order as *was your father a glazier?*; in short, semi-proverbial.

Westminster (Abbey) Shabby: rhyming s.

Westo A Devon or Cornish ship or seaman: nautical coll. Ex *West Country.*

wet, adj. Showing the influence, or characteristic, of drink. 'A *wet night.*' Hence, somewhat intoxicated: coll.—Prone to drink too much: coll.—'Soft', silly, dull, stupid, 'dud'; in *talk wet.*—Liquor. A drink: coll.—A dull, stupid, futile or incompetent person. Ex the adj.

wet, all All wrong: esp. 'You're all wet'.

wet behind the ears Untrained, inexperienced; youthful. A boy seldom dries himself behind the ears.

whack A heavy resounding blow: dial. > coll. Hence, its sound: coll.—A (full) share; esp. in *take* or *get one's whack*, and in *go whacks.* Ex the sound of the physical division of booty.—Hence, fig., 'My word! he did more than his whack.'—Anxiety; a rage; a bad state of nerves.

whack, v. To strike with sharp, resounding vigour: coll. and dial.

Echoic.—Hence, to defeat in a contest or rivalry: coll.—To share or divide. Also *whack up*. To sell illicitly: military. Suggested by the synonymous *flog*.

whack at, have or **take a**   To attempt; to attack: coll.: U.S. >, before 1904, anglicized. Perhaps ex tree-felling.

whack out of   Not working properly.

whack up   To increase the speed of (esp. a ship).

whacked; whacked to the wide (sc. *world*)   Utterly exhausted.

whacking, adj.   Unusually big, large, fine, or strong: coll. Often *whacking great*, occ. *w. big*.

whacko!   Splendid!: Australian.

whacky   See *wacky*.

whale of a . . . , a   'No end of a . . .': coll.: U.S., anglicized ca. 1918. Ex the whale's huge size.

whang, v.t.   To strike heavily and resoundingly: coll. Also n. Echoic.

whap, whapper, whapping   See *whop*.

what a life!   A c.p. expressive of disgust.

what all, . . . and I don't know   And various others unknown or unmentioned: coll.

what can I do you for?   A jocular c.p. variation of *what can I do for you?*

what did you do in the Great War, daddy?   A military c.p. (1917–18 and after) used 'scathingly in times of stress'. Ex a recruiting-poster.

what did Gladstone say in (date)?   An electioneering c.p., of no precise meaning.

what does that make me?   A c.p. expressing disinterest or a refusal to participate.

what-d'ye-call-'em, her, him, it; what's-his-name   A phrase connoting some thing or person forgotten, considered trivial or not to be named, or unknown by name: coll.

what it takes   Esp., courage, perseverance; ability; (in Australia) money: coll., adopted ca. 1935 from U.S.A. Lit., what the situation requires.

what hopes!; what a hope (you've got)!   I don't like (e.g., your) chance!: c.p.

what makes (someone) **tick**   (His) chief interest in life, his driving-force. 'I've never discovered what makes him tick.' Ex watches and clocks.

what's cooking?   What is happening?: Services' (esp. R.A.F.) since mid-1940. Ex 'What is that smell—what's cooking?': asked so very often by so many husbands. Adopted from U.S.A.

what's it or **what's this, in aid of?**   What's the reason, the purpose of it—of this, etc. ?: coll.

what's what; usually preceded by **know** To be wide-awake and much experienced: coll.

wheeze A theatrical 'gag', esp. if frequently repeated: circus and theatrical. Clowns often affect a wheezy enunciation. Hence, a catch-phrase, esp. if often repeated; hence, a frequently employed trick or dodge.

where I (or we) came in, this is; or which is where we came in We've gone full circle; I'm beginning to repeat myself; I, or we, have heard or seen this before; c.p. Ex cinema-goers realizing that a film has reached this point.

where's the fire? A c.p. addressed to someone in a tearing hurry: ironical.

where the flies won't get it (Of liquor) down one's throat: c.p.: orig. U.S., anglicized by 1912.

whiff, n. and v.i. A stink; to smell unpleasantly. Hence the adj. *whiffy*.

whip To steal.

whip the cat To vomit: low: mid-C. 19–20.

whiskers (on it), have (Of a story, an idea) to be well-known or known for years: jocular coll.

whistle The mouth or the throat: jocular coll. Ex *wet one's whistle*, to take a drink: likewise jocular coll.

whistle (and flute) A suit (of clothes): rhyming s.

whistle for To expect, seek, try to get, in vain; to go without; have a very slight chance of obtaining: coll.

white, adj. Honourable; fair-dealing: U.S. s., anglicized ca. 1885; by 1920, coll. Ex the self-imputed characteristics of a white man. The n. is *white-man*.

white-haired boy is an English, Australian and New Zealand variant of *white-headed boy*; usually *my, her,* (etc.) *w.-h. b.* Favourite, darling: coll.; the latter, orig. Irish >, by 1890, fairly gen. Ex the very fair hair of babies and young children.

white man's burden, the Work: jocular coll.

white satin Gin. By 1960, slightly ob.

whizz-bang A shell fired from a light field-gun, esp. the German ·77; occ. the gun: military: 1914–18. One only just heard, if at all, the whizz of its flight before one heard the bang of the explosion. Hence, the stereotyped field postcard (soon censored): 1914–18.

whizz (-game); whizz-boy or **-man,** also **whizzy; whizz-mob** (First and third, usually preceded by **the.**) Pocket pickers, a gang of pick-pockets, or pickpockets collectively: c. >, by 1930, also police and grafters' s. Ex the speed at which they operate.

who all, and I don't know And other persons unnamed: coll.

who(-)done it; usually **whodunit** A murder story; a detective novel; a murder-story cartoon: coll.: adopted, 1942, from U.S.A., where current since ca. 1934. Ex the gaping curiosity of the illiterate.

whoopee, make   To enjoy oneself, rejoice hilariously: coll.: U.S., anglicized by 1933 at latest. Ex *whoop with joy*.

whop or **whap**   To strike heavily, thrash, belabour: (low) coll.— Hence, to defeat (utterly); to surpass, excel greatly: coll.

whopper or **whapper**   Something, some animal or person, unusually large: (low) coll.—Hence, a 'thumping' lie: (low) coll.

whopping   A severe beating: (low) coll.

whopping, whapping   Unusually large or great: coll.

why keep a dog and bark yourself (or . . . *do your own barking?*)? A self-explanatory c.p.

wibbly-wobbly   Unsteady: coll.

wicked   Very bad, 'horrid', 'beastly': coll. Hence, expensive; very high. 'A wicked price.'

wickedly   Very badly; horridly: coll.

wide   Alert, well-informed, shrewd. Ex *wide awake*.

wide, to the   Utterly; esp. in *done* or *whacked to the wide*, utterly exhausted: coll.

wifey, wifie, rarely **wif(e)y**   Endearment for a wife: coll.

wigging   A scolding; a severe rebuke, reproof, reprimand: coll.; by 1960, slightly archaic.

wiggle   A wriggle; esp. in *get a wiggle on*, to hurry: Canadian. Ex to *waggle*, wriggle: coll.

wild-cat   A rash investor; a risky or unsound business-undertaking: U.S. coll., anglicized ca. 1880; slightly ob.—Hence, adj., risky, unsound (business or business enterprise): coll., orig. U.S., anglicized ca. 1880.

wild-catter, -catting   A person engaging in, an instance or the practice of, 'wild-cat' business: coll.: U.S., anglicized ca. 1900. Ex preceding.

Wilkie Bards   (A pack of) cards: rhyming s.

willies, the   A feeling of nervousness, discomfort, vague fear: U.S., anglicized ca. 1925.

willy-willy   A whirlwind: Australian.

win   To steal: c. >, in the Army, 1914–18 (and after), s., with the extension: 'to gain not quite lawfully or officially' .

wind-jammer   A sailing vessel: adopted ex U.S., by 1930, coll.

wind up, get or **have (got) the**   To get frightened or alarmed; to be so: military (1915) > gen. Perhaps ex the early days of aviation, when wind, if at all strong, precluded flight.—Whence *wind-up*, nervousness, anxious excitement.

wind up, put the   To scare or greatly frighten (a person): military >, by 1919, gen.

windy   Afraid or very nervous; apt to 'get the wind up': military (1915) >, by 1919, gen. Ex *wind up, get the,* q.v.—Applied to any place likely to induce fear: military.

wine   To treat (a person) to wine: coll. Whence *dine and wine,* the entertainments being either separate or combined.

winger   A steward at table: nautical.—Hence, a sneak, an underhand fellow: naval.

winking, as easy as   With great ease: coll.

winkle out   To hunt out, house by house or 'fox-hole' by 'fox-hole', esp. with rifle and bayonet: Army.—Hence, *winkling*: attacks by Typhoon aircraft on small enemy strong-points, 500-or-so yards ahead of the troops: R.A.F.: 1944–5.

winks   Periwinkles: streets' (mostly London).

winner   A thing—e.g. a play—that scores a success.

winter-time?, where do (the) flies go in the   A C. 20 c.p. from a popular song.

wipe (a person's) **eye**   In shooting, to kill a bird that another has missed: sporting. Hence, to get the better of (someone). To give (him) a black eye.

wire   A telegram: coll.—Hence also v.

wire in   To set-to with a will; v.t., *wire into.*

wise-crack   A smart, pithy saying: U.S. coll., anglicized by 1932. Also *wisecrack.*

wise up, v.i.   To 'get wise'; v.t., to 'put (a person) wise': U.S., anglicized ca. 1916.

wished on   As in 'I had this job wished on me', i.e., foisted upon me: coll.

with it   Alert, well-informed; sympathetic.

wizard, adj.   Excellent, first-rate. Ex S.E. *wizard,* magical.

wizzo   Usually exclamatory: splendid!: R.A.F. Ex preceding.

woffle, v.i. and t.   'To mask, evade, manipulate a note or even (a) difficult passage': music-halls' and musicians'. Cf. *waffle.* Hence, more generally.

wog   An Indian of India; an Arab; a dark-skinned native: orig. R.A.F. Ex *golliwog,* with ref. to the frizzy or curly hair; *wog,* indeed, is a nursery shortening of *golliwog.*—A germ or parasite; anything small (e.g., tea-leaf floating on cup of tea): Australian.—Hence, *the wog,* tubercular infection; whence, in turn, *wog,* a person with tuberculosis: Australian.

wolf   A philanderer: adopted, ca. 1944, ex U.S. servicemen.

women and children first   A jocular c.p. on an occasion of non-emergency.

wonder!, I   I doubt it; I can't believe it; I ask: coll.

wonder!, I shouldn't   I should not be surprised: coll.

Wood in front, Mr and Mrs   A theatrical c.p. = a bad house, i.e. empty seats.

wood in it!, put a bit of   Shut the door!

Woodbine   A Tommy: Australian and New Zealand soldiers': 1914–18. Tommies smoked so many Wild Woodbine cigarettes.

Woods; Wood   A Wild Woodbine cigarette.

woollies   Woollen underwear: domestic coll.

woop woop   The country districts: New South Wales jocular coll. Satirizing the Australian Aboriginal names, so often reduplicatory. —Hence, *woop*, a rustic simpleton: by 1939, slightly ob.

woozy   Fuddled (with drink); muzzy: U.S., anglicized ca. 1917.— Dizzy: Canadian.

wop   An Italian: from ca. 1931, via the 'talkies'. Ex U.S. *Wop*, an Italian immigrant in North America. Ex the Neapolitan and Sicilian *guappo* (often in greeting), itself ex Sp. *guapo*, bold, handsome; hence, It., a blusterer.

word   To warn or to prime (a person).

words   A wordy dispute or quarrel: coll.

work   To obtain, or achieve, illicitly, deviously, or cunningly.

work cut out, have (all) one's   To have all one can manage to do: coll.

work the oracle   To achieve (esp. if illicitly) one's end skilfully or cunningly: orig. low s. >, by 1930, coll.

works, give (a person) the   To manhandle; to kill, esp. by shooting: U.S. c., anglicized ca. 1930 as s. Probably short for *give the whole works*, i.e. everything, the ultimate—death.

world, dead to the   Utterly drunk; fast asleep: coll.

worry!, I should   I'm certainly not worrying, nor shall I worry about *that!*: coll., orig. U.S.

worse in gaol (jail), there are   A c.p., indicating that the person referred to might be worse.

worse things happen at sea   A vaguely consolatory c.p.

wouldn't it!   Short for *wouldn't it make you sick?*, angry Australian c.p.

would!, you; occ. he (etc.) would!   *For you* (etc.) *would go and do that, curse you!* or *that's the sort of thing you* would *do*: c.p.

wow, it's a   To be a great success or most admirable, 'really' excellent: U.S., partly anglicized by 1929, esp. in theatrical s.; by 1960, ob. Prob. ex a dog's bark: cf. *'howling* success'.

wowser   A person very puritanical in morals; a spoil-sport; one who neither swears nor drinks: Aus. s. >, by 1930, coll. Perhaps ex *wow*, a bark of disapproval + euphonic *s* + agential *er*; cf. the Yorkshire *wowsy*, 'an exclamation, esp. of surprise'.

wrap up   Usually in imperative. To cease talking; also, stop making a row or a noisy fuss: Services'. Prob. ex *wrapping up* preparatory to cold-weather departure. To crash-land (an aircraft): R.A.F.

wrapped(-)up Carefully arranged; carefully prepared; entirely in order: Services'.

wrinkle A cunning or adroit trick, device, expedient; a smart 'dodge': now 1860, coll.—Hence, a helpful or valuable hint or piece of information: sporting s. > coll.

write-off A complete aeroplane-crash: R.F.C.—R.A.F.: 1914 onwards. The machine could be written off as useless.

written off (Of aircraft) damaged, esp. crashed, beyond repair; (of a person) killed, esp. through carelessness.

wrong, get (someone) To mistake his spoken meaning or unexpressed intentions: coll.

wrong side, get up (on) the To rise peevish or bad-tempered: coll. To do this, lit., is supposed to be unfortunate.

wrong un (or **'un**) A 'pulled' horse: racing s. >, by 1910, (low) coll.—Hence, a welsher, a base coin or a spurious note, etc.: s. >, ca. 1910, (low) coll.—The wrong sort of ball to hit: cricketers' s. >, by 1920, their coll.

wrong with?, what's What's the objection to?; why not have?: coll. Ronald Knox, 1925, 'I want to know what's wrong with a game of bridge?' (O.E.D.).

Y

---

yabber, n. and v.   Talk; to talk, esp. if unintelligibly: Australian 'pidgin'. Ex Aboriginal.

yabbie   A fresh-water crayfish: Australian coll. Ex Aboriginal.

yakker or **yacker;** correctly **yakka**   To work; work at: Australian 'pidgin'. Ex Aboriginal. Hence n., hard toil.

yam, v.i. and t.   To eat; orig., to eat heartily: low and nautical. It is a native West African word (Senegalese *nyami*, to eat).

Yank   An American: coll. Ex *Yankee*, ditto—a misuse of correct American *Yankee*.

yap   To prate, talk volubly: coll. Ex S.E. *yap*, to speak snappishly. —Hence also n.

yard-arm, clear one's   To prove oneself innocent; to shelve responsibility as a precaution against anticipated trouble: nautical.

yarn   Orig. and often in *spin a yarn*, to tell a (long) story, hence to 'romance'. A story, usually long, and often connoting the marvellous: nautical s. >, ca. 1860, gen. coll. Ex the long process of yarn-spinning in the making of ropes and the tales with which sailors often accompany that task.—Hence, a mere tale: coll. Cf. the journalistic sense of *a good yarn*, a story that is not necessarily true—indeed, better if not.—Hence, v.—in both nuances.

yarn-spinner, -spinning   A story-teller; story-telling: coll.

year dot, in the   A long time ago: mostly Londoners'.

yellow belly   A coward. Ex U.S.

yellow jack   Yellow fever: nautical. Ex the yellow flag displayed from vessels in quarantine to indicate a contagious disease.

yellow silk, n.   Milk: rhyming s.

yen   A passion; intense craving; esp. in *have a yen for*: U.S. (orig. underworld): adopted in England ca. 1931. From the Chinese (Pekin dialect) *yen*, 'smoke'; hence, 'opium'.

yes man, yes-man, yesman One who always agrees: coll. Ex American *yes man*, a private secretary, an assistant (film-)director, hence a parasite.

Yid A Jew. Ex S.E. *Yiddish.*

yob A boy: back s. Hence, a youth. By 1940, ob. Hence, a lout, a stupid fellow.

yobbo A post-1910 variant of *yob.* An arrogant and resentful, loutish and violent Teddy boy: mostly Londoners'. An extension of, s. *yob*, as Anglo-Irish *boyo* is of S.E. *boy.*

yoke An apparatus; almost any gadget: Anglo-Irish.

Yorkshire tike (Often shortened to *Yorkshire.*) A microphone: rhyming on s. *mike.*

Yorkshire tike or, gen., **tyke** A Yorkshireman: coll. nickname.

you can take it from me! You may accept it as true: c.p.

you can't take it with you! A c.p. directed at one who, saving money, loses happiness.

you can't do that there 'ere! A c.p. that originated in derision at the illiteracy of the old-style police constable.

you can't think You cannot imagine it; to an incredible degree: a non-cultured c.p.

you couldn't fight (or **punch) your way out of a paper bag** A c.p. addressed to a man boasting of his strength or of his fist-fighting ability.

you don't say! A c.p. indicative of astonishment. Short for *you don't say so!*

you kill me! You're so funny!: ironic c.p.; since ca. 1935. Also, since ca. 1942, *you slay me!*

you make me tired! You bore me to tears: a c.p. introduced from U.S.A. in 1898 by the Duchess of Marlborough, 'a then leader of fashion' (Ware).

you never did You never did hear the like of it; you've never heard anything so funny: Cockney coll.

you never know! You never know what may come of it: c.p.

you'd forget your head if it wasn't screwed on (properly) Often preceded by *forget!* A c.p. addressed to a forgetful person.

you'd only spend it A c.p. reply to someone saying that he'd like to have a lot of money.

you pays your money & you takes your choice! You may choose what you like: c.p. Ex showmen's patter.

young (Of inanimates) small, diminutive, not full-sized: S.E. until it >, ca. 1850, coll. and jocular, as in Hornaday's 'Such a weapon is really a young cannon', 1885 (O.E.D.).—*The night's young yet*, it is still early: coll.: C. 20. Often *yet* is omitted, rarely is *day* (etc.) substituted for *night.*

young gentlemen, the The midshipmen: wardroom ironic coll.

your guess is as good as mine A c.p. applied to a situation where neither party knows the facts. Adopted ex U.S.

you're holding up production You're wasting time (own or others'): R.A.F. (mostly); since 1940.

you're telling me! I know that: American c.p. anglicized ca. 1933.

you're the doctor! Whatever you say, (for) *you*'re doing it; you're the authority or the expert or the man in charge—and the responsibility is *yours*: c.p., Canadian and English.

you've got something there You're onto something good; there's much to be said for it: c.p.

you've had it! See *have had it*.

yum-yum Excellent: esp., very attractive; loving: proletarian. Ex *yum-yum!*, an exclamation of animal satisfaction (with, e.g., delicious food).

Z

zack   Sixpence: New Zealand and Australian. Perhaps a perversion of *six*; but cf. Dutch *zaakje*, 'small affair'.

zat?   How's that?: cricketers' coll.

Zep   A *Zep*pelin airship: coll.: 1915–18.

ziff   A beard: Australian.

zip   An echoic word indicative of the noise made by (say) a bullet or a mosquito in its passage through the air: coll.—Hence, force, impetus, energy, spirit: coll.

zizz, n. and v.   A rest period; to rest, esp. to sleep. Services'. Echoic. Hence, *zizzer*, a bed.

zoo, the   The Zoological Gardens, London (N.W.1), hence, *zoo*, any such gardens elsewhere: coll.

zoom   An abrupt hauling-up and forcing-up of an aeroplane when it is flying at a low level: aviation. Also, a v.i. Echoic.

zoot suit   A flashy suit of clothes: U.S. Here, *zoot* is perhaps Dutch *zoet*.